Let's Build!

Why we need five million new homes in the next 10 years

James Heartfield
With a foreword by Robert Bruegmann

Edited by Kate Moorcock-Abley

audacity

Let's Build!
James Heartfield
Published September 2006 by audacity

audacity Ltd
8 College Close
Hackney
London E9 6ER
www.audacity.org

10 Digit ISBN 0-9553830-0-5
13 Digit ISBN 978-0-9553830-0-7

Front cover image copyright © ConstructionPhotography.com
Typeset and designed by Alex Cameron www.de-sign.org.uk
Printed in the UK by Alden Press, Oxford

Kindly sponsored by the **Modern Masonry Alliance**
They develop and promote masonry construction – the bricks, blocks, and stone; the cement and mortar which bind them together; the researchers and technicians advancing the industry; the men and women who build masonry homes, buildings and structures.
For more information visit www.modernmasonry.co.uk

ACKNOWLEDGEMENTS

Thanks are due to Ian Abley, Lynne Anderson, Dan Atkinson, Pat Bagshaw, Elenora Belfiore, Andrew Calcutt, Alex Cameron, Martin Clarke, Dave Cowlard, Dolan Cummings, Dan Damon, Amanda Dennison, Michael Driver, Larry Elliott, Ben Evans, Fiona Flynn, Grant Gibson, Alan Hudson, Patrick Hughes, Eve Kay, Penny Lewis, Liz Malone, Kevin McCullagh, Nico MacDonald, Munira Mirza, Kate Moorcock-Abley, Brendan O'Neill, Mick Owens, Peter Ramsay, Kryszia Rozanska, Vicky Richardson, Colin Searls, Becky Shaw, Eric Sorenson, Martyn Warren and James Woudhuysen.

As this book was being written, a number of excellent books and reports were published on its central theme, not all of which I have been able to give the attention they deserve; they include Wendell Cox and Hugh Pavletich's *Annual Demographia Housing Affordability Survey*, Ferdinand Mount's *Mind the Gap*, Alan Evans and Oliver Hartwich's trilogy of reports for Policy Exchange, Mischa Balen's *Land Economy* for the Adam Smith Institute, and Robert Bruegmann's *Sprawl: A Compact History*

Let's Build! is dedicated to Holly, in the hope that it will be a curious relic of the past by the time she strikes out on her own.

CONTENTS

FOREWORD
ROBERT BREUGMANN

LET'S BUILD! **PRESENTS AN ARGUMENT, OFTEN QUIRKY AND ECCENTRIC,**
but always forceful and ultimately convincing, for setting aside some
long-standing assumptions about city and country – for taking bold
steps to ensure the continuing vitality of urban Britain.

Following the argument isn't always easy. In his text Heartfield takes
us through a good deal of unexpected territory – from the bicycle craze
of the 1890s, through the Mad Cow Disease episode of the 1990s,
to a recent campaign to make Newcastle a center of international gay
tourism. And there is room for skepticism about some of the specific
recommendations that he makes.

But at the heart of the book is a ringing defense of the aspirations of
ordinary citizens and a confidence that there is no inherent contradiction
between these aspirations and a just and sustainable urban future.
That sets Heartfield apart from a great many of the hand-wringing
commentators on today's political right and left.

Heartfield's *Let's Build!* appears to be part of a growing international
literature attacking a set of ideas that in Britain could be characterized
as the '1947 Planning System', and that more generally we could call
the 'Northern European Post-war Planning Consensus.' This collection of
ideas was based on a particular set of circumstances, notably the crisis
caused by the Depression and World War II, but it has remained tremen-
dously influential long after the conditions that brought it into being
have disappeared. It still determines much policy in Europe and
throughout much of the affluent world, and it may be doing a good
deal of harm.

Heartfield gives us a vivid account of some of the ideas and forces that combined to form the British post-war planning system. From the mid nineteenth century through the early twentieth, as Britain and most of the countries of northern Europe became affluent, they expanded dramatically outwards at densities much lower than those of their historic cores. This allowed for the creation of an unprecedented amount of new housing for the less affluent part of the population, and a dramatic increase in their quality of life. It also provoked a reaction from individuals who already had the kind of life they wanted, and who bitterly resisted any undermining of what they considered to be their own rights and privileges.

In Britain the landed aristocracy was affronted by the way ordinary city dwellers were moving to the suburbs and invading what had been an aristocratic rural preserve. A group of these aristocrats made common cause with an artistic and intellectual elite and a rising professional group of urban planners. An elite who also felt besieged in a world where individuals in the rising middle and working classes no longer seemed willing to take instruction from their betters, or know their proper place in the great order of things. Ensconced in their great country estates, suburban villas and spacious London flats, the aristocrats and intellectuals fulminated against the way ordinary citizens were moving into the land around British cities; obliterating age-old distinctions between city and country, leveling long-standing class distinctions, and lowering artistic and ethical standards.

The twin crises of the Depression and World War II gave this coalition an unexpected opportunity. Immediately after the war the leaders of many European national governments decided that reconstruction was too urgent, and land use too important, to leave to individual citizens or developers or even local governments. They believed that they knew better and took matters into their own hands, delegating the day-to-day operations to a group of upper middle class urban professionals.

In Britain the central government seized control of the development process by nationalizing all development rights. The framework for control over land was the Town and Country Planning Act of 1947. This legislation allowed the planners to impose many of the ideas they had been formulating over the preceding decades. As Heartfield explains it, under this system the control over land once held by the aristocracy now passed to the State.

The most famous example of post-war planning was the Greater London plan of 1945, written by Sir Patrick Abercrombie. Abercrombie was the very prototype of the high-minded and paternalistic planner who disdained the real estate market, the taste of the ordinary citizen, and the messy reality of electoral politics. He proposed to take away from the real estate industry the power to shape the city by concentrating planning and most actual building in the hands of the state. He further wished to control the overall shape of the metropolis with a growth boundary or greenbelt, to give it the kind of simple geometric form seen in the illustrations in Ebenezer Howard's famous work on garden cities of 1899 – *To-Morrow! A Peaceful Path to Real Reform*. Where Howard's garden city was utopian and radical, however, Abercrombie's scheme was extremely conservative. He imagined some fairly radical changes at the beginning, but once these changes were made, the urban system would fall into a steady state requiring only minor adjustments. All of this process was to take place under the watchful eye of well-trained professionals like himself.

Although the means used were different, a similar process was visible throughout northern Europe. In the Nordic countries and northern Germany, for example, many cities bought up land at the urban edge as a way to control development. In Holland much of the land available for urban development in the highly urbanized west of the country was state-owned because it was the result of the filling in of land to create polders.

Likewise with the various attempts to impose specific shapes on cities. Planners in Copenhagen and Hamburg, rather than using the simple circles of Ebenezer Howard's diagrams, preferred a 'finger plan.' In this model, new development would mimic older growth by pushing outward following transit lines. The space between the fingers would be protected as green space. The pattern favored for the Dutch Randstad, the urban concentration in western Holland around Amsterdam, Rotterdam and Utrecht, was the 'Green Heart.' Here, ironically, the logic was completely the reverse of the British system. The center was to remain green with the dense urban area around it.

Whatever the local variations, contradictions inherent in this kind of top-down broad-brush planning regime were apparent from an early date. As the American writer Jane Jacobs observed, this kind of planning favored an '...easily manageable and static pattern', quite opposed to the

messy vitality that had always been the essence of cities. By focusing on
the ultimate form rather than the urban process, it tended to lock future
generations into the assumptions and aesthetic preferences of one
generation. It protected certain parts of the landscape because of where
they happened to be, rather than because of their intrinsic quality.
It meant that land with no great agricultural or scenic value within a
greenbelt was protected, but land outside with very high value was not.
It also had the effect of preserving in amber for all time to come an
extremely undemocratic countryside; one that had been divided up
among the aristocracy during the feudal era and cleared of much of its
population by this aristocracy in the years of the Enclosure Movement.

As the years went on practical problems with the British growth
management system became more apparent. In fact the greenbelt failed
to contain London, and population spilled over it, not into tidy new
garden cities as Abercrombie had imagined, but across the entire
South East of England. Because jobs did not move outward as quickly
as residences, it created some very long commutes and mounting
congestion. Moreover, the effect of the greenbelt, in taking away a large
amount of land that could have been developed adjacent to existing
settlements along with the time and money it took to get permission to
build on land outside, was to dramatically restrain the creation of new
houses and force up housing prices. This, as Heartfield so clearly argues,
has resulted in housing shortages and high prices that hurt families of
modest income.

Despite all of these problems, the post World War II European
planning consensus has shown remarkable tenacity. The tradition of
fulminating aristocrats and literati has been carried on by in contemporary Britain by individuals, like the architect Lord Rogers of Riverside.
Advocates of restricting growth have attempted to bolster their case by
alarming statistics about economic efficiency, energy use, sustainability
and environment.

They have been very successful. Many of the features of the northern
European post-war planning system are now being tried in places as
far-flung as Portland, Oregon, Toronto, Ontario, Sydney and Singapore.
In some cases in manifestations that are even more rigid and coercive
than in Britain. And they have already yielded many of the same
unintended consequences. But the problems with this kind of planning
system do not concern many advocates because of the very real benefits

many of these advocates derive from the system. The soaring prices created by artificial scarcity benefit them as homeowners and landowners. The entire system is designed to protect the kind of urban neighborhoods in which they live, and the country houses where they vacation, while the problems fall most heavily on other parts of the population.

Their worldview has started to come increasingly under attack, however, as the cracks and in the doctrine have become more apparent. Members of the libertarian right, particularly in the United States, have argued that in any system as volatile and complicated as the city, the market provides a more efficient and equitable way of deciding land use issues than any system of top-down planning. From the political left come voices that decry the way traditional town cramming schemes tend to hurt families of modest means by making it much more difficult for them to own their own homes, while piling them up in exactly the parts of the urban area that have the lowest levels of service. Others have shown that high density does not guarantee sustainability, and nor does low density necessarily result in increased energy use or environmental problems.

There has also been a growing recognition of another paradoxical development. While most of the old European city centers continue to decline dramatically in density, even when they have been subject to stringent regulations attempting to stem sprawl, many American cities, particularly those in the South and West, have become denser without the intervention of major growth management schemes. So, for example, the city of Paris has dropped from over 3 million to barely over 2 million since the 1920s, while the suburban population has shot up. The city of Barcelona, the poster child for many advocates of density, has lost over a quarter of a million people in last quarter century. This is one of the fastest reductions in urban density in history, and at the same time suburbs have exploded across the countryside around Barcelona. Los Angeles, on the other hand, one of the lowest density urban areas in the world in the early twentieth century, has, like many of the fastest growing cities of the American South and West, become significantly denser since the 1950s. Yet it has had very little in the way of growth management until very recently. With just over 7,000 people per square mile, it is now North America's densest urbanized area, and as dense as many urban areas of northern Europe.

Whether because of these apparent paradoxes or because of the growing debate, or simply because of the inherent problems in the system itself, there has been a widespread rethinking of the old planning consensus. The Dutch, for example, even though they inhabit a country more densely populated than Britain, have realized that they don't need all their agricultural land. This realization coincides with a growing acceptance of the fact that most Dutch families, just like most families everywhere, would rather live in a single-family house than an apartment. They also realize that the fight to preserve clear distinctions between urban and rural is probably not possible, or even desirable. So the planning regime in the Netherlands, while hardly as permissive as that seen in southern Europe or North America, has been relaxed in the latest revision of the national spatial planning policies document. This also calls for a less intrusive role for the national government.

In the United States the problems with anti-sprawl and 'Smart Growth' policies have perhaps been less apparent, in part because few of them have been put into practice until recently, and nowhere have they yet produced any substantial increase in density. Even so, there has been a growing recognition in the United States of the problems of 'Smart Growth' on the one hand, and, on the other, the benefits of sprawl. A number of the places with the most stringent growth management schemes, for example the states of Oregon and Maryland, have seen these schemes buffeted by major setbacks at the hands of voters and public officials in recent years. Opposition to top-down, inflexible growth management schemes also appear to be consolidating in Canada, Australia and New Zealand, where government schemes heavily favoring compaction have been introduced in recent years. The architectural and artist elite of all these places, once united in its disdain for suburbia and sprawl, has started to show increasing signs of interest in the new and unexpected aesthetic possibilities provided by sprawl.

There is no inherent reason why urban areas of the future should be like those of the past. After all, a few hundred years ago most of the population of Britain or North America lived scattered across the agricultural countryside at very low densities. The enormous and dense cities that followed in the wake of the Industrial Revolution came to be not because they were planned, or that anyone thought that they were particularly good places for most people to live. They decidedly were not. They came to be the way they were because of the stringent demands of industrial production. Now that many of these demands have been loosened by new technologies and communications systems, there is no reason why our cities couldn't function in ways very different from the way they have in the past. New technology might allow us to live and get around in ways that we can scarcely imagine today.

Unfortunately, many of the current policies aimed at stopping sprawl have the effect of trying to cut off any experimentation with new urban forms, and to turn the clock backward. Clearly, James Heartfield's *Let's Build!* takes its place in a growing literature of discontent with this reigning planning system. His book provides a strong argument for exploring new, more democratic decision-making that could provide enormous benefits for all urban citizens.

Robert Bruegmann
July 2006

Robert Bruegmann is an historian of architecture, landscape and the built environment. He is professor and chair in the Art History Department at the University of Illinois at Chicago, where he is also professor of Architecture and Urban Planning. His book *Sprawl: A Compact History* was published by the University of Chicago Press in November 2005.

CHAPTER ONE

LET'S BUILD!

LET'S BUILD. LET'S BUILD FIVE MILLION NEW HOMES. LET'S BUILD THEM NOW.
Buyers want them. Labourers want to build them. The capital is there.
There is more than enough land to put them on.

There are more people looking for homes. In England alone,
there are 175,000 new households every year.[1] Government officials
reckon that in Britain, the population will have increased by 6.5 million
between 2004[2] and 2030.[3] Since households are getting smaller,
we rather need 5 million additional homes in a quarter century.[4]

But the number of homes being built each year is less than the
200,000 families, or other households, that want them.[5] In 2001 the
number of house completions was at its lowest since 1946 – or since
1924 if you exclude the war years.[6] That is why we need to build new
homes – to meet the growth in households.

And there is another problem. Since 1981 the number of homes
built has fallen short of the increase in households. Since 1991 the
shortfall has accumulated to become a backlog of more than half
a million homes.[7]

Of course it is true that there is not the kind of homelessness crisis
today that there has been in the past. The number of families that local
authorities have been able to put into temporary accommodation has
been growing since 1997.[8] Overall there has not been a big increase in
the number of people sleeping rough, though homelessness charities
accuse the government of manipulating the figures, and put the
number without secure accommodation as anywhere between
100,000[9] and 500,000.[10]

1] Alan Holmans and Christine Whitehead, 'Housing the next generation – Housing growth, housing demand and housing requirements', Town & Country Planning, Town and Country Planning Association, October 2005, p 301 to 304

2] Office of National Statistics, 'UK Population grows to 59.2 million', www.statistics.gov.uk

3] Office of National Statistics, 'United Kingdom population set to pass 60 million next year', 30 September 2004, www.statistics.gov.uk

4] Ian Abley, 'If London is so great, why not build more of it?', Rising East Online, December 2005, Issue Number 3, www.uel.ac.uk

5] 'Housebuilding: permanent dwellings started and completed, by tenure, Great Britain', Live Table 203, www.communities.gov.uk

6] John Stewart, 'Building a Crisis – Housing undersupply in England', May 2002, www.audacity.org

7] 'Housebuilding: permanent dwellings completed, by tenure, Great Britain', Live Table 243, read against 'Household Estimates and Projections, Great Britain, 1961-2021', Live Table 401, www.communities.gov.uk

8] Joseph Rowntree Foundation, Britain's housing in 2022: More shortages and homelessness? (York, York Publishing Services, 2002) p6, www.jrf.org.uk

**HOMES BUILT
IN BRITAIN FOR
ALL TENURES**

**HOUSEHOLD
GROWTH IN
BRITAIN**

**ANNUAL
HOUSEHOLD
GROWTH IN
BRITAIN**

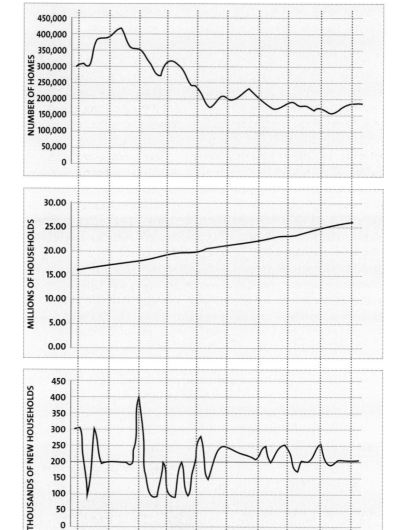

Source: Department of Communities and Local Government, Live Tables on
Housebuilding and Household Growth, www.communities.gov.uk

In past economic recessions people lost their livelihoods, and lost their homes, leaving them on the streets. Not so much today.

That is because the growing demand for homes is due to greater affluence, not recession. There are more people in work earning money to buy, up from 24 million in 1986 to 28.9 million in 2006.[11] People are living longer, with greater independence in old age. And more people are choosing to live alone. You might say that it is a good problem to have.[12] But still, the demand for homes is growing faster than the supply.

The reason that the shortfall in new house and flat construction does not lead to homelessness is that people just have to put up with their crowded living conditions. Parents get used to the idea that their grown up children are not moving out. People who would like to buy their own place share instead. And the overall number of houses is kept up because people prefer to repair them than replace them. Belgium apart, Britain's houses are the oldest in Europe. Over half in England were built before 1965 and over a third before 1945.[13] The House Building Federation's economic advisor, John Stewart, estimates that '... at current demolition rates in England, new homes built today will have to last 1500 years before it is their turn to be demolished.'[14] That is a lot of home improvements.[15] That is the short explanation for the growth in

9] Mark Townsend, 'Homeless total doubles as Labour backpedals on targets', Observer, 12 December 2004

10] Peter Hetherington, '50,000 homeless, claims charity', Guardian, 14 December 2004

11] www.statistics.gov.uk

12] Phil Mullan, The Imaginary Time Bomb: Why an ageing population is not a social problem (London, I.B Tauris, 2000)

13] 'Dwelling Stock: Year Built, by Region, England', DCLG, Live Table 110, www.communities. gov.uk

14] John Stewart, 'Building a Crisis – Housing Supply in Britain', July 2002, www.hbf.co.uk

15] James Woudhuysen and Ian Abley, Why is construction so backward? (Chichester, Wiley, 2004)

UK HOUSE PRICES: OVERVIEW (£ THOUSANDS)

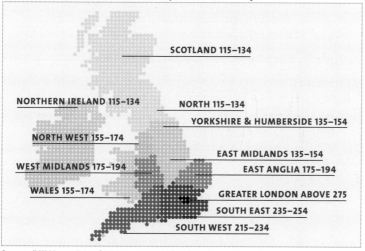

SCOTLAND 115–134

NORTHERN IRELAND 115–134

NORTH 115–134

YORKSHIRE & HUMBERSIDE 135–154

NORTH WEST 155–174

EAST MIDLANDS 135–154

WEST MIDLANDS 175–194

EAST ANGLIA 175–194

WALES 155–174

GREATER LONDON ABOVE 275

SOUTH EAST 235–254

SOUTH WEST 215–234

Source: 'UK House Prices', BBC News, posted on http://news.bbc.co.uk

16] ww.nationwide.co.uk
/hpi/

17] 'UK House Prices',
BBC News,
http://news.bbc.co.uk

18] Halifax, 'Halifax House
Price Index – January
2006', 9 February 2006,
www.hbosplc.com

19] Centre for Economics
and Business Research
Ltd, 'House prices to rise
6.0 per cent this year',
CEBR Forecasting Eye,
2 May 2006,
www.cebr.com

20] Ed Balls, 'On slippery
slopes', Building,
3 February 2006, p 22

21] Martin Pawley, Home
Ownership (London, The
Architectural Press, 1978)

22] Halifax, 'Value of UK
housing stock trebles over
10 years', 18 February
2006, www.hbosplc.com

23] Council of Mortgage
Lenders, 'Gross mortgage
lending by type of
advance', Table ML1,
www.cml.org.uk

house prices. House prices have grown so quickly that young families are struggling to get on the property ladder. In the year to May 2004 house prices rose by 19.5 per cent, or £24,000, giving a national average house price of £149,000.[16] Today it is £185,000. In the South East the average is £228,750, while in London, homes cost around £306,500.[17] Monthly payments on a mortgage of £150,000 at 5% are nearly £900. A typical first time buyer is now unable to afford the average house in 85 per cent of British towns.[18]

Demand is also fuelled by speculative investment in housing. Investors are always looking for a growing market into which they can put their money. The way that investment markets work means that growth begets growth. More investment increases demand, which in turn increases prices, increasing the value of investments. This investment spiral is unstable. And it migrates from industry to industry according to fashion. In the late nineties the investment market of choice was information technology. Before then investors were putting their money into the emerging markets of Russia and the Far East. The Dot.com bubble grew and grew, until it was out of all proportion to the earning potential of that market. Then the market slumped, and the investment cash moved on. The market that a lot of the investment moved into was housing.

The current structure of the housing market lends itself to speculative investment.[19] The shortage of new homes creates something like a monopoly.[20] Like the Dot.com shares, house prices look like a one-way bet to investors. Speculation in house prices is something that many people are involved in. It skews the market. But it need not be a bad thing. Though the Internet bubble got too big, it did put funds into new technologies that changed our lives for the better. The problem is that the massive investment in residential property is not giving rise to an increase in house building. Why is that?

The basic problem is that the housing market that is growing is a second-hand housing market.[21] The price increases are almost entirely accounted for by the growth in the cost of old houses, changing hands. In 2005 the value of the private housing stock in the United Kingdom stood at a staggering £3.4 trillion.[22] Total annual mortgage lending reached £288 billion in 2005. That year there were a million loans for house purchases, plus nearly 1.2 million remortgages and other secured loans,[23] but the number of new houses completed was just 167,000.[24] If all the mortgage money lent out each year were spent on new building, it would have paid for over one and a half million new homes.[25] Of course, redirecting resources from the second-hand housing market to building new homes would lead to a surplus, so that properties would lose their value as an investment.[26]

If the capital is available to build new homes, what about the labour? It is true that since the low in the early 1990s more people are working in construction. Around 2.5 million people work in the construction industry in 2006, across all occupations, including the professions. The Construction Industry Training Board says London alone needs 87 000 more construction workers each year.[27] Scaremongers like the British National Party warn about '...an emergency house building programme needed to provide extra accommodation because of the hundreds of thousands of immigrants arriving in Britain each year'.[28] But many immigrants are coming to Britain to build. The Housing Corporation's Yvonne Hutchinson knows that British recruitment fairs are looking for construction workers in the new Eastern member states of the European Union.[29] The Union of Construction, Allied Trades and Technicians has complained that foreign workers undercut their members, and in such high profile projects as the new Home Office Headquarters.[30] Even before we consider the potential for saving labour with new technologies, the potential for recruiting new construction workers is readily at hand.

But what about land: surely, there is not enough land to build the new homes on? The instinctive belief that Britain – and particularly the South East – is overcrowded is a very strong one. 'England is one of the most crowded countries in the world' according to the 2001 Green Paper; *Planning: Delivering a Fundamental Change*.[31] Seen from the ground it makes sense. Everywhere you look, there are other people. But then everywhere you look is already developed. Try taking to the skies. In a light aeroplane you can roam for hours over countryside that is empty of people.[32]

Just look at the numbers. Houses and roads take up almost 10 per cent of the landmass of Britain. Three-quarters of England is dedicated to farming.[33] Then consider that one third of that farming land is not needed to feed anyone.[34] In absolute terms there is a massive surplus of land. Developers are not even beginning to fill the vacuum left by Britain's shrinking farms.

24] 'Housebuilding: permanent dwellings started and completed, by tenure, Great Britain', DCLG, Live Table 203, www.communities. gov.uk

25] The National Housebuilding Council, 'Q4 2005 new house-building statistics UK', www.nhbc.co.uk

26] Jeremy Gates, 'Making housing affordable', Coventry Evening Telegraph, 11 February 2004, http://iccoventry.ic network.co.uk

27] Construction Industry Training Board, 'Blueprint for UK Construction 2006 – 2010', CITB, 2006, www.construction skills.net

28] Peter Young, 'Immigration forces Labour to build on the green belt', 11 February 2005, www.bnp.org.uk

29] Yvonne Hutchinson 'Where will we house the house builders?', Guardian, 20 May 2004, http://society.guardian. co.uk

30] 'Union denied access to foreign workers building new Home Office HQ', UCATT News Release, 7 November 2003, www.ucatt.org.uk

31] Department for Transport, Local Government and the Regions, 'Planning: Delivering a fundamental change' (London, TSO, 2001) p 1, previously posted on www.dtlr.gov.uk, www.communities. gov.uk

32] Peter Hall, Ray Thomas, Harry Gracey, and Roy Drewett, The Containment of Urban England: Urban and Metropolitan Growth Processes or Megalopolis Denied (London, George Allen & Unwin, 1973) Volume 1

33] R.M. Fuller, G.M. Smith, J.M. Sanderson, R.A. Hill, A.G. Thomson, R. Cox, N.J. Brown, R.T. Clarke, P. Rothery and F.F. Gerard, Land Cover Map 2000 – Module 7 Final Report (Huntingdon, Cambridgeshire, CEH, 2000) and posted on www.cs2000.org.uk

34] James Heartfield, 'Town and Country in perspective', in Ian Abley and James Heartfield, editors, Sustaining Architecture in the Anti-Machine Age (Chichester, Wiley-Academy, 2001) p 142 to 151

35] Alan Holmans and Christine Whitehead, 'Housing the next generation – Housing growth, housing demand and housing requirements', Town & Country Planning, Town and Country Planning Association, October 2005, Volume 74, Number 10, p 301 to 304

36] Building Research Establishment, 'LPS 2020:2006 – Loss Prevention Standard for Innovative Systems, Elements and Components for Residential Buildings (Garston, BRE Certification, 2006) www.redbooklive.com

With the decline in farm acreage land is readily available; with European enlargement there is no shortage of labour; with £288 billion of lending invested annually in homes there is no shortage of capital, and the unmet demand is driving up prices. Every factor of production is present. So what should we aim to build?

Experts say 200,000 new households need new homes every year. To that must be added some housing for families who have recently been frustrated from setting up homes on their own, and homes to anticipate a higher level of immigration than is being forecast.[35] Also, homes do not last forever. We must add the number of homes required for the replacement of existing properties as they age beyond repair. The Building Research Establishment recommends that innovative residential buildings should be designed to last for 60 years.[36] Georgian and Victorian housing has often lasted much longer than 100 years, but has required a lot of renovation. To replace the housing stock as it increases from 24 to 29 million on an average 100 year cycle requires us to build an average of 266,000 every year.[37] There are then three components to calculate the housing we need in Britain in the next decade:

> New household formation recognised at 200,000 per annum – currently

> Additional housing, to relieve overcrowded families and anticipate greater immigration, at, say, 34,000 per annum – an underestimation

> Housing stock replacement on a 100 year cycle at 266,000 per annum – a low rate of renewal

Building five million new homes in Britain in the next 10 years is not a problem: it is a tremendous opportunity. Whole new cities, towns, suburbs, conurbations, country mansions are waiting to be built. Architects – are you not bored with arts centres yet? Design homes. Planners – a blank page is waiting to be filled. Developers – are you not in the business of making money? Builders, there is plenty of work for everyone. Politicians – get popular, and leave a monument you can be proud of. Cynics, what is your problem? Life is not a rehearsal. These days, once they are over, are gone forever. Let's build, and let's start now.

THOSE FOUR MILLION NEW HOMES

In 1999, Lord Richard Rogers of Riverside, chairman of an Urban Task Force appointed by the new Labour government asked:

> *'How can we improve the quality of both our towns and countryside while at the same time providing homes for almost 4 million additional households in England over a 25 year period?'* [38]

The question was interesting because it was already quite a revision of the original proposition made by the (Tory) environment secretary John Selwyn Gummer in 1996. Gummer called for an additional 4.4 million homes to be built in England by 2016, but counted from 1991.[39] Gummer based his proposal on the projected increase in the number of households. 'This is indeed the lowest figure which one can safely present', he said, explaining: 'I chose the lowest number I could truthfully support'.[40] In fact, after Gummer's officials prepared the statistics on which the projection was based, it was revised upwards. In 1998 the statisticians reckoned they had underestimated household growth as a consequence of migration to the South East of England. Actually, we needed 5.5 million new homes.[41]

Lord Rogers' brief, set by Prime Minister Tony Blair, overseen by his Deputy John Prescott, was for 3.8 million new homes. But this was not just a moderation of previous expectations. It knocked them into the long grass. The target date for this smaller increase was 2021 – five years later than John Gummer's. In 2021, Sir Richard will be 88, John Prescott will be 83, and even our youthful Prime Minister will by three years past retirement age. Back in 1999 it seemed unlikely that any of them would be held to his promise of – nearly – four million new homes. But very quickly the mood began to shift. In 2004 the Prime Minister told Labour MPs that a pledge to boost house building would form a centrepiece of Labour's general election manifesto – though in the 2005 election it faded from view.[42] Already in October 2002, Deputy PM Prescott told an Urban Summit that '...we're building fewer new homes than at any time since the 1920s. That has to change'.[43] Even the 'prudent' Chancellor Gordon Brown made clear in his annual Mansion House speech of 2004 that the government was going to tackle '...to tackle the large and unacceptable imbalance between supply and demand in the British housing market'.[44]

37] Ian Abley, 'If London is so great, why not build more of it?', Rising East Online, University of East London, December 2005, Issue Number 3, www.uel.ac.uk

38] Lord Richard Rogers, chairman of the Urban Task Force, Introduction, Towards an Urban Renaissance – Final Report of the Urban Task Force (London, HMSO, Spon, 1999) p 7

39] John Gummer, Secretary of State for the Environment, Foreword, Household Growth – Where shall we live? (London, Department of the Environment, 1996)

40] John Selwyn Gummer, 'Those four million homes', in Anthony Barnett and Roger Scruton, editors, Town and Country (London, Jonathan Cape, 1998) p 180. (Gummer gives the year of 2006, not 2016, but this is a proofing error in the book)

41] 'UK household growth expected to rise', BBC News, 19 January 1998, http://news.bbc.co.uk

42] Paul Waugh, 'Blair: Housing as important as health', Evening Standard, 17 June 2004, www.thisislondon.co.uk

43] John Prescott, Deputy Prime Minister, 'Speech to the Urban Summit', 31 October 2002, www.communities. gov.uk

44] Gordon Brown, Chancellor of the Exchequer, 'Mansion House Speech', 16 June 2004, www.hm-treasury.gov.uk

45] Kate Barker, Barker review of housing supply – delivering stability: securing our future housing needs – Final Report and Recommendations (London, HMSO, 2004), www.barkerreview.org.uk

46] Nick Mathiason, 'The scourge of the nimby brigade', Observer, Business, 21 March 2004, http://observer.guardian.co.uk/business/

47] 'Housebuilding: permanent dwellings started and completed, by tenure, England', DCLG, Live Table 204, www.communities.gov.uk

48] Shaun Spiers, 'Curb demand for Housing', Guardian, 28 February 2005, http://society.guardian.co.uk

49] George Monbiot, 'Britain's Most Selfish People', 25 May 2006, www.monbiot.com

The government signalled its new course with a *Review of Housing Supply* by the Bank of England's Monetary Policy Committee member Kate Barker, a former chief economic adviser to the Confederation of British Industry and chief economist at Ford Europe. In 2004 Barker reported that between 200,000 and 250,000 new homes for sale should be built each year in England, with up to an additional 30,000 housing association homes for rent.[45] Rather than depending on household projections, Barker took the empirical evidence of prices. 'The question we ought to have asked is: can people in a locality afford to live in houses there?'[46] Once again, the target was modest. At these rates, it would take until between 2018 and 2021 to build four million new homes. None the less Barker's review became a signal of a new willingness to build as well as a focus for opposition to development.

It is not hard to understand the renewed urgency around housing. The exponential rise in house prices is hurting. And politicians who are keen to get back on to a domestic agenda after the long distraction of the war in Iraq recognise the appeal of a bricks-and-mortar issue. What is harder to explain is why was the housing question allowed to drift for so long? After all, Gummer's original target of 4.4 million new homes by 2016 is only a decade away, and since 1991 some 2,640,000 should have been built by now. Since 1991 about 2,285,000 homes have been built in England.[47] If that carries on to 2016 we will have built 590,000 fewer homes than the Department of the Environment calculated would be needed for household growth alone. Yet Gummer's 4.4 million over 25 years always underestimated the housing needed in England, and was silent on that more widely needed in Britain. (See Box: Why we need five million new homes in the next 10 years)

This is a problem of supply, not demand. Shaun Spiers of the Campaign to Protect Rural England thinks we need to curb the demand for housing. Against all the evidence he thinks that more than enough homes are being built. Spiers' solution is to reduce demand, by increasing the tax on home ownership and mortgages – as if house prices were not high enough already.[48] *Guardian* columnist, George Monbiot thinks that the reason that there are too few homes is because of the number of second homes.[49] Two hundred and fifty thousand second homes is about the same number as the homeless. But the shortfall in homes built **each year** exceeds the number of second homes. And the only reason that second homes are an investment is because of the artificially high

WHY WE NEED FIVE MILLION NEW HOMES IN THE NEXT 10 YEARS

>> Between 2004 and 2030 the population of Britain is expected to increase by 6.5 million, to about 64 million.

>> Over a quarter of a century the number of households is expected to rise by 5 million, to 29 million.

>> That translates to a demand for 200,000 new homes each year just to meet estimates of household growth.

>> On top of that, we need to build 266,000 homes each year, to demolish and replace the most dilapidated British housing stock.

>> Together, new households and replacement stock add up to a demand for 466 000 new homes each year.

>> Since 1990 the number of new homes built in Britain has not once exceeded 200,000, and has been as low as 161,000 in 2001.

>> That means that the shortfall in construction has been between 266,000 and 305,000 homes a year, every year.

>> Just to meet the increased number of households and replace worn out existing stock, we need to build 4,660,000 homes in the next 10 years.

>> To address the shortfall in the preceding years, to relieve overcrowded families, and anticipate greater immigration, we need to build more than that: an additional 340,000 is probably an underestimate.

>> We need five million new homes in the next 10 years.

50] David Miliband, Minister of Communities and Local Government, interviewed by James Heartfield, 'People, not architecture, make communities', in Ian Abley and Jonathan Schwinge, 'Manmade Modular Megastructures', AD magazine, January/February 2006, Wiley-Academy, p 20 to 23

51] www.communities. gov.uk

52] Michael Winter, replying to the author at Rural Futures, University of Plymouth, 5 to 7 April 2006, www.ruralfuturesconfere nce.org

53] www.thames-gateway.org.uk

54] Eric Sorensen, discussing the Thames Gateway with the author at the Shanghai Administration Institute Programme, Oxford University Department for Continuing Education, 10 June 2006, www.conted.ox.ac.uk

55] Paul Barker, 'Prescott Speaks But Does Anything Happen?' Evening Standard, 11 August 2005

56] Ian Abley, 'A lack of commitment in the Labour 'commitment' of a decent home for all', 12 October 2003, www.audacity.org

prices, caused by the lack of supply. Forcible redistribution or billeting might be a solution in extreme circumstances, like war, or revolution. But a less dramatic option might be to build more homes, so that unequal distribution is less onerous. Monbiot's editor at the *Guardian* can rest easy: Alan Rusbridger's second home will not have to be confiscated yet.

WHAT TO DO?

The Labour government has often said that it would get the homes built. Former Communities and Local Government Minister David Miliband counters the anxieties people have over mass-building by saying '...there is an anxiety among parents that their children will not have somewhere to live'.[50] Like Prescott, Miliband said that there needed to be a 'step change' in the building of new homes. But according to Michael Winter of the South West Rural Affairs Forum it is Miliband's old department, now with Ruth Kelly and renamed the Department for Communities and Local Government,[51] which is stopping new homes being built.[52] And Eric Sorensen, chief executive of the Thames Gateway London Partnership,[53] says there has been no step change in building new homes. According to Sorensen it was typical of the problem that housing agencies have with government that just as Miliband understood the need for a change of gear, he was moved.[54]

The government's problem is that even when it recognises the need for change, as Kelly also seems to, change is against its nature. Scoffing at fears that the Deputy Prime Minister will '...concrete over the South East', sociologist Paul Barker offers the motto: 'Prescott Speaks But Does Anything Happen?'[55] This government is too nervous of letting go to let homes get built. Once, the government aimed to build half a million homes a year, and contractors built in the hundreds of thousands.[56] But now they do not. If private developers are to build houses, they need to be allowed to do it.

In a trilogy of reports for the think tank Policy Exchange, Alan Evans and Oliver Marc Hartwich explained how the Planning Law has become a barrier to building new homes.[57] They do not go so far as Mischa Balen writing for the Adam Smith Institute, who makes an excellent argument that '...there is a strong case for the planning process to be abolished'.[58] I agree with him. Abolish the Planning Law. But even that does not go far enough.[59]

Yes, government must stop putting barriers in the way of new house building. But it would be naïve to imagine that once the restraints were lifted, developers would spring into action. It is funny to hear people worrying about a free for all if there was no Planning Law. What country are they living in? This is not East Europe or China. Our developers are not red in tooth and claw. They are tired, risk averse, 'Timid Corporations'.[60] British developers are 'Cowardly Capitalists'.[61]

Developers will have to be persuaded to build the housing we need. They will need to be persuaded by government subsidy. Do not go all coy about it. We know that this is how things happen. Governments subsidise industry all the time. They provide credits, and invest in infrastructure. Instead of trying to put a leash on the developers, who are hardly straining at it, they should try and tempt them with a juicy bone or two.

Government could commission road and rail links to make new areas of development attractive. They could provide incentives to first time buyers, like tax relief, or for that matter they could restore mortgage interest tax relief for every mortgage on a new home.

And yes, government could frame national priorities for areas of development. That is legitimate – as long as those priorities are expressed in rewards, not restraints. Unfortunately, the Planning Law does not represent a considered policy of national priority.[62] Instead it is a farrago of Not-In-My-Back-Yard prejudice. This book will examine how Planning Law empowers the prevention, but not the building of houses. In the routine negotiation of Planning Law new housing is presented only as a problem – so that people never connect their own difficulties buying with the determination to stop new homes being built in their back yards, or the countryside.

This book is a case for building five million new homes – the least that we will need by 2016. But it is also an attempt to understand what is getting in the way of building those homes. In the following pages we look more closely at some of the barriers to growth.

57] Alan Evans and Oliver Marc Hartwich, Unaffordable Housing – Fables and Myths (London, Policy Exchange, 2005), Bigger, Better, Faster, More – Why some countries plan better than others (London, Policy Exchange, 2005), Better Homes, Greener Cities (London, Policy Exchange, 2006)

58] Mischa Balen, Land Economy: How a rethink of our planning policy will benefit Britain (London, Adam Smith Institute, 2006) p.13, www.adamsmith.org

59] Jonathan Hughes and Simon Sadler, editors, Non-Plan: Essays on freedom, participation and change in modern architecture and urbanism (Oxford, Architectural Press, 2000)

60] Ben Hunt, The Timid Corporation: Why business is terrified of taking risk (Chichester, Wiley, 2003)

61] Daniel Ben-Ami, Cowardly capitalism: the myth of the global financial casino (Chichester, John Wiley & Sons, 2001)

62] Kate Barker, Barker Review of Land Use Planning: Interim Report – Analysis (London, HMSO, 2006) p 6, www.communities. gov.uk

CHAPTER TWO

NOT IN MY BACK YARD

'GREY SKIES OVER GREEN AND PLEASANT LAND', AND 'PLANS FOR 250,000 homes in the South will be the greatest destruction since the Luftwaffe'.[63] 'Suburban sprawl,' [64] 'Prescott's concrete countryside,' [65] 'Plan looms to concrete 1000 miles of Britain',[66] 'The rape of rural life by urban politicians' – these are just some of the headlines responding to the Barker *Review of Housing Supply*.[67]

It was John Mortimer, the former barrister and creator of the television hit *Rumpole of the Bailey*, who saw rural life raped by urban politicians, during a lifetime '...spent on the edge of the Chiltern Hills.' A lifetime commuting in to London to work, one assumes. 'No to Mr Prescott's tide of concrete', writes an emotional Mortimer: 'Our green and pleasant land simply cannot accommodate it.' As so often in this kind of rhetoric, the contrast is between rural idyll, and urban depravity – '... these fields and forests are havens of peace and sanity, refuges from the disintegrating chaos of the modern world, and now they are to be sacrificed,' to 'New Labour's mania for concrete'. Mortimer's view is apocalyptic: 'Southern England is to be a land concreted with up to one and a half million new houses, all well supplied with supermarkets and service stations but with absolutely no room for any glorious Jerusalem.'[68]

Nevertheless, John Mortimer's fears are echoed by the Campaign to Protect Rural England's head of planning, Henry Oliver, objecting to plans to develop the M11/Cambridge area: 'Growth on this scale could engulf many of our most beautiful historic towns and villages,' so that they become '...part of a continuous suburban swath of housing, business parks, new roads and runways.'[69] TV historian Tristram Hunt

63] Duncan Campbell, 'Grey skies over green and pleasant land', Guardian, 8 May 2004

64] Evening Standard, 19 December 2003

65] Daily Mail, 31 July 2003

66] Observer, 16 May 2004

67] Kate Barker, Barker review of housing supply – delivering stability: securing our future housing needs – Final Report and Recommendations (London, HMSO, 2004), www.barkerreview.org.uk

68] John Mortimer, Daily Mail, 31 July 2003

69] Henry Oliver,
Guardian, 22 October
2003

70] Tristram Hunt,
Observer, 8 December
2002

71] Sir Sandy Bruce
Lockhart, Observer,
21 March 2004

72] Finian Davern,
'Suburban Sprawl',
Evening Standard,
19 December 2003

warned of '...a massive construction programme set to engulf what remains of Britain's rural heritage'.[70] Meanwhile Sir Sandy Bruce Lockhart, leader of Kent County Council worries that government plans would lead to an '...increase in national housebuilding that equals the loss of greenfield land the size of Manchester'.[71] Another Manchester: God forbid! Nigel Kersey, London director of the Campaign to Protect Rural England warns '...if this plan goes ahead, in 20 years time that green belt won't be there.'[72] That would be a turn up for the books indeed, since as Kate Barker shows in the interim report of her *Review of Land Use Planning*, nearly 13 per cent of England is Green Belt, and much more than is developed. (See Box: How much of Britain is developed?)

DESIGNATED LANDSCAPE	NUMBER OF SITES	HECTARES	% OF LAND
Sites of Special Scientific Interest (SSSIs)	4110	1,072,540	8.2
Special Protection Areas (SPAs)	77	609,249	4.7
Special Areas of Conservation (SACs)	229	809,199	6.2
Area of Outstanding Natural Beauty (AONB)	35	2,040,000	15.6
Green Belt		1,678,200	12.9
National Parks		994,000	7.6
Total of Designated Landscape		7,203,188	55.2
Urban Areas		1,100,000	8.3

Source: Kate Barker, *Barker Review of Land Use Planning: Interim Report – Executive Summary* (London, HMSO, 2006) Table 1: Designations and other land uses in England, posted on www.hm-treasury.gov.uk

73] Max Hastings,
quoted in press release,
Campaign to Protect
Rural England, 'Battle of
Hastings – Sir Max says
Mobilise to Save the
Countryside', 17 June
2004, www.cpre.org.uk

In June 2004, launching the annual report of the Campaign to Protect Rural England, its president Sir Max Hastings objected that '... in recent years, the word Nimby – not in my backyard – has been given a pejorative meaning, by housebuilders and politicians whom local democracy does not suit.' He continued:

> *'Yet it seems to me a fundamental and absolutely proper right that local people should have a real voice in what is done to their own community. Why should not people object to horrible things being done in their backyards?'*[73]

The former *Daily Telegraph* and *Evening Standard* editor called on his army of Nimbys '... to fight to secure the English countryside for future generations'.

Sir Max also expressed alarm at the massive increase in house building recommended by Kate Barker in her *Review of Housing Supply* for the Treasury. 'If Barker's proposal is implemented,' said the military historian, '...it will provoke the most reckless invasion of the rural environment staged by any government in history.'[74] Over at the *Guardian*, economics editor Larry Elliott was sceptical:

'It takes real chutzpah to be pictured by the Sunday Times lolling against the gates of your country estate while asking insouciantly: "Do we not owe it to our descendants to check our obsession with house-ownership before it devastates what is left of rural England?"'[75]

Sir Max's one-time Brussels correspondent, now Tory MP for Henley,

74] Max Hastings, Guardian, 17 June 2004

75] Larry Elliott, Guardian, 25 March 2004

76] 'Land cover by Broad Habitat and Standard Statistical Regions, 1998', Table 11.11, www.statistics.gov.uk

77] ODPM, 'The South East: Land Use Statistics for 2001', 28 February 2005, www.visionofbritain.org.uk

78] Office of National Statistics, 'Woodland Increasing – Amounts and conditions of habitats in Britain', 14 August 2002, www.statistics.gov.uk

79] www.cs2000.org.uk/Report_pdf/exec.pdf

80] R.M. Fuller, G.M. Smith, J.M. Sanderson, R.A. Hill, A.G. Thomson, R. Cox, N.J. Brown, R.T. Clarke, P. Rothery and F.F. Gerard, Land Cover Map 2000 – Module 7 Final Report (Huntingdon, Cambridgeshire, CEH, 2000) and www.cs2000.org.uk

81] Department of the Environment, Food and Rural Affairs, Accounting for nature: assessing habitats in the UK countryside (London, DEFRA, 2000) www.defra.gov.uk

HOW MUCH OF BRITAIN IS DEVELOPED?

In reality, in the South East of England, more than three quarters of all land is woodland (9.7 per cent), arable and horticulture (41.8 per cent), or grassland (27.5 per cent). The extent of the South East estimated to be developed is between 7.3 per cent,[76] and 10.7 per cent.[77] The South East is certainly no more developed than the rest of the country. Britain is 23.5 million hectares, used in 2002 as follows:

> intensive agricultural land 10.8 million hectares or 45.96 per cent
> semi-natural land 7.0 million hectares or 29.78 per cent
> woodland 2.8 million hectares or 11.91 per cent
> settled land accounts for 1.8 million hectares or 7.65 per cent
> water bodies 0.3 million hectares or 1.28 per cent
> sundry other categories 0.8 million hectares or 3.42 per cent[78]

If settlements are added to most of the 'sundry' component of largely transport infrastructure, such as roads and railways, then the total developed area is about 2.3 million hectares, or almost 10 per cent of Britain.[79] The three countries of Britain differ markedly, with intensive agricultural uses affecting nearly three-quarters of England and about half of Wales; in Scotland, less than a quarter is intensively farmed or developed.[80] About 90 per cent of Britain as a whole, and the South East of England in particular, remains undeveloped.[81]

82] Boris Johnson,
Hansard, 13 Jan 2004

Boris Johnson is more cautious about adopting '... the ancient vice, endemic to our country, of nimbyism'. He told the House of Commons that '...the very people who demonstrate, who write passionate letters to me, who fill the town halls of our market towns demanding that local hospitals be kept alive and who want more nurses, policemen and bus drivers in the area, are, alas, all too often the very people who oppose the construction of houses in which such people could live'. But Johnson's caution was only preliminary to his own exercise of 'good nimbyism' in opposition to new homes in South Oxford.[82] 'Shame on you Nimbys,' Johnson is saying, '...but not in my back yard'.

'Not in my back yard' is a cry of despair. The whole point is that it is not your back yard. If it was, you could refuse to let them build there. 'Back yard' is a euphemism for the land you do not own, but that forms part of your environment. The desire to control one's 'back yard' is a desire to control not the physical, so much as the social environment. It would be naïve to think that the ownership of a house was just the possession of a thing. The value of the property is dependent on its location – which is to express in spatial terms, a social relationship. Buying a property relatively isolated from volume built homes or 'social housing' estates is a way of establishing a relationship to others. The attraction of greenery, views, and air is not really to do with the exhalations of plants or aesthetics alone; it is about establishing distance from other people, or, more precisely, about establishing control over one's relations to other people. To be really isolated would be a disaster. A house with no driveway, or access to shops would be unattractive, but so would one hard up against a busy highroad, or overlooked by a supermarket car park.

In taking possession of a house, the owner hopes to own more than the bricks and mortar; he hopes to take hold of his relationship to his neighbours. The net of relations between homeowner and neighbourhood are extensive, including immediate neighbours, local shopping, transport, nearby schools, nearby nightlife – and all are full of advantages and pitfalls. But relationships are not things, and not so easy to keep in one's possession. The home you bought can be changed in just a short time, from a 'Des-Res' to a 'home-from-hell'. New developments nearby are a great source of anxiety for people who are struggling to maintain control over their situation.

Unfortunately, the way that the debate over housing is being played out makes a Nimby out of everyone. That is because all sides are being set against each other in a contest over land as **if it were in short supply**. But the truth is urban areas account for no more than 10 per cent of the entire country. 'The conventional map shows a country dominated by agriculture', say statisticians Daniel Dorling and Bethan Thomas.[83] Eighty-nine per cent of all Britons live in urban areas. Who is the countryside being saved for? Britain's elite has considered the country-side their personal fiefdom ever since they drove the peasants off of it and into the towns.[84] In Patrick Wright's account '... country-folk view the city as the nightmare domain of a mongrel population that should be confined at all costs, stacked up in tower blocks and further walled in, if at all possible, by the green belt'.[85]

Successive attempts have been made to keep the proles in the towns, where they belong, reserving the green and pleasant land for the nobs. Unfortunately that was never an easy ambition to reconcile with democracy. For Britain's growing middle class, like John Mortimer's father, the rural life was a model to imitate. Lacking the same resources, but with far greater numbers they populated the first suburbs in the early twentieth century.[86] Working people, too, aspired to take back the countryside. On 24 April 1932 the Manchester Communist Benny Rothman led 200 on a trespass on Kinder Scout, the highest hill in the Peak District to establish rights of access – which were only granted in the Countryside and Rights of Way Act two years before he died.[87] Families from the East End of London started to live in the holiday huts they made at Pitsea and Laindon in Essex, such that '...by the end of World War II there was a settled population of about 25,000 on 75 miles of grass-track roads, mostly un-sewered and with standpipes for water supply'. In 1949 it was designated a new town; Basildon.[88] In fact most of the new towns in the South East were built on top of unplanned developments of pattern book bungalows, self-built shacks, and converted railway carriages, that ordinary people had made between the wars.[89]

The flight from the city is a contradiction whichever class is making it. It is often driven by disdain for the city, and yet it tends to urbanise the countryside in turn. Broadcaster Rod Liddle is aware of the paradox. The former *Today* editor told Lyn Barber: 'We need space. We crave it. And that's why so many people wish to move out of London.'[90] Once in his castle, the Englishman raises the drawbridge against anyone who might be tempted to follow him. According to novelist Christopher

83] Daniel Dorling and Bethan Thomas, People and Places: A 2001 Census Atlas of the UK (Bristol, The Policy Press, 2004)

84] Arnold J Toynbee, The Industrial Revolution in England (Newton Abbot, Devon, David and Charles, 1969) first published 1884

85] Patrick Wright, 'An Encroachment too Far', in Anthony Barnett and Roger Scruton, editors, Town and Country (London, Jonathan Cape, 1998) p 32

86] Simon Gunn and Rachel Bell, 'Building Middle England – Suburbia between the wars', Middle Classes: Their Rise and Sprawl (London, Orion, 2002)

87] Benny Rothman, obituary, Guardian, 25 January 2002

88] Peter Hall and Colin Ward, Sociable Cities: the legacy of Ebenezer Howard (Chichester, John Wiley, 1998) p 76

89] Dennis Hardy and Colin Ward, Arcadia for All: The Legacy of a Makeshift Landscape (Nottingham, Five Leaves, 2004)

90] Lynn Barber, 'Liddle at large', Observer, 5 October 2003

91] Christopher Hart, Guardian, 12 August 2000

92] David Blackmore, 'Are You Local?' Guardian, 13 February 2002

93] Duncan Campbell, 'Grey skies over green and pleasant land', Guardian, 8 May 2004

94] Anthony Barnett, Iron Britannia (London, Allison and Busby, 1983) p 102

95] Angus Calder, The Myth of the Blitz (London, Pimlico, 1992) p 182 to 183

96] Patrick Wright, 'An Encroachment too Far', in Anthony Barnett and Roger Scruton, editors, Town and Country (London, Jonathan Cape, 1998) p 24

97] Iain Sinclair, London Orbital: A walk around the M25 (London, Penguin, 2003) p 328

Hart, suburbanites can quickly turn into Nimbys: 'Once installed in Rose Cottage it is then the townies who are the most vociferous campaigners against any new, low-cost, and probably rather ugly housing in the village: squat, grey, pebble-dashed, and proudly boasting aluminium window frames.' Which Hart observes are, '...precisely the kind that the low-waged locals need to buy or rent'.[91]

Home ownership can bring out the worst in people. Development plans drafted by New Forest Council refuse planning permission to all dwellings not earmarked for people who can show a local connection for at least seven years.[92] Eastleigh and Winchester Councils, too, have succumbed to pressure from the Nimbies, and stopped planned housing developments. In 2002 Kent County Council wanted to plan for fewer homes than the target for the county set in the South East regional planning guidance. Meanwhile in Apsley Guise, the Bedfordshire village just off the M1, Pat Clarke insists: 'Obviously we want local houses for local people, but there isn't the infrastructure for more than that. The hospitals are full already. We don't want the parish to be swallowed up.' Alf Murray, chairman of the nearby Mid Bedfordshire District council planning consortium wants to set limits: 'We have never said no to housing here, but we do not want housing built for commuters.' You can hear the drawbridge coming up: 'If they want to double Milton Keynes in size, surely to God they do not want to come to small villages.'[93]

The enduring theme of the invasion of rural England – with the implication that the invading forces are foreign, like the 'Luftwaffe' draws upon war propaganda. Frank Newbould's poster 'Deep England' in the *Your Britain* series for the Army Bureau of Current Affairs pictures an idealised village green, complete with picnicking cyclists and church, echoing Stanley Baldwin's nostrum 'England is the country'.[94] Though most of the casualties were from the cities, Britons were called upon to protect their countryside from the invading horde.[95] In 1944, Lady Eve Balfour, founder of the Soil Association likened the 'conquest of nature' in the English countryside to '...the Nazi conquest of Europe'.[96] In fact it is a fantasy that goes at least as far as 1871, when novelist George Chesney published *The Battle of Dorking*, which imagines '...the Home Counties ravished by cruel Huns'.[97]

In the contest over an artificially-restricted supply of land, the competing parties are wont to see the worst in each other. Author Melissa Jones writes: 'Because people are sick of the city, they should not be allowed to poison the country, too.'[98] People are cast here as toxic. It is a hostility to others that is shared by Rod Liddle: 'I don't want any more people in this country...I'd rather people left. I don't care what colour they are, I just think the density of population is too great... I just don't want the South East of England paved.'[99]

Let it be said that there is no danger whatsoever that the South East of England will be paved. Still, it is striking that in the Nimby mentality urban growth is a disease. Sir Crispin Tickell, director of the Centre for Environmental Policy, University of Oxford and a member of Lord Rogers Urban Renaissance Taskforce, told BBC2's *Newsnight* that Britain's cities were a source of overpopulation:

'You have cities that are expanding which require water and materials of different kinds, and you can degrade the environment thereby. You also have to dispose of the wastes of the product of the city including all the pollution...with immigration you are in fact increasing the population...constantly increasing growth is the doctrine of the cancer cell. You just get out of control.[100]

Sir Crispin was promoting a conference organised by the Optimum Population Trust, which believes the UK must set an example to the world and reduce its population from nearly 60 million to 30 million by 2121.[101] The OPT argues that, as the birth rate is already very low, the only way to do this is to all but stop immigration. Patrons include Sir Crispin Tickell, and Jonathan Porritt, the former head of Friends of the Earth, and now chairman of the Government's Sustainable Development Commission.[102]

Crispin Tickell, a former guardsman and career diplomat was Chairman of the Sustainable Development Panel that was subsumed into the Commission under Porritt. Then he summed up the prejudices of the age when he urged the government not to build new homes arguing that '...if you build more houses,' all that will happen is that '...more people will live alone rather than live in couples with granny upstairs'.[103] John Mortimer agrees: 'With fewer houses being built some people who had thought about divorce might stay together because they could not afford two homes.' What is more, 'Teenagers might, reluctantly, accept that they have to stay with their parents for longer.'[104] Sir Crispin's residence is listed in *Who's Who* as a Somerset farmhouse, while John Mortimer lives near Henley-on-Thames in a house built by his father, a divorce lawyer.

98] Melissa Jones, Blueprint, February, 2002

99] Lynn Barber, 'Liddle at large', Observer, 5 October 2003

100] Sir Crispin Tickell, Newsnight, BBC2, 20 August 2003

101] www.optimum population.org

102] Juliette Jowit, 'Alarm at plan to halve UK population', Observer, 28 September 2003

103] Sir Crispin Tickell, Telegraph, 6 February 1998

104] John Mortimer, Daily Mail, 31 July 2003

105] Steven Morris,
'Campaigners rekindle
spirit of Newbury',
Guardian, 9 July 2003

But there are other reasons that Nimbyism has taken off recently. As one environmentalist protester against the Arundel by-pass in West Sussex put it:

'After Newbury, John Major's government realised its plans had managed to bring together an unlikely alliance between scumbuckets like us and Middle England. When they understood that, they realised they had big trouble. It looks as if the Labour government is going to have to learn the same lessons that we taught the Conservatives.' [105]

This activist's recollections of the anti-road protests are rather better than his prospects for recreating it. An alliance of shire Tories with grungy eco-warriors combined to oppose housing developments and motorway extensions, such as those at Oxleas Wood or the Newbury by-pass. This kind of activism drew on a purposeful minority, but rarely won the support of all locals, since many were themselves the users of the facilities that were being protested against. But beyond the local countryside, such road protesters articulated an inchoate disappointment with modern living, the misery of congested roads and box-like developments. The Major government responded by suspending new road building and transport minister Stephen Norris declared retrospectively that the protesters 'were right' – a concession that made them even more self-righteous than they already were.

Can the anti-road protests be recreated ten years later? It seems unlikely that they could achieve the same impact. Younger protesters are now occupied with other issues, like the anti-war movement. But a deep-seated scepticism with mainstream politics certainly does give a ready formula to the Grunge-Nimby axis. No sooner does the Deputy Prime Minister float the prospect of building new homes than he is greeted with outrage in Tunbridge Wells, and pretty much the rest of the Home Counties too.

The real tragedy of the debate over housing, though, is that it has been established as a zero-sum game. It ought to be one in which all sides can win. The assumption that this is a small island with just a few green spaces left is wildly inaccurate. Of course, that is how it looks, as you are walking, or driving around, surrounded by buildings that are much higher than your eye-level. But then very few of us spend that much time in the vast tracts of open countryside that dominate Britain.

Instead we usually prefer built-up places with the amenities that make life comfortable, and draw the wrong conclusion that the whole country looks like that. As we will see, there is not a shortage but a massive surplus of land in Britain, and even in the South East, that could be developed without leading to the abolition of England's green and pleasant land.

The reason that the argument over building houses has turned so bad-tempered is not because of an absolute shortage of land, but because the government has set out to restrict the land available for development. Adopting a long-term policy of constraining new building into tightly defined areas, the area of land legally available for development is indeed in (artificially) restricted supply. It is this constraint on the available land that makes a jealous, small-minded Nimby out of everyone. Policies that are designed to restrict development lead – unnecessarily – to people being crammed into areas that are too small to house them. Post-war policies of easing overcrowding have been reversed to make **higher** population densities a goal of public policy. The destructive consequence of this policy is to make each resident the enemy of his potential neighbour, as every new development is experienced as an infringement on your personal living space.

One consequence of the government policy of restricting building in the countryside is ever greater pressure on already built-up inner cities. The London Planning Advisory Committee '...identified small leftover spaces, urban backlands and larger windfall sites', and calculated that, in all, '...London has room for the creation of 570,000 extra homes'. 'At a stroke', says Urban Task Force chair Richard Rogers, '...this would absorb almost the whole of the capital's projected demand for new housing'[106] Do we really want every inch of London packed with houses, instead of parks, squares, playgrounds and other amenities? Residents in Hillside Estate and Hazellville Road, North Islington have been told that they must have a fifth estate in Pilgrim's Way dropped into the spaces in between the other four. The first thing developers told one house-owner was that they were going to take her roof off. The council's reasoning is that amongst the other estates, one more will not make much difference. Developments like these are taking place throughout the already built-up towns and cities of Britain. Their effect is to make our cities into a dull monoculture of continuous housing, as every small park, sports ground, derelict cinema or remaining patch of scrubland sprouts three or more storeys of 'in-fill' flats.

106] Richard Rogers and Richard Burdett, 'Let's cram more into the city', in Marcial Echenique and Andrew Saint, editors, Cities for the New Millennium (London, Spon, 2001) p 13

107] Lynne Anderson, interviewed by author, 27 November 2004

108] 'Anger at "sneaky" plans to expand Cambourne', Cambridge News, 10 January 2003

109] www.cambourne-uk.com

Residents who object are cast in the role of the Nimby. But that is only because the authorities are withholding planning approval on so much vacant land that could be developed.

Cambourne is a new settlement outside Cambridge, on the way to Bedford. It is part of a positive expansion of that city to house the many families recruited to work in the new science park, as well as commuters to London. Since 1989 it has grown up from surplus farmland to 1200 new homes. Lynne Anderson is headmistress of Monkfields Primary School, which has grown from five to 420 students. 'The families see this new village as an opportunity to work together in creating this new community,' she says.[107] But last year, her school building was full of angry residents protesting at plans to increase the village to 5,000 homes in '... response to the Government's wish to see homes built more densely in new developments'.[108] Like those Londoners objecting to urban infill, the people of Cambourne have been cast as Nimbys. But all they really want is not to be overcrowded.[109]

The contest over resources makes it seem inevitable that residents will be in conflict with incomers. This mutual antipathy helps to reinforce a generalised hostility to change, or a preference for the status quo, even when the status quo means storing up new problems for the future. Set at each other's throats, we all become more conservative. But there really is no reason that it should be so. On the contrary, it is only because the availability of land is being artificially constricted that new residents and those already settled are thrown into conflict. While country-folk and established suburbanites are jealously hanging on to the village green, the authorities lord it over a 'back yard' the size of Wales. It is not the Nimbyism of ordinary people that is the problem: it is the Nimbyism from above. The mood of hostility to change is more than a mood: it is an institution.

CHAPTER THREE

THE GREEN BELT: OFFICIAL NYMBYISM

'WE HAVE A CLEAR DUTY TO DO ALL WE CAN TO PREVENT THE FURTHER
unrestricted sprawl of the great cities', said Duncan Sandys.[110]

There are nearly 1,680,000 hectares that are designated 'green belt' in England, or around 13 per cent of the land. That is an increase since 1993 of 125,000 hectares, which is almost as much as the further 164,000 hectares of green belt in Scotland. The first green belt in modern times was created by the London and Home Counties Green Belt Act of 1938. Since then green belts have been established around Glasgow, Edinburgh, Aberdeen, Greater Manchester, Merseyside and the West Midlands, as well as many other smaller towns, under Duncan Sandys' 'historic circular' of 1955 '...inviting local planning authorities to consider the establishment of green belts'.[111]

Green belts are '...areas of land intended to be left open and protected from inappropriate development'. There purpose is '...to check the sprawl of largely built-up areas, safeguard surrounding countryside from encroachment', and to '...prevent neighbouring towns from merging', according to the Government.[112] Under government guidelines, local authorities withhold planning permission to buildings that contravene the green belts. 'Once the general extent of a green belt has been approved it should be altered only in exceptional circumstances,' with the permission of the Secretary of State.[113] The green belts consolidate the restrictions imposed upon development in the Town and Country Planning Act of 1947 (updated in 1990). It was the 1947 Act that made all building subject to planning permission, abolishing the right to freely develop privately owned land. The Town and Country Planning Acts

110] Duncan Sandys, HC Debs, col. 45W, Hansard, 26 April 1955

111] Department of Communities and Local Government, 'Planning Policy Guidance 2: Green Belts', first published by ODPM, 2 July 2001, www.communities. gov.uk

112] Britain 2000 – the official yearbook of the United Kingdom (London, HMSO, 2000) p 344

113] Office of the Deputy Prime Minister, Planning Policy Guidance 2: Green belts (London, HMSO, 2001) section 2.6, p 5

114] Alan W. Evans,
Economics and Land Use
Planning (Oxford,
Blackwell, 2004) p 6

115] Edward Heath,
The Course of My Life
(London, Hodder and
Stoughton, 1998) p 291

116] Stephen Dorril and
Robin Ramsey, Smear:
Wilson and the Secret
State (London, Fourth
Estate, 1991)

117] Edward Heath,
The Course of My Life
(London, Hodder and
Stoughton, 1998) p 418

have made it possible to introduce government goals by circulars, instead of further Acts of Parliament.

PERMISSION REFUSED!

When 11-year old Anna Bennett's dad built her a tree house in her grandmother's garden, Sheffield Road, Glossop, he thought he was doing a good thing. Daniel Bennett is a Conservation Biologist, and was pleased to encourage his daughter and her friends to get in touch with nature. High Peak borough council, however, objected that no planning permission had been granted for the 1.5 x 1.8 metre tree house, calling it 'visually intrusive'. Despite a last minute appeal to the Deputy Prime Minister, the borough council were granted an enforcement order to have the tree house removed on 9 December 2003.

Although the language of planning indicates proactive government, the Act and subsequent guidance works by stopping development. Land economist Alan Evans explains that the 1947 Act was passed under Attlee's post-war Labour administration, when it was presumed that most development would be government development. But such 'statist' visions did not survive, especially after the return of Conservative government in 1951, and most development was undertaken by the private sector:

> *'Since there were no powers to force development to be undertaken, planning became to a large extent negative so far as it affected the private sector. The system could prevent development by refusing planning permission, but it had no positive powers.'* [114]

Churchill's son-in-law, the Conservative MP Duncan Sandys (pronounced Sands) was a dubious champion of England's green and pleasant land. A supporter of capital punishment, restrictions on immigration,[115] and an opponent of colonial liberation, he was widely blamed for wrecking the British aviation industry;[116] he was called '...the unpleasant and unacceptable face of capitalism' by former Conservative Prime Minister Edward Heath, after he was rewarded with an offshore payment of £100,000 while chairman of Lonrho;[117] and in 2000 he was finally

named as the 'headless man', photographed in a sex act with the
Duchess of Argyll in a Polaroid that was the subject both of her divorce
and a Cabinet investigation.[118]

Sandys' purpose in creating the green belt was directed against the
city-dwellers as much as it was for the countryside. According to Alan
Evans, '...in Britain, one of the main concerns leading to the creation of
a comprehensive planning system was the way in which the private car
allowed development to occur outside the boundaries of existing built-up
areas'. He says that '...for the first time people other than the very rich
did not have to live within walking distance of jobs, shops, or public
transport'.[119] Alfred Marshall, founder of the school of 'neo-classical' economics proposed a 'national fresh air tax' in 1899:

> 'We need to increase the playgrounds in the midst of our towns.
> We need also to prevent one town from growing into another, or
> into a neighbouring village; we need to keep intermediate stretches
> of country in dairy farms ... as well as public pleasure grounds.'[120]

The Restriction of Ribbon Development Act (1935) came about as a result
of the complaints of prominent architect Clough Williams-Ellis,[121] and
the Council for the Preservation of Rural England, formed in 1926, only
changing its name in 2003 to the Campaign to Protect Rural England.
As Colin Buchanan observed, the very title of the Ribbon Development
Act indicated '...the sense of panic which engendered it'.[122]

The modern green belt owes its origins to Ebenezer Howard, whose
Garden Cities of To-Morrow of 1902 was the model of urban planning.[123]
Influenced by the utopian socialism of John Bellamy, Howard drafted
plans for the city as if it was a single project. The key to his city, and his
contribution to the case for the green belt was the plan for a city made
up of concentric rings, with a park at the centre, surrounded by houses,
with industry relegated to the outer ring, but surrounded by agriculture
and the countryside. Howard's scheme was embraced as the positive
proposal that nevertheless accommodated the negative hostility to the
roadside ribbon development of the 1920s. The template was reproduced
so that a central city of around 60,000 people could be ringed by
smaller cities of around 30,000.

Howard's Garden Cities caught the imagination of the middle classes
– though it was not always clear whether he was satisfying the desire
to move out to the suburbs, or to arrest suburban sprawl. Probably

118] Guardian, 11 August
2000

119] Alan W. Evans,
Economics and Land Use
Planning (Oxford,
Blackwell, 2004) p 59

120] Alfred Marshall,
quoted in Lewis
Mumford, The City in
History (Harmondsworth,
Penguin, 1991) p 574

121] Clough Williams-Ellis,
England and the Octopus
(London, Geoffrey Bles,
1928)

122] Colin Buchanan,
quoted in Alan W. Evans,
Economics and Land Use
Planning (Oxford,
Blackwell, 2004) p 59

123] Ebenezer Howard,
Garden Cities of
To-Morrow (London,
Swan Sonnenschein,
1902)

124] Helen Meller, Patrick Geddes: Social Evolutionist and City Planner (New York, Routledge, 1990)

125] Frederic J Osborn and Arnold Whittick, The New Towns; The Answer to Megalopolis (London, Leonard Hill, 1969) first published 1963

126] Richard Crossman, Diaries of a Cabinet Minister, Volume One, Housing Minister (London, Jonathan Cape, 1975) p 87

127] Phil Macnaghten and John Urry, Contested Natures (London, Sage Publications, 1998) p 39

Howard's appeal was that it reconciled both the ambition to move out, and the revulsion at unplanned ribbon development. Here was an orderly creation of discrete suburbs, with any subsequent growth arrested. The plan inspired developments at Letchworth (1903), Hampstead Garden Suburb (1915), Welwyn (1919) and Wythenshawe in Manchester (1930). Raymond Unwin was architect at Letchworth, Hampstead Garden Suburb and Wythenshawe, and it was he who proposed the green belt idea that became law in 1938. Another influence was Patrick Geddes, inspired by Howard to warn of the danger of 'conurbations' in his Cities in Evolution, an essay on the growth of cities of 1915.[124] Between the wars the London County Council took up the Garden Cities approach as part of its slum clearance programme, building cottage estates at Acton, Beacontree, Dagenham and St. Helier (near Morden).

It was after the war, though, in Sir Patrick Abercrombie's 1944 Greater London Plan, and the 1946 New Towns Act that followed it, that Howard's Garden Cities, and the green belt were formalised. The plan envisaged a depopulation of London, through the creation of new towns. In the act there were three categories: Mark I towns, Stevenage, Harlow and Crawley, essentially London overspill accommodation; Mark II towns Redditch, Runcorn, Washington and Telford, attempts to revitalise depressed areas of the country; and Mark III towns, of which Milton Keynes was the paradigm.[125] It was hoped that the bungalows that characteristic of ribbon development had been contained, and conurbations barred. Instead, Garden Cities neatly hemmed by extensive green belt would control the outward splurge. But when Labour Housing Minister Richard Crossman tried to meet aspirations for new homes in the 1960s he was forced to conclude that '...the green belt can be the strangulation of a city'.[126]

The green belt is one of a long series of official measures to rein in city dwellers that have persisted since the time of Elizabeth I, right up to the 1994 Criminal Justice Act's ban on 'Ravers' taking over barns with their 'repetitive beats'. The rationale behind the creation of the green belts was, according to researchers Phil Macnaghten and John Urry, '...to protect town and country distinctions'.[127] The green belts were a kind of barricade to prevent the ugly troglodytes escaping from their cities into the fragrant countryside preserve of the elite.

Sir Richard Rogers, chair of the Urban Task Force, takes a somewhat

PROCLAMATION OF ELIZABETH I, 1580

'The Queen's Majestie perceiving the state of the city of London and the suburbs and the confines thereof to increase daily, by access of people to inhabit the same, in such ample sort, as thereby many inconveniences are seen already, but many of greater necessity of like to follow, being such as her majesty cannot neglect to remedy ...where there are such great magnitude of people brought to inhabit in small rooms, whereof a great part are seen to be very poor, yea, such as must live of begging, or by worse means, and they heaped up together, and in a sort smothered by many families of children and servants in one house or tenement ... plague ... would also be dispersed through all other parts of the realm, to the manifest danger of the whole body thereof ... her majesty, by good and deliberate advice of her council, and being also moved by the considerate opinions of the Lord Mayor, aldermen, and other the grave wise men in and about the city, doth charge and strictly command all manner of persons of what quality soever they may be, to desist and forebear from any new buildings of any house or tenement within three miles from any of the gates of the said city of London, to serve for habitation or lodging for any person, where no former house hath been in the memory of such as are now living...'

The proclamation, which was made an act of Parliament in 1592, and also forbade sub-dividing of houses, was enforced by threat of imprisonment: 'For the reformynge of the great mischiefs and inconveniences that daily grow and increase by reason of the pestering of Houses with diverse Famylies, harboringe of inmates and converting of great Houses into several Tenements or Dwellings and erectynge of New Buildings within the Cities of London and Westminster and other Places nere thereunto adjoining ...many idle vagrant and wicked persons have harboured themselves there and divers remote places of the Realme have been disappointed of workmen and dispeopled'.

Further royal proclamations against London's growth followed in 1602, 1603, 1604, 1607 and 1615. Henry VIII had made the first in 1548. More followed under James I. The Commonwealth Parliament passed laws '...hindering the increase of buildings in and outside the suburbs of London within a distance of ten miles from the city'. [128]

128] Steen Eiler Rasmussen (London, Jonathan Cape, 1937) p 63 to 75

129] Richard Rogers and Anne Power, Cities for a Small Country (London, Faber and Faber, 2000) p 66

130] Marcial Echenique and Rob Homewood, The Future Of Suburbs And Exurbs; Report for The Independent Transport Commission (Cambridge, The Martin Centre for Architectural and Urban Studies, 2003) p 4

131] Ferdinand Mount, Mind the Gap: The New Class Divide in Britain (London, Short Books, 2005)

132] Polly Toynbee 'An electable Tory voice', Guardian, 3 September 2004

133] Paul Barker, 'Edge City', in Anthony Barnett and Roger Scruton, editors, Town and Country (London, Jonathan Cape, 1998) p 208

134] Shaun Spiers, CPRE, Guardian letters, 7 September 2004

135] Ros Coward, 'A green light to the developers', Guardian, 18 December 2004

different view of the tenor of public policy towards suburban development. He sees the post war new towns as part of a policy to build over the countryside.[129] It is true that after both wars there was governmental support for new building beyond existing boundaries. But as researchers at the Martin Centre for Architectural and Urban Studies, Marcial Echenique and Rob Homewood point out that the UK government '... has adopted, for over half a century, a policy of urban containment to reduce the intake of greenfield land for urban development.'[130] The two interpretations are not as contradictory as they seem. The expansions under Stanley Baldwin's government in the 1920s, and under post-war governments, all attempted to reconcile the pressure for outward expansion with regulation of that growth. More suburbs were built, but the growth was reined in by the creation of the green belt.

Guardian columnist Polly Toynbee got into trouble in 2004 when she wrote the following: 'The shortage of affordable housing, especially in the south, is due to the astronomic price of land'. Toynbee, who took these arguments from Conservative politician Ferdinand Mount's *Mind The Gap*,[131] went on to argue that '...forty per cent of the cost of a new house in the south-east is the price of the land'. She applauded Mount, saying '...here's a conservative willing to argue against a landscape frozen in time by the 1947 Town and Country Planning Act'.[132] Toynbee ought to have known that this was an argument that would have brought the wrath of the liberal-minded *Guardian* readership down upon her head. Paul Barker one-time editor of *New Society*, columnist for the New Statesman, wrote in 1998 about 'those who are hostile to sub-urbs' that '...the leftish *Guardian* is their citadel', adding '...it becomes the task of the rightish *Daily Telegraph* to note that, in the words of the headline on one commentary in early 1998, "Green belts suit the rich" '.[133] Shaun Spiers of the CPRE duly wrote in to inveigh against Toynbee, Mount and '...owner occupied housing sprawl over the countryside': 'Building houses over rural England would destroy much of what people most value about this nation – its countryside.'[134] Government proposals to 'streamline planning proposals' a few years earlier were shot down in flames by another *Guardian* columnist, Ros Coward, as '...a green light to the developers', protesting '...there is virtually no mention of environmental protection, nature conservation, or green belt'.[135] Forty years earlier, housing minister Richard Crossman '...began to realise what a sacred cow the green belt had become in progressive circles', when he agreed the development of a model village, Ash Green in Hartley, Kent.[136] Though quite why progressives are so determined to protect the status quo is hard to understand.

It might seem as if modern society could do without this archaic institution, but the monopoly over land ownership has been central to the authority of the British elite since they first cleared people from it. The Acts of Enclosure in England from the fifteenth century onwards broke up the commons, and distributed them amongst those whose legal claims were recognised by the courts. Laws of Enclosure did not just suit the elite in the countryside. It was also a necessary condition of the reduction of England's yeomanry to a landless proletariat. The proprietor of the land clears '... the land of its excess mouths, tears the children of the earth from the breast on which they were raised'.[137] Arnold Toynbee said of the clearances that '...a person ignorant of our history...might surmise that a great exterminatory war had taken place'.[138] For that reason the enclosures were wholly endorsed by the new industrial ruling classes as well. Once robbed of their ability to subsist on the land, the 'surplus populations' had no choice but to take employment in the mill. As Karl Marx, the best-known critic of the industrial system said, in his Germanic way, this new Capital needs '...landed property which it includes as its antithesis'.[139] It was for this reason that the Marx scholar Roman Rosdolsky insisted, against expectations, that '...modern landed property' was '...a creation of capital', not the other way around.[140] To keep the hands from escaping the factory to live on the land, the landlords punished poaching and squatting. From the Levellers of seventeenth century England, to the Hoovervilles of twentieth century America, any attempted return to the land has been punished with force.

Britain's landed aristocracy owes its authority to the service it performed the rising industrial classes of maintaining a monopoly over the earth, which is to say the original means of subsistence. The aristocracy's role was formalised in the law of Strict Settlement in the eighteenth century, which said that land could only be sold once in each generation, and then only if a landowner and his heir agreed.[141] The influence of that original monopoly over land still echoes down the ages. Kevin Cahill has listed the top landowners in the UK and the Republic of Ireland: Historian John Saville has written that '...it is hardly surprising that for

136] Richard Crossman, Diaries of a Cabinet Minister, Volume One, Housing Minister (London, Jonathan Cape, 1975) p 93

137] Karl Marx, paraphrasing Sir James Stuart's 'An Inquiry', Grundrisse (Harmondsworth, Penguin, 1973) p 276

138] Arnold J Toynbee, 'England in 1760 – The Decay of the Yeomanry', in The Industrial Revolution in England (Newton Abbot, Devon, David and Charles, 1969) first published 1884, p 59

139] Karl Marx, Capital, Vol. III (London, Lawrence and Wishart, 1984) p 879

140] Roman Rosdolsky, The Making of Marx's 'Capital', Vol. I (London, Pluto Press, 1989) p 39

141] Dominic Hobson, The National Wealth (London, Harper Collins, 1999) p 78

	Title	Landowner	Home county	Acreage	Value £
	TOP TWENTY LANDOWNERS IN UK AND THE REPUBLIC OF IRELAND, BY ACREAGE, 2001				
1	Duke of	Buccleuch and Queensbury	Dumfries	270,900	282,500,000,000
2	Dukedom of	Atholl (trustees)	Perth	148,000	430,000,000,000
3	Prince of	Wales	Cornwall	141,000	125,000,000,000
4	Duke of	Northumberland	Northumberland	132,200	800,000,000,000
5	Duke of	Westminster	Cheshire	129,300	11,500,000,000,000
6	Captain	A.A. Farquharson	Aberdeen	106,500	28,000,000,000
7	Earl of	Seafield	Banff	101,000	104,000,000,000
8	Viscount	Cowdray	Aberdeen	93,600	120,000,000,000
9	Mr	Robert Fleming	Argyll	88,900	40,000,000,000
10	Mr	Edmund Vesty	Sutherland	86,300	40,000,000,000
11	Countess of	Sutherland	Sutherland	83,239	15,000,000,000
12	Mr	Paul Fentener van Vlissingen	Ross and Cromarty	81,000	35,000,000,000
13	Baroness	Jane Willoughby d'Eresby	Perth	78,200	121,000,000,000
14	Colonel Sir	Hamish Cameron of Lochiel	Inverness	76,000	15,000,000,000
15	Duke of	Devonshire	Derbyshire	73,000	435,000,000,000
16	Queen	Elizabeth Windsor	Aberdeen	73,000	3,000,000,000,000
17	Earl of	Lonsdale	Cumbria	70,000	325,000,000,000
18	Mr	John Mackenzie	Ross and Cromartie	67,000	12,500,000,000
19	Duke of	Roxburghe	Berwick	65,600	150,000,000,000
20	Sheik	Mohammed bin Rashid al Maktoum	Ross and Cromarty	63,100	30,000,000,000

Source: Kevin Cahill, Who owns Britain (Edinburgh, Canongate, 2002) p 379

so long the landed class remained the richest group in an industrialising Britain'. Saville goes on to count the ways that landowners turned their landed property to industrial property. Landlords profited from the building of industrial towns, railways and coalmines on their lands, as well as shifting their considerable funds into the new ventures.[142] Confirming Saville's point, Shirley Green looked at who owned London in 1986, and found that after the royal family of England, and the Church, '...the Howard de Waldens, the Grosvenors, the Portmans, the Cadogans...between them these long-established and titled families own most of what is worth owning in Central London'.[143]

The executive director of Friends of the Earth, Charles Secrett, argues that the upper classes have a special feeling for nature: 'Among the aristocrats there is a sense of noblesse oblige...a feeling of stewardship towards the land'.[144] It was a sentiment rehearsed by Prince Charles in his Reith Lecture when he spoke of '...a sacred trust between mankind and our Creator, under which we accept stewardship of the Earth.' [145] The future King of England has accepted a considerable burden of stewardship: 128,189 acres with a rental value of £10 million a year, with a further income of £2 million from stocks valued at £45 million, plus, of course, the proceeds from the organic beef and lamb produced by his Highgrove™ farm, along with its 'Duchy Original' biscuits.[146] Charles' duties of stewardship did not extend to the 60 travellers who set up camp at his Poundbury model village in Dorset – The Duchy of Cornwall's spokesman Simon Conibear announced that '...we are in the process of putting in an application in to get them moved',[147] and vowed to secure the site against further occupation.[148]

The landed gentry did good service in keeping the **hoi polloi** off the land. But in time this class decayed to the point that it could no longer be wholly trusted to carry out its policing role. Increasing debts led the lords to press for the right to sell up. The Settled Land Acts of 1882 reversed the restrictions on land sales (apart from the family seat). 'The aristocratic share of the acreage of the British Isles fell from four-fifths in the 1880s to no more than a quarter a century later'.[149] In the first instance land was bought by its farmers, as the pressure for more land under tillage grew in the twentieth century. Later, though, intensive farming would release land from cultivation. The historic function of the landlords in preserving the monopoly over land had to be maintained, even without the landlords. It was

142] John Saville, The Consolidation of the Capitalist State 1800-1850 (London, Pluto, 1994) p 50

143] Shirley Green, Who Owns London? (London, Weidenfield and Nicholson, 1986) p 36

144] Charles Secrett, Guardian 5 May 2000

145] Prince Charles in his BBC Reith Lecture, 17 May 2000

146] Dominic Hobson, The National Wealth (London, Harper Collins, 1999) p 29

147] The Sun, 12 August 2004

148] 'Travellers leave Prince's village', BBC News online, 13 August 2004, and posted http://news.bbc.co.uk

149] Dominic Hobson, The National Wealth (London, Harper Collins, 1999) p 79

150] James Mill, Elements of Political Economy (London, 1821) p 198, cited in Karl Marx, Theories of Surplus Value, Vol. II (London, Lawrence and Wishart, 1992) p 152

151] www.greenpeace.org.uk

152] James Heartfield, 'The Economics of Sustainable Development', in Ian Abley and James Heartfield, editors, Sustaining Architecture in the Anti-Machine Age (Chichester, Wiley-Academy, 2001) chapter 7, p 99

153] Dominic Hobson, The National Wealth (London, Harper Collins, 1999) p 118 and 121

the economist James Mill, preoccupied with the ready supply of labour to the factories, who first observed that production could continue undisturbed if the landed proprietor disappeared and the state took his place.[150] The green belt campaign was part of the increasing move to nationalise the land. Other facets of this general change were the creation of the National Trust, national parks and heritage sites. Nationalisation did not mean opening up the countryside to the people, though. It meant the preservation of the land from the people, in the name of the nation – or the planet.

On 16 August 1996 Norfolk farmer and Greenpeace director,[151] Lord Peter Melchett wrote to Prime Minister John Major appealing for restrictions on nature's bounty: 'So long as nature is available to be treated as a free good which can always be opened up, good steward-ship elsewhere will be undermined'.[152] Today the role of policing the boundaries is done more in the name of conserving the environment than preserving aristocratic privilege. The National Parks, originally created in 1949, with the help of Clough Williams-Ellis, cover one tenth of England and Wales, and are the responsibility of the Countryside Commission. The National Trust owns 603,265 acres of land, (and recovered £19 million in rent from tenant farmers in 1996/1997), the National Trust for Scotland owns 187,873 acres, the Royal Society for the Protection of Birds controls some 245 000 acres, the Woodlands Trust 40 269 acres. Between them English Nature, the Countryside Council for Wales and Scottish Natural Heritage control 5.1 million acres, or nearly one tenth of the 56 million acres of Britain.[153]

PRESERVING NATURE – BUT WHO FOR?

In 1998 the Pembrokeshire National Park Authority were surprised to discover a thriving eco-community in the forests. Tony Wrench, himself a former planner, and Jane Wrench built the solar-powered, turf-roofed Round House, around which the Brithdir Moor community revolved – without planning permission. In January 2004 Tony was fined £1000, and in April the Authority got their way and the Round House at Brithdir Moor was demolished. The sanctity of the land had been preserved against invasion by ordinary people.

In September 2004 the *New Statesman* initiated a '...campaign to tackle Britain's astonishingly unequal distribution of land', adding that '...the lopsided distribution of land is the single most important reason for Britain's chronic housing shortage and for the high prices that prevent so many from buying homes'.[154] All well and good, so far. But on developing the argument it became clear that the *New Statesman* had no intention of making land available to all for development. On the contrary, their ambition was to transfer the control of land from the landed aristocracy to the state. Noting that the ambition was only as modest as could be supported by the Liberal Party in the nineteenth century, Tristram Hunt demanded to know when Prime Minister Blair would end the landlord's monopoly.[155] In 1982 Dave Wetzel, then the Greater London Council's Head of Transport, stood trial at Lavender Hill Magistrates Court for refusing to pay his bus fair as a protest against the government's overturning of his cheap fairs policy. But in 2004 here was Wetzel, now chair of the Labour Land Campaign, demanding higher taxation on the land as a part of the *New Statesman*'s campaign to address the 'Great British Land Scandal'.[156] Taking from the landowners to give to the government is hardly a radical policy. In fact it is a gradualistic version of the nationalisation policy that James Mill had proposed two centuries earlier; a policy that has for the most part, already been accomplished. After all, where are the country estates that the *New Statesman* rails against? Are they in the South East of England, where the greatest pressure for new homes is? No. For the most part the larger landed estates are in Scotland and Northumbria, in the depopulating areas of the country. The monopoly that stands in the way of building housing where it is wanted is for the most part, government regulations, green belts, and national parks. The *New Statesman*'s campaign would only enhance the constraints that the state puts upon new development.

THE CONSULTATION CHARADE

In the 1960s radical critics of the big housing developments pointed to the lack of consultation amongst local people as the reason for the presumed failures of the high rises. In 1968, plans to demolish Covent Garden were overturned after public protest (though the mix of working and middle class residents did not survive the vacation of the fruit market as was hoped by the conservationists). Local consultation was

154] 'The Great British Land Scandal', New Statesman, 20 September 2004

155] Tristram Hunt, 'A revolutionary who won over Victorian liberals', New Statesman, 20 September 2004

156] Dave Wetzel, 'The Case for Taxing Land', New Statesman, 20 September 2004

157] People and Planning - Report of the Committee on Public Participation in Planning (London, HMSO, 1969)

158] Alan W. Evans, Economics and Land Use Planning (Oxford, Blackwell, 2004) p 8

159] Gordon Cherry, quoted in Alan W. Evans, Economics and Land Use Planning (Oxford, Blackwell, 2004) p 8

officially identified as a necessary part of the planning process from the Skeffington Report of 1969 onwards.[157]

The consequences of making public participation in the planning process compulsory, however, were less than radical. 'Although this critique of planning was, politically, from the left', writes Alan Evans, '...the effect of "public participation" was to reinforce the status quo and the position of those in possession'. What Evans means is that where new developments are proposed, the 'public' that is consulted, is the public that already lives there. Those who want to move in are not yet resident, and so do not figure. The consultation has a built in conservative bias to the status quo.

> 'If, for example, a housing development was proposed near to a village, the residents of the village could participate in the process (and would inevitably object to the proposal), but the future residents who would live in the houses if the development went ahead did not and could not participate because they were unidentified and unidentifiable.'[158]

It was a case of the legislation favouring insiders over outsiders. The late Gordon Cherry, historian of urban planning, wrote in 1996 that it had become '...clear that the biggest beneficiaries of the planning system were the special interest groups and the lobbies, particularly when they were in harmony with environmental values relating to countryside protection.' What is more '...the fact that the same values sought to protect conservative interests in maintaining residential exclusivity in suburban locations made them extremely powerful.'[159] Here was the legislation that empowered the Nimby lobby to prevent development, disguising selfish interests as care for the environment.

Consultant Miffa Salter was a Senior Fellow at the Office for Public Management, where she dealt with public participation in the planning process. In a paper written in 2001, Salter looked at the problems of public consultation, of misunderstanding, manipulation and so on, before getting to the nub of the matter: 'most importantly', she said, consultation '...assumes that the public want to get involved in the first place'. But, Salter tells us, research for the former Department of the Environment, Transport and the Regions, and the Social Exclusion Unit, shows that '...in terms of public participation in local government, informal networks do still dominate, and those who know how the system works are the ones who get most out of it'. Furthermore, the '...assumption inherent in contemporary thinking is that the public will, given enough time, speak and act as a collective', when '...the reality is that often nothing could be further from the truth'.[160] The practical effect of the elevation of public participation is a long way from democratic control of development. On the whole it works simply as a brake on development.

BROWNFIELD DEVELOPMENTS

Planning Policy Guidance 3: Housing (PPG3), enshrines the principle that local authorities should '...give priority to re-using previously-developed land within urban areas, bringing empty homes back into use and converting existing buildings, in preference to the development of greenfield sites'.[161] The case for the priority of greenfield over brownfield development is that land left derelict from previous development is preferable to greenfield development because of the encroachment of developed land into the countryside. As we have seen, there is no such shortage of greenfield land in absolute terms. Nonetheless, the perception that there is has led to PPG3. In its practical application, however, PPG3 acts as a partial constraint upon new development, rather than a redirection of development to available brownfield sites. Indeed, the principle is simply unworkable in a dynamic society, since it has the effect of constraining new development within the already established pattern.

The history of PPG3 begins with the previous administration. North Wiltshire's Tory MP James Gray made clear in parliament that there was a '...seamless continuation of the policies of the previous government, at least since 1992, when my right Hon. Friend the Member for Suffolk, Coastal (Mr. Gummer) came to the Department of the Environment'. John Gummer's Department of the Environment indeed set the standards that the current government follow, by throwing the brakes on new development. James Gray is right that '...PPG3 is merely a revision of a previous PPG'.[162] One person who took Gummer's message of preferring recycled land to greenfield development was Lord Rogers of Riverside, the chair of the Urban Task Force. It was he who popularised the target of 60 per cent development on brownfield sites, in his report *Towards an Urban Renaissance*.[163] Rogers has since called for 100 per cent brownfield development, prompting the planner Peter Hall to resign from the Urban Task Force and publish *The Land Fetish*.[164]

160] Miffa Salter, 'Engaging the Stakeholder in the Development Process', in Ian Abley and James Heartfield, editors, Sustaining Architecture in the Anti-Machine Age (Chichester, Wiley Academy, 2001) chapter 8, p 104 to 110

161] DETR, The Government's Response to the Environment, Transport and Regional Affairs: Seventeenth Report – Planning Policy Guidance 3: Housing (London, HMSO, 2000)

162] James Gray, MP, Hansard, 24 March 2000, column 1239

163] Richard Rogers, chairman, Towards an Urban Renaissance; Final Report of the Urban Task Force (London, Spon, 1999) p 174

164] Peter Hall, The Land Fetish (London, Town and Country Planning Association, 2005)

165] Iain Sinclair, London Orbital: A walk around the M25 (London, Penguin, 2003) p 82

166] 'Ministers "must push for greenfield housing"', Guardian, 20 March 2002

Though it seems to make sense to use up the spare land before you build on the new land, in practice matters are quite different. The injunction to build on already developed land means much higher costs to developers. Designing within sites deteermined by other criteeria in earlier times, clearing and cleaning-up previous uses, keeping existing infrastructure working, and accomodating existing utility connections all add costs to development. In shifting the cost of clearing sites from local authorities to developers, it raises the cost of new investments.

Author Iain Sinclair highlighted the contrast between the ideal of brownfield development in the Millennium Village in Greenwich, with the less glamourous housing development on a former armaments factory:

> 'Greenwich Peninsula was show-business brownfield, Peter Mandelson as Kubla Khan. Enfield was left to Fairview Homes plc. They picked up the Royal Small Arms Factory makeover: land contaminated 'with an arsenic to zinc range of chemical substances, plus explosives, oils and tars and the by-products of five gas works.'[165]

Not surprisingly, the residents campaigned to have the site de-contaminated once they started to find out the mix of chemicals they were living on.

In principle there is no reason why building should not be on brownfield sites. The difficulty with PPG3, though, is that in prioritising brownfield over greenfield it raises the bar to new housing just at the moment when houses are in desperately short supply. Nor does it follow that enough brownfield land will become available in the right place at the right time. As Joseph Rowntree Foundation Director Richard Best put it in 2002 '...we have got to be honest and accept that not all of the necessary housing can be built on recycled land'.[166]

Looked at in the round, the general principle could never be adhered to. It implies that all development is merely the replacement of previous development. But in fact, the additional homes are needed because of the way the country is changing: the way it is becoming more populous, more affluent, is raising its expectations, is shifting its centre of gravity towards the South East, and is becoming more mobile. Like the green belt, the priority of greenfield over brownfield development is actually an attempt to arrest development, or at least constrain it, by imposing the model of the past onto the future. If there really were a shortage of land one might understand it. But there is not a shortage of land. PPG3 exists only to put the brakes on the development that people need to give them the homes they want.

Another effect of putting brownfield development before greenfield development is that the option of using newly derelict land to create new green spaces in cities is closed off. Instead, as dwellings get larger and increase in number, on roughly the same ground, they would squeeze out all land uses but housing, leading to a monocultural environment, with nothing but green on one side of the divide, and nothing but brown on the other. It is pointed that the large parks that were envisaged for cities in the early century are almost impossible now. Instead we have pocket parks. At the same time hundreds of trees are threatened by the new west London tramway from Uxbridge to Shepherd's Bush.[167]

HERITAGE BRITAIN

Just as the green belt preserves the countryside, listing preserves buildings. In 1987, the art historian Robert Hewison wrote about the ubiquity of listed buildings:

> 'Since the principle of listing buildings in order to inhibit their demolition or alteration was first introduced in 1947 the number has steadily grown, and is expected to reach half a million in 1988, double the number in 1982. The latest changes to the system mean the potential number is infinite. The cut-off date will no longer be 1939, but a rolling period by which any building more than thirty years old may qualify for protection.'[168]

In fact there are 440,000 listed building in the UK, more than half a million if you include Ancient Monuments. There are 370,000 listed buildings in England, a further 46,000 in Scotland, 22,000 in Wales.[169] In Northern Ireland 8,500 buildings are listed, which, improbably '...is about two per cent of all buildings' in the province.[170] Apart from listed buildings and ancient monuments, there are a further 20,000 properties held for the nation by the National Trust. Hewison was right to point to the accelerating rate of listing. Today there are twice as many listed buildings as in 1980 and three times as many as in 1970. When the National Audit Office visited English Heritage, the body responsible for most of the listing, the list had grown to 2,000 volumes.

167] Guardian, 17 September 2004

168] Robert Hewison, The Heritage Industry: Britain in a climate of decline (London, Methuen, 1987) p 24

169] English Heritage; Historic Scotland; Auditor General for Wales, Protecting and Conserving the Built Heritage in Wales (London, HMSO, 2000) p 2

170] Environmental and Heritage Service, '30 Years of Listed Buildings in Northern Ireland', 7 November 2004, posted on www.ehsni.gov.uk

171] www.nao.org.uk

172] Dominic Hobson, The
National Wealth, London,
Harper Collins, 1999, p 91
and 92

173] Robert Hewison,
Office of Arts and
Libraries, Press Release, 27
November 1986

174] www.museums
association.org

The NAO concluded that this '...makes it difficult to identify and use the information they contain'.[171] Voluntary historical societies have driven the listing of historical buildings since the Society for the Protection of Ancient Buildings was formed in 1876, with William Morris as secretary. The Georgian Society, formed in 1937, followed by the Victorian Society of the 1960s, made the case for more recent buildings. They were followed by a Thirties Society, then a Forties society, and eventually a Fifties, Sixties and even a Seventies Society – all eventually amalgamated into a Twentieth-Century Society. The past has caught up with us. The National Trust, responding to the demand for the protection of recent history, bought the childhood home of John Lennon in 1995. The financial journalist Dominic Hobson mocked some of the mundane objects that could be listed in the new climate: 'Pigsties modelled on the Bank of England, urinals in Liverpool, a Butlins chalet, a railway signal box, a bus garage, shelters for London taxi drivers, a reinforced concrete silo, a corrugated iron church, bollards and telephone boxes'.[172]

Robert Hewison related the growth in listed buildings to the growth in the 'heritage industry'. He was reacting to a comment by the Arts Minister Richard Luce in 1986:

> 'One of the most impressive facts in the art world today is the astonishing vitality of museums. Over the last 15 years the number has doubled in the United Kingdom. There are about 2000 of them – a great majority privately funded. Once every fortnight, somewhere in the United Kingdom a new museum unfolds its treasures to the public gaze.'[173]

Today the Museums Association Yearbook lists 2,500, but the Association estimates that the total might be as much as 3,000.[174]

Hewison connected Britain's declining industrial base to its expanding heritage industry. 'Instead of manufacturing goods, we are manufacturing heritage, a commodity which nobody seems to be able to define, but which everybody is eager to sell'. He suggested that the trend towards 'Industrial Heritage', and industrial archaeology was emblematic of a society mired in the past. The National Trust endorsed the growing interest in industrial archaeology in 1960, when it first accepted 26 miles of the Stratford-upon-Avon canal. By 1987 there were 464 museums of industrial equipment. In 1973, the Wigan Corporation offered to pay British Waterways to demolish 'unsightly premises' – warehouses opposite Wigan Pier, an offer they did not take up. But when in 1982, British Waterways asked for permission to '...demolish the decaying buildings and develop the site' the Corporation refused, and instead got the buildings listed. In 1984 the Wigan Pier Heritage Centre opened, recreating the site of 1900, supported by an English Tourist Board grant of £150,000. The site, that George Orwell made a symbol of industrial decline in *The Road to Wigan Pier*, was now a heritage museum, complete with cloth-capped dummies. Other industrial heritage sites include Abraham Darby's foundry at Coalbrookdale, where the Ironbridge Gorge Museum opened in 1968. The foundry is now under glass: 'The cradle of the industrial revolution is also its reliquary', wrote Hewison, '...treated with the reverence of a shrine'. 'The reconstructed industrial village has all the authenticity of a film set.'

According to Hewison, '...the urge to preserve as much as we can of our past is understandable, but in the end our current obsessions are entropic: that is to say, as the past solidifies around us, all creative energies are lost'. Neil Cossons, then Director of the Science Museum, looked at the expanding number of museums in 1986 and said '...you can't project that growth much further before the entire country becomes one big open air museum, and you just join it as you get off at Heathrow'.[175] There is a worry that Britain is turning into a 'museum society'.[176] When he took office, Prime Minister Blair, too, argued that '...often people have an image of Britain that is stuck in the past – good at pageantry, less good at new technology'.[177] The entropic imposition of the past over the present that Robert Hewison first warned us of, however, has not abated since then. On the contrary, more and more of the built environment is Listed, and more and more of the countryside is protected. The past is secured a thousand times over; only the future is precarious.

THE CONSERVATIVE QUANGOCRACY

While the government commits itself to building new homes, it has to cope with a powerful lobby against development. On top of its own Urban Task Force, there is the CPRE,[178] English Heritage,[179] and the expanding design watchdog, the Commission for Architecture in the Built Environment.[180]

Eighty years old in 2006, the CPRE is today a campaigning charity with 59,000 members, who donate around £3 million, on top of the

175] Robert Hewison, The Heritage Industry: Britain in a climate of decline (London, Methuen, 1987) p 9, 10, 16-19, 24, and 93

176] Dominic Hobson, The National Wealth, London, Harper Collins, 1999, p 90

177] Prime Minister Tony Blair, Financial Times, 18 September 1997

178] www.cpre.org.uk

179] www.english-heritage.org.uk

180] www.cabe.org.uk

181] Campaign to Protect Rural England, Annual Review (London,, CPRE, 2004) p 22

182] 'Housing Sprawl: What is the solution?', viewed on 15 December 2004, www.cpre.org.uk

183] English Heritage, People and Places; a response to Government and the Value of Culture (London, English Heritage, 2004

184] F. Chernov, 'Cosmopolitanism and its reactionary role', in Bolshevik: Theoretical and Political Magazine of the Central Committee of the ACP(B), Issue #5, 15 March 1949, pp. 30 to 41, posted on www.cyberussr.com, viewed on 15 December 2004

£200,000 it receives in grants. Calor Gas, Langhams and Tesco were among its biggest private contributors; the Community Fund, the Heritage Lottery Fund and the Countryside Agency its biggest public fund sources. Its patron is the Queen of England and its President the military historian and former *Telegraph* editor Max Hastings. Vice Presidents include Jonathan Dimbleby, Viscount Esher, Dame Jennifer Jenkins, Lord Marlesford and Lord Putnam.[181] These venerable men and women look down on the hoi polloi from their country mansions to proclaim 'sprawling housing estates...must not be allowed'.[182]

English Heritage received £115.2 million from the government, plus an additional £38.4 million from other sources, spending £44 million on wages. Its main practical activity is maintaining historic sites, like Stonehenge (which it has fenced off from the general public), but it is also heavily engaged in educational and propagandistic work with an understandable bias against new developments. English Heritage works to the Department for Culture Media and Sports, which appoints its seventeen commissioners and chairman. Appearing to have put his anxieties about an open-air museum aside, the appointed chairman is now Sir Neil Cossons. English Heritage looks positively space age, next to the CPRE, with commissioners like writer Bill Bryson and popular historian David Cannadine. But its post-modern case for heritage belies a conservative fear of the alienated masses. 'As people's lives come to be less constrained by beliefs, traditions and customs and more subject to individual choice, the importance of the historic environment features increasingly in those choices', runs their response to a DCMS consultation. 'Characterless, anonymous places produce rootless, unattached people', warns English Heritage.[183] 'Rootless Cosmopolitanism' was a preoccupation of the Soviet regime under Stalin.[184]

Founded in 1999 to replace the Fine Arts Commission, the Commission for Architecture in the Built Environment has an annual budget of £11 million to promote good new architecture rather than preserve old buildings. It has a staff of over 100 based at its central London headquarters, directed by 16 commissioners. But CABE is around 350-strong if you include the professionals who provide an advisory and review service on planning applications. CABE acts as a non-statutory consultee in the land use planning system, or as another break on new development, although for the most part it has been criticised for being too cavalier. Chairman Stuart Lipton resigned in June 2004 to forestall criticisms in an independent auditor's report on potential conflicts of interest. Lipton is majority owner of the property firm Stanhope PLC, and many of his developments would be going before CABE for approval.[185] Of course, a body that has the authority to hold up new developments is necessarily open to the charge of having conflicts of interest.[186] Once CABE approval was made decisive it was bound to be thought of as a commodity in its own right, even if that suspicion proved to be unfounded. Councillor Adrian Dennis' preference for the Arrowcroft development at Croydon Gateway led him to suspect that CABE's championship for the rival Stanhope bid might be influenced by Stuart Lipton's private interests.[187] It is characteristic of the stranglehold of the heritage industry over development that CABE was accused of favouring new building, when its principle activity is to raise the bar higher on new projects, as well as promoting brownfield over greenfield developments.

There is nothing wrong in principle with the work of the CPRE, English Heritage or CABE. Often they do good things. But the problem is that all of the weight is on the side of not building, while the bodies that might once have been lobbying in the other direction are largely silent. Developers are cautious in the extreme, and politicians of the left have decided that yielding to public demands for more resources is too 'Old Labour'. The net impact is that the planning bureaucracy and its supporting cast of conservation campaigns and quangos have succeeded in stifling new growth to the point that there are not enough houses to meet demand.

185] 'Nooks and Corners', column in Private Eye, 8 July 2004 and 22 July 2004

186] Nick Mathiason, 'How pillar of society was laid low', Observer 20 June 2004

187] Evidence to the Urban Affairs Sub-Committee, Office of the Deputy Prime Minister, 'Effectiveness of CABE', 1 November 2004, Q 51

CHAPTER FOUR

HATING THE SUBURBS

'New homes spread like so much detritus discarded across thousands of hectares of southern England. Plots of land the size of handkerchiefs, crumpled into the nowhere lands of the Thames Gateway, the m11 corridor and greater Milton Keynes. Hundreds of thousands of new homes: red-tiled, upvc windowed, developers' junk.'

ARCHITECTURAL CRITIC JONATHAN GLANCEY, IMAGINING THE YEAR 2020,
gave vent to his hatred of suburbia, and the nowhere people of the Thames Gateway, the m11 corridor and Milton Keynes.
'This is what most of us fear when we think of future housing. An England made more subtopian than suburban. ...Ever more cul-de-sac estates linked together by raging arterial roads lined with chain stores...Superstores. Multiplexes. Distribution depots. An England 100% England Free. A getting-and-spending logoed and baseball-capped land chock full of call centres and staffed by customer service facility managers.' [188]

Hostility to the suburbs has been a vice of Britain's moaning classes ever since there were suburbs. To William Morris in 1884 London was '...a spreading sore...swallowing up with its loathsomeness field and wood and heath without mercy and without hope' [189] H.G. Wells thought '...the whole of Britain south of the highlands seems destined to become an urban region'. [190] Late Victorian historian Sir William Beasant thought that the '...suburbs epitomized the narrow-mindedness, isolation and dull respectability of middle class life'. [191]

188] Jonathan Glancey, 'Where we will live', in '2020', a supplement to the Guardian, 25 September 2004

189] William Morris, quoted in Stephen Inwood, A History of London (London, Macmillan, 1998) p 588

190] H.G. Wells, quoted in Tristram Hunt, Building Jerusalem: The Rise and Fall of the Victorian City (London, Weidenfeld and Nicholson, 2004) p 331

191] Sir William Beasant, quoted in Stephen Inwood, A History of London (London, Macmillan, 1998) p 588

192] Tristram Hunt, Building Jerusalem: The Rise and Fall of the Victorian City (London, Weidenfeld and Nicholson, 2004) p 330

193] William Wordsworth, quoted in Keith Thomas, Man and the Natural World: Changing Attitudes in England 1500-1800 (Harmondsworth, Penguin, 1984) p 267

194] William Wordsworth, quoted in James Winter, Secure from Rash Assault: Securing the Victorian Environment (Berkely, University of California Press, 1999) p 176

195] Keith Thomas, Man and the Natural World: Changing Attitudes in England 1500-1800 (Harmondsworth, Penguin, 1984) p 248

196] Simon Gunn and Rachel Bell, Middle Classes: their rise and sprawl (London, Phoenix, 2002)

197] John Carey, The Intellectuals and the Masses: Pride and Prejudice among the literary intelligentsia, 1880-1939 (London, Faber and Faber, 1992) p 46

198] Tristram Hunt, Building Jerusalem: The Rise and Fall of the Victorian City (London, Weidenfeld and Nicholson, 2004) p 331

Historian Tristram Hunt echoes the theme of spiritual failings regretting that '...there was no attempt to inculcate the urban spirit' in the new suburbs.[192]

Intellectuals loathed the popular invasion of the countryside even before anyone had the temerity to set up homes there, objecting to the day-trips that were becoming more popular amongst the middle classes. As early as 1800 the poet Samuel Taylor Coleridge would complain that the Lakes were over-run with tourists. And in 1844 Wordsworth opposed the Kendal-Windermere railway extension, which he thought threatened to flood the Lake District with '...the whole of Lancashire and no small part of Yorkshire'.[193] 'Is then no nook of English ground secure from rash assault?' he wrote in a sonnet to the *Morning Post*.[194]

It was the suburban homes, though, that really provoked the snobs. As early as 1754 an article in the *Connoisseur* mocked the weekend villas that London tradesmen had built in Turnham Green or Kentish Town.[195] In the early nineteenth century it was possible to stop 'living over the shop' as suburbs in Clapham, Edgbaston, by Birmingham, and Ardwick near Manchester housed tradesmen's families, while they worked in town.[196] Surrounding London with acres of suburbia, warned the *Times* in 1904 '... is to produce a district of appalling monotony, ugliness and dullness. And every suburban extension makes the existing suburbs less desirable. Fifty years ago Brixton and Clapham were on the edge of the country ... Now London stretches to Croydon. It is no longer possible to escape from the dull suburbs into unspoiled country.'[197]

The real growth, however, took place between 1920 and 1939, when house building averaged at 300 000 a year, with a peak of 350 000 in 1936. All in all four million homes were built between the wars, nine tenths in newly developed or existing suburbs – Becontree to the east of London, Kirkby near Liverpool, Longbridge on the outskirts of Birmingham.[198]

Reaction to this fantastic expansion of human civilisation was brutal. It has already been noted that architect Clough Williams-Ellis (1883-1984) supported the founding of the CPRE in 1926, and two years later published an alarmist tract *England and the Octopus*, in which he set out his dread of suburbia. 'In the late War we were invited to fight to preserve England,' wrote Williams-Ellis, regretting that '...we saved our country that we might ourselves destroy it.' The problem was 'Urban beastliness':

'Having made our towns with such careless incompetence, those of us who have the means to be choosers are calmly declining to live in them and are now proceeding with the same recklessness to disperse ourselves over the countryside, destroying it and dishonouring it with our shoddy but all-too permanent encampments.'

The problem was that 'as the Joneses fly from the town, so does the country fly from the pink bungalow that they have perched so hopefully on its eligible site. And '...the Joneses have brought the blight of their town or suburb with them'. It is not hard to see that Williams-Ellis' arguments are not really about geography or even architecture, but about other people. Despite the immense surplus of land in Britain, to Williams-Ellis it seemed that '...our island is inconveniently, if not dangerously overcrowded'. And though his book is in the form of a plea to the public, he had little faith in them. 'This great majority – the unburied dead – are a perpetual drag on all progress whatsoever.' [199]

In a follow up to *England and the Octopus*, a compendium edited by Williams-Ellis called *Britain and the Beast*, and published in 1937, Howard Marshall wrote that '...a gimcrack civilisation crawls like a giant slug, across the country, leaving a foul slime behind it'.[200] C.E.M. Joad, who later established a reputation as the Brains Trust resident philosopher on BBC Radio, published *The Horrors of the Countryside* in 1931, cataloguing the spread of 'drab and squalid' bungalows south of London, a '...scurf of villas and bungalows' that has polluted practically the whole coast of Kent and Sussex, and the '...purulent beastliness of Worthing'.[201] It was the bungalow that '...constitute[d] England's most disfiguring disease',[202] and the 'Gloomy Dean', William Ralph Inge, coined the phrase 'Bungaloid growth' for it. Williams-Ellis' judgment endures to this day in the many pronouncements of the CPRE; and in the views of people like Tristram Hunt, who detest the '...nefarious breed of suburbia, which came to swamp inter-war Britain' [203] By an odd twist of fate, Williams-Ellis' best known work, the fake village at Portmeirion in Wales, was made to stand for the lifeless conformity he criticised, when it was used as the setting for Patrick McGoohan's eccentric TV series, *The Prisoner*.

Williams-Ellis campaigned against suburbia, and many other authors deplored it. In the popular children's story *Wind in the Willows*, published in 1908, Kenneth Grahame has '...the stoats and weasels of

199] Clough Williams-Ellis, England and the Octopus, (Uckfield, The Beacon Press, 1996) first published 1928, p 20, 31, 39, 40, 43, and 97

200] Howard Marshall, quoted in Peter Hall and Colin Ward, Sociable Cities: the legacy of Ebenezer Howard (Chichester, John Wiley, 1998) p 75

201] C.E.M. Joad, quoted in John Carey, The Intellectuals and the Masses: Pride and Prejudice among the literary intelligentsia, 1880-1939 (London, Faber and Faber, 1992) p 50

202] Clough Williams-Ellis, England and the Octopus, (Uckfield, The Beacon Press, 1996) first published 1928, p 141

203] Tristram Hunt, Building Jerusalem: The Rise and Fall of the Victorian City (London, Weidenfeld and Nicholson, 2004) p 328

204] John Carey, The Intellectuals and the Masses: Pride and Prejudice among the literary intelligentsia, 1880-1939 (London, Faber and Faber, 1992) p 49

205] Tristram Hunt, Building Jerusalem: The Rise and Fall of the Victorian City (London, Weidenfeld and Nicholson, 2004) p.333

206] John Carey, The Intellectuals and the Masses: Pride and Prejudice among the literary intelligentsia, 1880-1939 (London, Faber and Faber, 1992) p. 23-70, 48, 51, and 57

207] John Betjeman, Slough, 1937, posted on www.pmms.cam.ac.uk

modern suburbia ... destroying the England of his childhood'. In her story Fortunatus Rex and Co another children's writer, Edith Nesbit, attacked speculative builders who buy up '...all the pretty woods and fields' and '...put streets there, and lampposts and ugly little yellow houses'. E.M. Forster stayed with the Nesbits when Edith produced models of factories and suburban villas, made of cardboard and brown paper, and everyone set light to these effigies of urban encroachment, in a little ceremony in the garden.[204] George Orwell, who often let his misanthropy get the better of him, saw the suburban street as '...just a prison with the cells all in a row', or '...a line of semi-detached torture chambers'.[205] In E.M. Forster's *Howard's End*, Helena Schlegel points over the meadows to a 'red rust', which were houses on the horizon: 'London's creeping', she warns. Q.D. Leavis stigmatised the '...emptiness and meaningless iteration of suburban life' in *Fiction and the Reading Public*. Cyril Connolly thought that '...slums may well be the breeding-grounds of crime, but the middle-class suburbs are incubators of apathy and delirium'. Graham Greene described suburbia as '...a sinless, empty, graceless, chromium world'. In 1905, the poet T.W.H. Crosland dedicated a whole volume to The Suburbans, '...a low, inferior species', 'soulless', 'stingy', and tinned salmon eating. In *The Intellectuals and the Masses: Pride and Prejudice among the literary intelligentsia*, critic John Carey argues that the expanding white-collar suburbs were symbolic for intellectuals of the degradation and cultural mediocrity wrought by mass culture under the influence of universal education.[206] Along with bungalows, Carey remarks that tinned food seemed to be particularly repugnant to England's intellectuals, standing as it did, for the kind of people that ate it. In 1937 the poet John Betjeman brings the two markers of mediocrity, suburbs and spam together in Slough:

'*Come friendly bombs, and fall on Slough,*
It isn't fit for humans now

Come, bombs, and blow to smithereens
Those air-conditioned, bright canteens,
Tinned fruit, tinned meat, tinned milk, tinned beans
Tinned minds, tinned breath.'[207]

H.J. Massingham, '...a townee journalist who became a country dweller' thought the countryside was properly '...a source of our daily bread and the indispensable foundation of our national well-being'. Suburbia, by contrast was '...detached from all other cultures, detached from everything', though Angus Calder thought that '...probably suburb dwellers formed part of the large public for Massingham's books, which between 1930 and 1950 he published at a rate of more than one per year'. Seeing his Buckinghamshire landscape developed Massingham descended into melodrama:

> *'Only a handful of Englishmen regard this phenomenon as a*
> *catastrophe for England, but a truth is not cheated by evading it,*
> *and one day by no means in the distant future that tragedy will*
> *close, like Hamlet, in a harvest of catastrophe.'* [208]

The journalist Ian Nairn prepared a special issue of *Architectural Review* titled 'Outrage' in 1955. Seeing only 'Subtopia', the title of a book he published two years later,[209] he wrote there is '...the annihilation of the site, the steamrollering of all individuality of place to one uniform and mediocre pattern'. Nairn's fear of uniformity was echoed by the American architectural writer Lewis Mumford in 1961, who saw:

> *'A multitude of uniform, unidentifiable houses, lined up inflexibly,*
> *at uniform distances, on uniform roads, in a treeless communal*
> *waste, inhabited by people of the same class, the same income,*
> *the same age group, witnessing the same television performances,*
> *eating the same tasteless prefabricated foods, from the same*
> *freezers, conforming in every outward and inward respect to the*
> *common mould.'* [210]

Mumford warned that '...if what is called development is allowed to multiply at the present rate, then by the end of the century Great Britain will consist of isolated oases of preserved monuments in a desert of wire, concrete roads, cosy plots and bungalows'.[211] At the end of the century, Nairn's anxieties were not realised. Britain's green spaces are, thanks to the retreat of the plough, even more extensive than they were in 1955, but the anxieties are, if anything even greater.

In the 1980s the nostalgic conservative hatred of the suburbs was given a radical twist. Margaret Thatcher's victory in the 1979 election had stunned supporters of the old Labour Party, who found it difficult to believe that she had succeeded in winning popular support from working class people. The intellectuals of the left started to manufacture

208] Angus Calder, The Myth of the Blitz (London, Jonathan Cape, 1991) p 182 to 183

209] Ian Nairn, Subtopia (London, Architectural Press, 1957)

210] Lewis Mumford, The City in History: Its origins, its transformations, and its prospects (Harmondsworth, Penguin, 1991) p 553

211] Lewis Mumford, quoted in Anthony Barnett and Roger Scruton, Town and Country (London, Jonathan Cape, 1998) p 23

212] Thurrock Urban Development Corporation, 'Atlas, Thurrock: A Visionary Brief in the Thames Gateway', 2004, paragraph 2.3

213] Stuart Hall and Martin Jacques, editors, The Politics of Thatcherism (London, Lawrence and Wishart, 1983)

214] Dennis Hayes and Alan Hudson, Basildon: The mood of the nation (London, Demos, 2001) p 21, 24, and 29

215] Michael Danielson, The Politics of Exclusion (New York, Columbia University Press, 1976)

216] Dan Lazare, America's Undeclared War: What's killing our cities and how we can stop it (New York, Harcourt, 2001) p 157 and 288

217] Mike Davis, City of Quartz: Excavating the future in Los Angeles (London, Vintage, 1992) p 6

theories to explain the corruption of the masses, and Mrs Thatcher's supposedly unique appeal. It was difficult to avoid the evidence of the election results – Conservative support in the suburbs and throughout the South-East was solid. 'I think Essex Man will vote for a Conservative Government' said Thatcher, in April 1982. [212] Though radicals like Peter Hall and Colin Ward had celebrated the working class colonisation of Pitsea after the war, 'Basildon man' became an archetype of the Tories' success in winning over the aspiring working classes. In his 1983 book *The Politics of Thatcherism*, Stuart Hall argued that Thatcherites had won wide support for their powerful images of a new, share-owning, home-owning democracy from individual consumers. [213] By the end of the 1990s, Britain's New Labour Party wooed Middle England, though it has proved a patchy marriage. For much of the urban intelligentsia, the suburbs remain intrinsically foreign territory. Two academics who did take the time to ask Essex Man what he really thought, Dennis Hayes and Alan Hudson, found that Basildonians thought of themselves overwhelmingly as working class, though they had little use for trade unions; they were generally optimistic about their own conditions, but pessimistic about the country as a whole – not very different from the rest of the country, in fact. [214]

The British left's reaction against the suburbs had its model on the other side of the Atlantic. Just as Britain's leftists feared the judgement of Essex Man, in the United States the suburbs of California filled America's radicals with trepidation. Finding solace in city hall politics, American Democrats felt the suburbs slipping away from them. Starting with Michael Danielson's *The Politics of Exclusion* in 1976, [215] America's committed politicos heaped scorn on the country's burgeoning suburbs. To Dan Lazare the suburb is '...a bottomless black hole that sucks up energy and wealth in order to sustain an increasingly uneconomical existence'. But it is the threat to the cities as much as the countryside that animates the radical case against the suburbs. Like Ancient Rome, says Lazare '...the Fordist suburb draws parasitically off the cities'. The migration of wealth to the suburbs, he thinks '...was not urban decay but a form of urban manslaughter' which would '...reduce one city after another literally to rubble'. And for good measure Suburbia is '...boring to its depths'. [216] Mike Davis elaborates the theme writing of '...sterilized sites stripped bare of nature and history, master-planned only for privatized family consumption'. [217] Lazare also charges that suburban communities were '...middle class redoubts whose raison d'être was to screen out blacks, Jews...' It is of course true that the way that the suburbs expanded in the US – and in Britain – was exclusive socially, and racially. But it was the failing of the political system that made racial exclusion central to Western societies in the twentieth century. Damning the suburbanites as racists tells us more about the radicals' alienation from the greater mass of the American people than it does about suburbs.

In the face of such a deluge of anti-suburban hostility it is difficult not to succumb. After arousing such animosity, surely the suburbs have done something to earn our wrath? No doubt many people remember glum childhoods and stultifying moralism in the suburbs. But it is worth considering that inner cities and countryside can be stultifying too. John Carey is surely right when he argues that the suburbs are just too broad to earn the collective judgement set out for them. Put another way, decrying the suburbs is just a rhetorical device for decrying modernity and change. Think about Notting Hill. First celebrated as countryside under the threat from suburban encroachment; then as original suburb, threatened from outer suburban development; and finally as inner city, drained by suburban flight.

The common note in all of these reactions is a fear of change. Further, the case against the suburbs reads like a case against most of us. The suburbs – usually creeping or sprawling suburbs – are generally defined against other populations that are in decline: the elegised country-folk, or lately, the abandoned inner-city dwellers. In this rhetoric, the contrasting population are invoked not for any original characteristics they have, but to serve to show the shortcomings of suburbia. The qualities that intellectuals moan of in the suburbs – vulgarity and a lack of community and spirituality – are the qualities that they find missing in society at large. 'Suburbia' is just a shorthand for 'Anywhere' in these screeds.

The lack of community in particular is a compelling concern. In Thurrock in 2004, the Secretary of State for Culture, Media and Sport, Tessa Jowell chose a presentation on development to launch her department's latest document *Culture at the heart of regeneration*. [218] But is the belief that new suburbs are uncultured really justified? Simon Gunn and Rachel Bell think that '...the pace at which the associational life of the suburbs grew was vigorous'. Their study of the suburbs near

218] Department of Culture, Media and Sport, Culture at the heart of regeneration (London, DCMS, 2004) posted on www.culture.gov.uk

219] Simon Gunn and Rachel Bell, Middle Classes: their rise and sprawl (London, Phoenix, 2002) p 79

220] Sarah Ivens, 'The Mother of All Essex Girls', Observer, 3 October 2004

221] Stevie Smith, quoted in The Intellectuals and the Masses: Pride and Prejudice among the literary intelligentsia, 1880-1939 (London, Faber and Faber, 1992) p 68 to 69

Morden, South London found that the Stoneleigh Residents Association grew in membership from 600 in 1936 to 1,400 in 1939, and '...a whole gamut of activities and organisations was set up under its auspices: whist drives, dances, cricket club, motoring club, cycling club, an orchestra and choral society'. They argue that '...it is clear that the suburb was not the isolated, private place that critics such as the writer George Orwell or the architect Clough Williams-Ellis described'. [219]

John Carey makes the case that the suburbs are far from un-cultured, producing such talents as the poets Stevie Smith, Philip Larkin and, even, John Betjeman – one could add film-maker John Boorman, and, though he resented it, angry young man John Osbourne. Anti-suburban snobs derided 'Essex Girls' in the 1980s, but they ought to include actresses Helen Mirren, Maggie Smith and Sheila Hancock, singers Sade and Alison Moyet, commentators Germaine Greer and Julie Burchill in their list. [220] Indeed one might stretch the point to say that much of the criticism of suburbia was consumed by a largely suburban audience. Stevie Smith was untypical in singing the praises of the suburb:

'In the high-flying outer northern suburb the wind blows fresh and keen, the clouds drive swiftly before it, the pink almond blossom blows away. When the sun is going down in stormy red clouds the whole suburb is pink, the light is a pink light, high brick walls that are still left standing where once the old estates were hold the pink light and throw it back. The laburnum flowers on the pavement and trees are yellow, so there is this pink and yellow colour, and the blue-grey of the roadway, that are special to this suburb. The slim stems of the garden trees make a dark line against the delicate colours. There is also mauve and white lilac.'

Smith liked the '...briskness, shrewdness, neighbourliness' of Palmers Green in North London, where she lived most of her life. Like the romantic poets, she enjoyed rugged nature, but knew her self well enough to know '...only those who have the luxury of a beautiful, kindly bustling suburb...can indulge themselves in these antagonistic forest thoughts'. [221] In fact Smith's Palmers Green was far from being without cultural life. The Women's Social and Political Union was active there, as was the Fabian Society, which Mrs Pankhurst and her daughters Christabel and Sylvia addressed, while Lady Constance Lytton addressed the Palmers'

Green literary society. According to Smith's biographer 'Societies and clubs flourished', and a cinema opened in 1912. [222]

John Boorman paints a characteristic picture of growing up in suburbia. He combines condemnation of insularity and snobbery, but also a sense of the aspirations that moving out expressed. 'Was there ever such a stealthy social revolution as the rise of this semi-detached suburbia?' he asked, and. '...where did they come from, these millions?' Boorman's answer is:

> 'We were convalescents from the Industrial Revolution and needed several generations of fresh air and proper food to recover'.

Then '...half the population was wrenched from the land and into city slums ...And now here were the survivors fleeing to these new suburban streets, fugitives from not only the shock of the Industrial Revolution, but also of the unspeakable horrors of the First World War and the privations of the Depression.' 'It was a massive migration.' Boorman's account of the charms of middle class life in Carshalton is sarcastic:

> 'On Sundays the car ['the Morris 8 or the Austin 7'] was ceremoniously wheeled out from the garage, washed and polished and the parents, with their two little tots in the back, would motor off to the seaside or to Box Hill or to the zoo at Whipsnade'.

But does it really sound so bad? Boorman remembers a '...comfortably snug void', 'with the bonds of traditional society severed':

> 'Filling that emptiness was the wireless. It played all day, banishing the dread silence, yet I never heard a reference to the semi-suburbs in those BBC programmes.' [223]

For those moving to the suburbs there was a disconnection from the social bonds that were created in industrial cities. But these bonds could be romanticised just as easily as the suburban home. In *Family and Kinship in East London*, their paean to the 'extended family', sociologists Michael Young and Peter Wilmott divined a 'sense of belonging' that was 'so deep because it is rooted in a lasting attachment to their families'. [224] The truth was that life in industrial cities was for most people hard, and for some, penury. The clubbable nature of London that Dr Johnson celebrated, the society of the eighteenth century

222] Francis Spalding, Stevie Smith: A Critical Biography (London, Faber and Faber, 1998) p 12

223] John Boorman, Adventures of a Suburban Boy (London, Faber and Faber, 2003) p 7 to 9

224] Michael Young and Peter Wilmott, Family and Kinship in East London (Harmondsworth, Penguin, 1980) first published 1957, p 187

225] Terry Eagleton, The Function of Criticism, from the Spectator to Post-structuralism (London, Verso, 1997)

226] Gordon Cherry, quoted in Harley Sherlock, Cities are Good for Us: the case for close knit communities, local shops and public transport (London, Paladin, 1991) p 148

227] 'Supercities', Channel 4, posted on www.channel4.com

228] Will Alsop, Supercity (Manchester, Urbis, 2005)

coffee houses was restricted to a relatively small circle of people. [225] And though the suburbs might seem insular their growth coincides with a growth in the cultural life of the population, whether measured in newspaper readership, library membership, the growth of new media like radio and television, or the expansion of education. The new, red-brick universities of the 1960s are characteristically suburban in their setting, and in their recruitment: Essex in Colchester, Sussex in Brighton, Kent in Canterbury, Southampton, and the Open University based in Milton Keynes.

In 1972 Gordon Cherry proposed loosening the bounds of city-dwelling in his *Urban Change and Planning*: 'Urban areas will not have a setting of a green belt surrounding a circular, compact area, but will be loosely dispersed with belts of green between.' Anticipating much of the actual development of the South-East, Cherry argued that '...within this polyform type of area, not one but a number of central concentrations where specialist activities take place will be located at junctions of the circulation system.' [226] Cherry's optimism seems out of place today, but that might be a reprimand to us, rather than him.

A contemporary architect who embraces the disaggregation of the city is Will Alsop, who show-cased his idea of *Supercities* on Channel 4 in 2003. Alsop sketched out Supercities, which are already coming into existence.

> '*In contrast to conurbations of the past which grew out in a sprawling mass from the centre, these new cities are linear and relatively narrow, stretching out along communication routes, like motorways.*' [227]

Alsop's supercities are:
> Coast to Coast city route, a 130-mile long, 20-mile wide strip of the M62 from Liverpool to Hull. For its 15.4 million residents, high-tech, high-rise living would mean that no-one was far from the outskirts of the city or from its central line.
> The Diagonale, from Birmingham in the centre of England to London and Southend on the Essex coast.
> Wave, looping along the South coast from Hastings to Poole in Dorset. [228]

Another visionary, Martin Pawley attacks the urban-country divide:
*'Today, because of motorways, electronic communications, scientific
agriculture and the globalisation of the food industry, the old
Ebenezer Howard diagram of the relationship of town and country
as radial and concentric no longer describes reality. The corrected
version would be a distributed network in which the 11 per cent
of the land surface already urbanised is shown as becoming
progressively less densely developed, by means of selective demolitions.
While the 89 per cent of non-built-up countryside is shown as
becoming more densely developed, by means of dispersed new
housing and related services. The whole programmed to reach
an Arcadian mean in which the arbitrary distinction between
agricultural and building land is removed, and a uniform network
of low density settlements served by appropriately sized distribution
centres is growing up to replace it.'* [229]

Marcial Echenique, whose plans for enlarging Cambridge have helped
the city change itself from a sleepy university town to Britain's Silicon
Valley, is similarly optimistic about the prospects for dispersed living.
'It seems to me', he writes, '...that we should not force people back
into high density environments in order to reuse brownfield sites'.
Rather, '...we need to think of innovative options, such as transforming
brownfield sites into parks and other recreational areas':
*'Then, we can entice households back into these areas with their
spaciousness and accessibility by car. In other words, we should
suburbanise these brownfield areas.'* [230]

Far from being necessarily de-humanising, dispersed settlements are
an opportunity for an enlargement of the human spirit. To imagine that
there is anything in physical proximity that is essential to community
is to confuse animal warmth with civilisation, and an unfortunately
deterministic view of architecture's relationship to society. But worst
of all it misses out the great alternatives that are waiting to be made in
new communities across the country.

229] Martin Pawley, 'The sand-heap urbanism of the twenty-first century', in Ian Abley and James Heartfield, editors, Sustaining Architecture in the Anti-Machine Age (Chichester, Wiley-Academy, 2001) chapter 13, p 152 to 161

230] Marcial Echenique, 'Mobility and space in Metropolitan Areas', in Marcial Echenique and Andrew Saint, editors, Cities for the New Millennium (London, Spon, 2001) p 35

CHAPTER FIVE

THE CULT OF NATURE

ONE OVERRIDING FEELING IN THE CASE AGAINST DEVELOPMENT IS THE LOVE
of nature. In the countryside, nature is threatened by new building.
But nature is often seen rather childishly as something that is pure,
in contrast to the dirty city. This is nature as an ideal, or a cult. It is
a romantic picture of nature that is hard to sustain. There really is
precious little nature that is not already the outcome of man's work
on it, and especially not in the English countryside. More than that,
our idea of nature is one that is changing all the time, in keeping with
our changing social position. [231]

Keith Thomas argues that '...in Renaissance times the city had been
synonymous with civility, the country with rusticity and boorishness.'
Then, '...when men thought of heaven they usually envisaged it as a city,
a new Jerusalem.' In 1802 the romantic poet, Wordsworth, who went on
to craft our contemporary idea of nature, thought that Earth had
nothing to show fairer than the sleeping city of London seen from
Westminster Bridge. But in time the prejudice took root that 'God made
the country, man made the town'. Quaker William Penn, who founded
the state of Pennsylvania, preferred the country life, '...for there we see
the works of God, but in cities little else but the works of men'. [232]
'God made the country, man made the town and the devil made the
suburbs', in William Morris's version. [233]

What's more, the **kind** of countryside that is in vogue changes
over time, expressing different attitudes, and changing relationships
between man and land, and man and man. 'Throughout the eighteenth
century and beyond, the improvers continued to praise this regular

231] Nan Fairbrother, New
Lives, New Landscapes;
Planning for the twenty-
first century (New York,
Alfred A Knopf, 1970)

232] William Penn, quoted
in Keith Thomas, Man and
the Natural World:
Changing Attitudes in
England 1500-1800
(Harmondsworth,
Penguin, 1984) p 243 and
250

233] Fiona MacCarthy,
William Morris: A life for
our time (London, Faber
and Faber, 1994) p 541

234] William Cobbett and Hugh Blair, quoted in Keith Thomas, Man and the Natural World: Changing Attitudes in England 1500-1800 (Harmondsworth, Penguin, 1984) p 257 and 259

235] Keith Thomas, Man and the Natural World: Changing Attitudes in England 1500-1800 (Harmondsworth, Penguin, 1984) p 250 and 264

landscape of opulence and productivity and to deplore the uncultivated waste.' Thomas quotes the early-nineteenth century reformer William Cobbett, who detested the 'rascally heaths': 'I have no ideas of picturesque beauty separate from the fertility of the soil', he said, summarising a central idea of enlightenment utilitarianism. But by the end of the eighteenth century conventional tastes in landscape had already turned through 180 degrees. Now it was the un-kept – or at least the illusion of the un-kept – that held the imagination. 'What are the scenes of nature that elevate the mind in the highest degree and produce the sublime sensation?' asked critic Hugh Blair lecturing in Edinburgh. 'Not the gay landscape, the flowering field or the flourishing city; but the hoary mountain, and the solitary lake; the aged forest and the torrent falling over the rock.' [234] This is the nature of the Lake Poets, the romantics, Wordsworth, Keats, Shelley and Coleridge. It is very much our own time's view of nature – but it is not a natural attitude. Rather it is one that was crafted for us, by them. Their idealisation of unadorned nature has a purchase because it appeals to something in our social, not our natural, condition.

Thomas thinks that '...the growth of a sharp division between town and country...encouraged this sentimental longing for rural pleasures and the idealization of the spiritual and aesthetic charms of the countryside'. Citing Hugh Blair, Thomas argues that '...a taste for the pastoral **depended on the prior growth of the towns,** for men did not pine for the countryside so long as they lived on terms of daily familiarity with it.' Furthermore, the celebration of uncultivated nature, '...this ability to derive pleasure from scenes of relative desolation represented a major change in human perception':

> 'Inevitably it was more likely to be found among those who, by virtue of their social and economic position could contemplate with equanimity the prospect of leaving land uncultivated which might otherwise have produced food. Only when the threat of starvation receded could such an attitude prevail.' [235]

The towns changed the countryside itself. Before the growth of the industrial cities, the countryside was full of cottage industries. The first mills were water mills, and places like picturesque Cromford in Derwent, were the birthplace of the industrial revolution. But, says ecological historian James Winter '...industry, including cottage industry, gradually departed from the country, when steam energy came to be applied to machinery, thus leaving the countryside more agrarian than it had been before or ever would be again'. [236] The countryside that seems original to us is one that has had all the industry sucked out of it, into the towns.

But the real transformation that makes the romantic countryside is the expulsion of the peasantry that once worked those fields intensively. Political commentator, Anthony Barnett makes the point, quoting the historian Martin Wiener's groundbreaking study of the decline of the industrial spirit in England:

> 'The country was, "available for use as an integrating cultural symbol" precisely because it was virtually empty and hence safe. "The vision of a tranquilly rustic and traditional national way of life (which) permeated English life" originated with massive depopulation of the actual countryside. Vacant land is sacred.' [237]

Thomas insists that seeing '...the countryside as a symbol of innocence rested on a series of illusions', involving '...that wholly false view of rural social relationships which underlies all pastoral' – 'The cult of the countryside was...a mystification and an evasion of reality.' [238]
Barnett agrees:

> 'The English consciousness with its gentrified repression of urban and industrial reality regards the tiny village as somehow central and the towns – in which 90 per cent of the population lives – as artificial.' [239]

But the countryside, too, has been made by man. As the historical geographer Henry Clifford Darby explained, the English countryside in general, '...is as artificial as any urban scene'. [240] The late historian Roy Porter gently mocks the modern environmentalist: 'What passes these days in England for nature – the chequerboard fields, hawthorn hedgerows and coppices which conservationists defend against developers – is largely the product of Enlightenment agri-business, landscape gardening and peasant-cleansing.' [241]

The meaning of the romantic ideal of nature can be seen in the Victorian contest between the Lakes and the City. In 1876 Britain's romantics were angered by plans to dam Thirlmere in the Lake District, to give water to sprawling Manchester. Robert Somervell, son of

236] James Winter, Secure from Rash Assault: Sustaining the Victorian Environment (Berkeley, University of California Press, 1999) p 166

237] Martin Wiener, English Culture and the Industrial Spirit (Cambridge, Cambridge University, 1981) quoted in Anthony Barnett, Iron Britannia (London, Allison and Busby, 1983) p 102

238] Keith Thomas, Man and the Natural World: Changing Attitudes in England 1500-1800 (Harmondsworth, Penguin, 1984) p 250 and 251

239] Anthony Barnett, Iron Britannia (London, Allison and Busby, 1983) p.102

240] Henry Clifford Darby, 'On the Relations of Geography and History', Transactions of the Institute of British Geographers, 19, 1953, p 6, and reviewed in Michael Williams, The Relations of History and Geography: Studies in England, France and the United States (Exeter, University of Exeter Press, 2002)

241] Roy Porter, Enlightenment: Britain and the Creation of the Modern World (London, Allen Lane, 2000) p 297

242] Robert Somervell, John Ruskin, and John Graves, quoted in James Winter, Secure from Rash Assault: Securing the Victorian Environment (Berkely, University of California Press, 1999) p 179 to 180

243] www.thecumbria directory.com

244] Phil Macnaghten and John Urry, Contested Natures (London, Sage Publications, 1998) p 35

a shoemaker from Kendall, and inspired by John Ruskin, wrote a pamphlet – *Water for Manchester from Thirlmere*. Somervell won support from his mentor Ruskin, as well as the great man of letters, Thomas Carlyle, and reformers Octavia and Miranda Hill. Ruskin wrote that the best solution would not be that the '...Lake of Thirlmere be brought to the top of Manchester, but that the town of Manchester...should be put at the bottom of Lake Thirlmere'. Ruskin thought it the special claim of Thirlmere that it had kept itself free of '...villas and all that is villainous'. The Chairman of the Waterworks Commission, John Graves demanded who had given these priests, romantics, intellectuals, art critics, poets and agitators the right to sneer at villadom? [242] Indeed, some have suggested that Ruskin and Carlyle's campaign was '...less purely environmentalist than it was anti-Manchester and what that city represented'. Somervell's campaign held back the damming of Thirlmere till 1891, and it is today a site of great beauty. According to the Cumbria Directory '...the area around the lake offers walking trails' and recommends itself, ironically, because '...it's a peaceful, quiet spot to get away from it all ...devoid of human habitation and visitor facilities'. [243] Where once it was the sign of the victory of industry over nature, today the casual visitor to Thirlmere would easily take it for precisely the romantic setting that the poets were trying to defend.

Victorian preservation societies, like the National Trust and the Royal Society for the Protection of Birds were '...established during the latter stages of the (nineteenth) century, largely because of perceived concerns about the negative impact of industrialism and urban growth'. [244] The romantic ideal of nature in the mid-Victorian age concealed some unattractive prejudices against mass man, but these were tempered at least by an attention to the loss of human scale in the industrial revolution. But as it grew old, the romantic ideal of nature grew sourer, and less generous in its impulses.

In the 1930s the rural reviver Rolf Gardiner promoted '...organic farming and forestry, Morris dancing, communal singing and the recovery of seasonal rituals like beating out the bounds', all from his Springhead estate in north Dorset. His prototype youth movement was premised on a strongly anti-urban attitude. In 1935 Captain George Pitt-Rivers, another Dorset landowner, fought the general election as the Wessex Agricultural Defence Association, though during the war he was interned as a Nazi sympathiser and servants recall swastikas displayed in his manor house. Viscount Lymington founded an 'English Array', organised as 'musters' scattered around the country under the slogan 'English Food in English Bodies'. 'Their theorists wrote vile things about the urban working class – perceived as hideously fecund, hybrid and degenerate in every way'. Lady Eve Balfour formed the Soil Association '... on the inspiration of Lord Lymington's alarmist tract *Famine in England*'. [245]

Today's urban elites are possibly a little more sceptical about the romantic ideal of the countryside. Experimental writer Iain Sinclair, considering the nature cult of painter Samuel Palmer passes this judgement:

> 'As with pre-Raphaelites, Arties and Crafties, hippies, the paradigm was lost in the past: medieval, Gothic – without plagues, torture, hunger, and ice. Discretionary poverty. Cider. Bread. Cheese. Nuts, Green tea. Optional peasants bringing in the hops. Poverty which, in Palmer's case (as with so many of Notting Hill's countercultural elite of the sixties), was underwritten by a small private income and a property portfolio.' [246]

But as we shall see, it is not only the countryside which has been mythologized; the city too has its romantics.

245] Patrick Wright, 'An Encroachment too Far', in Anthony Barnett and Roger Scruton, editors, Town and Country (London, Jonathan Cape, 1998) p 30

246] Iain Sinclair, London Orbital – a walk round the M25 (London, Penguin, 2003) p 416

CHAPTER SIX

THE DECLINE OF RURAL BRITAIN

'IT'S THE DIDS', SAYS FARMER BARBARA, AN IMPRESSIVE SERGEANT MAJOR'S daughter-type. 'Dids?' 'Diddicois, travellers you probably call them. They are behind all the crime around here.' Everybody agrees. In fact it is the only thing that they talk about. 'You find them in the middle of the night driving across your farm and they just say "have you got any work?", but you know that they are looking for stuff to steal', says Dick. 'They steal farm equipment, diesel fuel, anything they can find. You want to go after them, but what if you go armed and they are not? Or what if they are armed and you aren't?'

'The police won't follow them into their camps', says terry, jumping off his combine harvester in dark glasses and pipe. 'I'd send the troops in. That would soon sort them out.' It is true, of course, that travellers are a law unto themselves. It is also true that the police are cautious about taking on travellers' camps. But the farmers' crime panic is not really about crime, which is no great problem.

Farmers are feeling insecure for other reasons. In particular they are worried about 'the Dids' because they used to give them work, but now, with the rural economy faltering, there is none. 'They're not the same as the old travellers we used to get', says Barbara, echoing the then home secretary Jack Straw's distinction between 'real' Romanies and travellers. 'We used to give them work on the fields, but these lot are different. They don't want to work.' What she means is that there is no work to give them. As surplus labour, hanging around hare coursing, 'the Dids' make the farmers nervous.

247] Interviews by the author, September 1999

248] Guardian, 11 September 2003

249] Guardian, 12 August 2000

250] Guardian, 19 September 2003

But then Jeremy from the Farmers' Union started to get a bit nervous, too, nervous that the farmers have been too explicit. 'Not all crime is committed by travellers, and not all travellers are criminals', he says. Barbara, Terry and Dick, meanwhile, are all looking at him as if he has been out in the sun too long. When Tony Martin shot a 16-year old boy dead on his farm, he became a hero among Norfolk farmers. 'I warned them that something like this would happen on the very day he was shot', Martin's local councillor told me. 'Now they admit that Norfolk has the lowest police funding in the country.' Norfolk also has one of the lowest crime rates in the country, but that does not seem to cut much ice with the local farmers. [247]

'From my young days, I can remember it being a lively village', Donald MacKay told Gerard Seenan of Calbost on the Hebridean Island of Lewis. *'There were 14 crofts, and croft nine had five families on it. It was small but fruitful. Then, one by one, the families left. The depopulation is across this area. Before the First World War, there was a population of 1900 on the Pairc estate, now it is down to 400.'* [248]

Scotland's population has fallen two per cent since 1981: in 2002 only 51,270 babies were born in Scotland, the lowest number since records began in 1851, and the average number of children in a family is 1.48, the lowest in Britain. Depopulation is felt most keenly in the barren stretches of rural Scotland. The Western Isles are depopulating. Between 1981 and 2001 the islands lost 16 per cent of their population. On some islands the figure is 40 per cent.

The problems of the Scottish crofters can be seen throughout Britain's countryside. Novelist and countryman Christopher Hart writes that:

'In a few years time, many of these people and their "economically marginal" farms – the small sheep farms of the wild and beautiful uplands of Cornwall and the Pennines, of the moorlands of Wales and the wide chalk downs of Wessex – will go the same way as the shipyards on the Clyde.' [249]

Sparsely populated land deteriorates, without people on hand to look after it. In September 2003 a blaze which started at Fylingdale burned off four square miles of tinder-dry heather then sparked more fires, cutting off the Lyke Wake Walk and Cleveland Way. [250]

The total number of full-time farmers dropped from 173,000 in 1995, to 169,000 in 1997; the total number of farm labourers dropped from 248,000 in 1995, to 243,000 in 1997. In 2001 the government announced plans for the countryside that envisage one quarter of all farms will have closed or merged, with 50,000 people forced to leave the industry. The Ministry of Agriculture, Fisheries and Food predict that the number of farm workers of all kinds could fall below 300,000 by 2006, a drop of 100,000 since 1994. Farmers' earnings in the year to February 2001 were just £5,200 a year, or just £3,500 for a hill farmer. [251] The damage done to the countryside in recent years has spurred mass demonstrations called by the Countryside Alliance, [252] on the issue of parliament's proposed ban on fox-hunting – a reform seen as emblematic of the town's failure to understand the countryside.

The problems faced by the countryside are difficult to separate from two successive farming disasters, epidemics first of Bovine Spongiform Encephalitis (BSE), or 'Mad Cow disease' in the period from 1994 to 1997, and then of foot-and-mouth disease in 2002.

The first was particularly debilitating because of its impact on public trust of farmers. BSE remains a poorly understood disease to this day, transmitted by prions, which cause a build-up of protein in the brain, eventually disrupting brain functions, leaving diseased cattle stricken with motor-neurone disease. Public alarm – the town's distrust of the countryside – was focussed on the possibility of cross-species infection. Environmentalist critics of 'agri-business' incited disgust amongst consumers, pointing out that the disease was spread by the use of beef remains in cattle feed. The existence of a similar disease in humans, Creutzfeld Jacob Disease (CJD) led to the belief that this was the 'human form' of BSE. The Leeds-based scientist Richard Lacey first proposed that Bovine Spongiform Encephalitis, entering into the food chain, caused CJD. Lacey was reported as saying that virtually a whole generation of people might die. [253] On the basis of Lacey's estimates One World reported that '...it was estimated that 34 million people could be infected by 1997.' [254] In the event annual deaths from CJD were negligible, and generally lower than those caused turning off a radio alarm clock (20) or falling out of bed (20).

No matter how overstated fears of cross-species infection through the food chain, the impact of the Mad Cow panic was devastating to British farmers. They were believed to have put consumers at a terrible

251] www.maff.gov.uk

252] www.countryside-alliance.org

253] Richard Lacey, Nature, 13 May 1990, issue 345, p 648, posted on www.nature.com

254] One World, April 1996, and posted on www.oneworld.org

255] The BSE Inquiry, 'Statement No 625 Professor Philip Thomas', posted on www.bseinquiry.gov.uk

DEATHS FROM VARIANT CREUTZFELD JACOB DISEASE (VCJD)

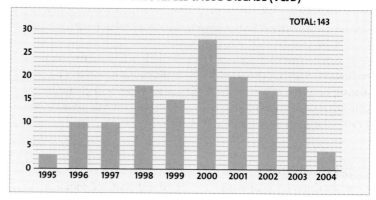

risk just to cut costs. Initial attempts to shore up public confidence had the opposite effect – not least because the Conservative government doing the persuading was already deeply distrusted. When Environment minister John Gummer had himself filmed feeding his children beef burgers, the message was supposed to be 'beef is safe'. But sceptical voters only assumed that Tory politicians would sacrifice their own children to cover up the crisis. A draconian culling policy seemed to be the only way to win back lost markets. During 1998 some 890,000 cattle were slaughtered under the Over Thirty Months Slaughter Scheme, making a total of 2.9 million since it was introduced in May 1996. In 2000 government adviser Professor Philip Thomas was a lone voice in the wilderness, when he said '...we told the government more than a year ago that there would be no epidemic of new-variant CJD and that spending billions on slaughtering cattle would save only a few lives'.[255] It seemed that things could not get worse for British farmers, but within four years there was another livestock disaster: foot-and-mouth disease.

Foot-and-mouth disease affects cows, pigs, sheep and goats and, though not fatal, its flu-like symptoms prevent livestock from fattening-up while infected. In more sedentary societies, foot-and-mouth would not stop the raising of animals for food, especially where mutton as well as lamb is acceptable. The infection is virtually harmless to humans (only one or two slaughter men ever contracted the disease). But where farmers' capital is tied up in livestock the increase in the time it takes to turnover his capital effectively reduces the returns below a profitable level. Furthermore, the threat that foot-and-mouth (much more virulent that BSE) represents to farmers' returns means that only certificated foot-and-mouth free stock will be bought.

The last outbreak of foot-and mouth was in 1967, when widespread culling was adopted as to create a firewall against infection, on the assumption that British livestock needed a 100 per cent guarantee to command consumer confidence. Then 400,000 animals were culled. In 2001 the numbers were even greater:

256] Times, 31 January 2002

THE DEATH TOLL
» Total number of animals slaughtered with foot-and-mouth or on contiguous farms - 4,080,001
» Total number of animals slaughtered under the Animal Welfare Disposal scheme and the Light Lamb Disposal Scheme, set up for farmers not hit by foot-and-mouth but whose stock was suffering from movement restrictions – 2,573,317
» None of the above, including all piglets, calves and lambs, as estimated by Farmers Weekly – 2,000,000
» Total – 8,653,318
» Total number of premises where animals have been slaughtered – 9,996
» Number of farms affected by the outbreak – 10,124
» Number of confirmed cases of foot and mouth – 2,030

Source: *Times*, 31 January 2002

Conscious of the political damage done by acting slowly in the BSE crisis, the Blair government culled pre-emptively and extensively, slaughtering thousands of uninfected animals on adjacent farms. This time it was not the public outrage against the farmers, but small farmers outrage against the culling policy that was felt. 'The government has made it clear that we are totally expendable – they want to cull us', one farmer's wife told Ann Treneman of *The Times*. [256] Conspiracy theories abounded in the countryside. Farmers told Treneman that a phial of the virus was stolen from Porton Down germ warfare centre to infect sheep, cattle and pigs, and the army dropped ears from these animals on to fields from helicopters. In the year to June 2000, 5,300 more farmers and farm workers lost their livelihood.

THE HEALTH CRISES IN CONTEXT

With the countryside reeling from one crisis – BSE – to the next, foot-and-mouth, it is easy to lose sight of the way that the infections only hastened the underlying trends in agriculture: overproduction, falling prices, bankruptcy and the concentration of farms into larger agri-businesses. The two successive infections and the policies adopted to deal with them brought these trends out into the open.

The major impact of the various regulations and the subsequent EC ban on British produce has been to accelerate the restructuring of European farming. For decades European beef production has outstripped effective demand. Politically motivated subsidies to farmers have glutted the market with unwanted beef, accumulated in 'beef-mountains' of Euro-legend, and distributed free to pensioners, the famine-struck, and social security claimants. Under the guise of health measures, Britain's beef farms were concentrated in the hands of a few big agri-businesses, and smaller farmers forced out.

The BSE panic was informed by hostility to agri-business: a growing environmental lobby helped undermine public confidence in farmers by highlighting the less attractive features of industrialised farming – not least the use of beef remnants in cow-pellets, widely held to be the cause of the BSE outbreak. But ironically, agri-business actually enhanced its domination over small farmers through the very process of regulating the industry. The trend towards fewer but bigger farms and abattoirs is being forced along by new rules on hygiene brought in by the EC. For MAFF there is an excess capacity in abattoirs, and they expect the smaller less efficient firms will be forced to close.

In 1997, following the public BSE crisis, total farm incomes fell by 35 per cent, and for farmers and their spouses (i.e. exclusive of partners, directors and workers) by 45 per cent. The value of beef production fell by six percent, or £111 million; the fixed capital stock of farms fell by £230 million between 1996 and 1997. Between 1993 and 1997 the number of small-holdings (1-19 beef cows) fell from 45,500 to 42,200, while larger herds (over 50) rose over the same period from 9,500 to 10,700. The small herds accounted for a steady 339,000 cows, while large herds increased from 842,000 to 983,000.

In other words, the BSE culling, regulation and ban had helped
a reduction in the number of farms and farm workers, as larger businesses
swallowed up the smaller. The unintended consequences of the new
regulations on agri-business have been bigger agri-businesses,
and fewer family farms.

There is an historical parallel. In 1906 Upton Sinclair's book
The Jungle drew attention to the dirty and repressive conditions in the
meat packing industry,[257] leading to a meat inspection law that broke
the Beef Trust – or at least that is how the official version runs.
Reflecting on the storm over *The Jungle*, Sinclair wrote that he was
primarily moved by the condition of the workers, not the meat: 'I aimed
at the public's heart, and by accident I hit it in the stomach. I am supposed
to have helped clean up the yards and improve the country's meat
supply – though this is mostly delusion. But nobody even pretends that
I improved the condition of the stockyard workers.' Historian Gabriel
Kolko explained: 'The reality of the matter, of course, is that the big
packers were warm friends of regulation, especially when it primarily
affected their innumerable small competitors.'[258]

In 2001 the government forecast that one quarter of all farms will
have closed or merged with 50,000 people forced to leave the industry.
Amongst hill farmers, even with subsidies averaging £33,000 a year,
their incomes averaged at just £3,500 in 2001.[259] The Hill Farms Task
Force, chaired by David Arnold Forster, called for subsidies to be directed
to funding early retirement and diversify the local economy. In 1999,
a quarter of hill farmers were over 60. On 9 April 2001 agriculture
minister Nick Brown told MPS '...the big decision for farmers who have
received compensation payment is whether to restock the farmholding
...or pause and think very carefully what the future holds for them.'
MAFF predicts that the number of farm workers could fall below
300,000 after 2006, and already a drop of 100,000 since 1994. The fall
in the existing number of farms, on top of existing trends, could be
15-20 per cent, although some may be merged into larger businesses.
In 1999, 75 per cent of the sheep and cattle holdings were responsible for
98 per cent of output. The largest ten per cent of holdings are responsible
for 35 per cent of output. Most smallholdings – 17 per cent in 1999 – are
in Cumbria, which was worst hit by foot and mouth.[260]

On 20 April 2001 the Hill Farms Task Force report argued that hill
farmers could become 'land stewards'. Grants would be focused on

257] Upton Sinclair, The
Jungle, 1906, and posted
on
http://sunsite.berkeley.ed
u/Literature/Sinclair/TheJ
ungle/

258] Gabriel Kolko, The
Triumph of Conservatism
(New York, Free Press,
1963) p 103 and 107

259] Guardian, 18
February 2002

260] Guardian, 11 April
2001

261] DEFRA, Task Force For
The Hills (London, HMSO,
2001) p 4, posted on
www.defra.gov.uk

262] History of
Agriculture, 'Post-war
Agriculture', posted on
www.ecifm.rdg.ac.uk/pos
twarag.htm

issues such as animal density, the length of field boundaries and the
cost of maintaining the landscape, including dry-stone walls. There
would also be additional payments to special areas of conservation or
common land. The report suggested that the foot-and-mouth crisis:

> '...could provide an opportunity to encourage a less intensive and
> more environmentally friendly way of farming. The future could
> be one in which animals do not have to travel so far, local markets
> reduce the roles of the middle man and the big chains, and the
> environmental output of the hills – which underpins tourism and
> quality of life for society – is properly rewarded.' [261]

That all sounds marvellous. But actually it means that the government
wants to edge people out of farming. The alternative they have in mind
is perverse. Rather like the ex-miners who became guides in Sheffield's
Earth Museum, the farmers are to be made into custodians of the land
they no longer farm: from farmers to park-keepers, in fact.

The argument to turn farmers into land custodians goes to the heart
of the official reaction to the contraction of farming. Their overriding
concern is not farming, but the defence of the monopoly over land.
The mythical status of the English countryside disguises the way it has
changed over time. Today, three quarters of Britain is farmland, but the
extent of agriculture is not set in stone for all time.

It was the war years that made what is called 'food security' a priority,
and the fear of disruption of imports meant that policy was skewed
towards increasing output both during and after the war. At the end
of the war in 1945 Britain needed to maximize food production – food
rationing did not end until 1953. Generous guaranteed prices were
continued for major agricultural products. The 1947 Agricultural Act
was passed and supported by all political parties, and stated:

> 'The twin pillars upon which the Governments agricultural policy
> rests are stability and efficiency. The method of providing stability
> is through guaranteed prices and assured markets.' [262]

Annual price reviews were instigated and prices fixed for the main
crops (wheat, barley, oats rye, potatoes and sugar beet) for eighteen
months ahead. Minimum prices for fat-stock, milk and eggs were fixed
for between two and four years ahead. An agricultural expansion plan
aimed to raise output from agriculture by 60 per cent over pre-war levels.

Without that commitment of the government to price support, farmers would never have agreed to relinquish their development rights on freehold land, as the 1947 Town and Country Planning Act required. Or put the other way, the price exacted for agricultural subsidy was the denial of the freedom of farmers to sell their land for development. Without the Agricultural Act of 1947 there would be none of the Planning Law that stops farmers selling up to developers and retiring today. After nearly 60 years of increasing agricultural output, it is worth recognising the predicament facing farmers in 1947.

There are two ways of increasing agricultural output: either extensively, by putting more land under cultivation, or intensively, by getting higher yields from existing land. In the first instance the policy promoted extensive growth. W Robertson Scott, editor of *The Countryman* wrote in 1947, '...I could not have believed that between 1924 and 1947 the countryside would have got more than three-quarters of a million new cottages'.[263] The British Agricultural Act gave way to the wider European Common Agricultural Policy, which also favoured extensive growth as it subsidised prices. The CAP empowered an Intervention Board to buy up surpluses to guarantee a healthy return. The effect was to artificially boost prices, and to reward farmers for increasing their output. The effects of extensive growth can be seen today in the over-extension of farmland. In March 1988 the Intervention Board held half a million tonnes of barley and 100,000 tonnes of beef. Wartime fear about self-sufficiency turned the country into a vast agricultural estate.

CAP subsidies went to big and small farmers alike, putting off the day of final reckoning one would expect in a more open market. Though protected against competition from abroad, the bigger agri-businesses still introduced economies of scale and mechanisation to increase output by intensive methods of growth, even if smaller farmers did not. The impact of the advances in output has been remarkable.

In 1955 Jacob Roisin of the Montrose Chemical Company and *Readers Digest* editor Max Eastman published the classic exposition of the green revolution, *The Road to Abundance*:

> 'The time has come to recognize that our dependence for food on the dilatory and inefficient plant is a cruel bondage. We have given the plant almost the entire floor space of our planet and devoted to it by far the largest part of our energies. And in return we have not got enough food to go round.'

263] www.countryman magazine.co.uk

264] Max Eastman, Jacob Roisin, The Road to Abundance (London, Rider, 1955) p 23, 122, and 144

265] Robin Page, 'Restoring the Countryside', in Anthony Barnett and Roger Scruton, editors, Town and Country (London, Jonathan Cape, 1998) p 101

266] Chris Haskins, Guardian, 7 March 2001

Roisin and Eastman complained that '...our social and political scientists often deal astutely with problems concerning distribution of resources, but the thought of creating new resources such that these problems may be made obsolete is alien to their minds.' Citing the application of pesticides and fertilisers to increased yields Roisin and Eastman say that '...chemistry has already rescued agriculture'. And they anticipate that '...its ultimate destiny...is to replace agriculture altogether, except as a pastime'. [264]

The agricultural writer Robin Page explains the impact of the improvements on patterns of land use:

> 'Advances in animal and crop husbandry; breakthroughs in botany, biology, chemistry and technology have for years meant higher yields. Consequently, just as more land was being brought into production, agricultural sciences were rapidly increasing yields and making self-sufficiency attainable in any case.'

And on joining the European Common Agricultural Policy, '...we quickly drifted from a situation of food deficiency to one of surplus.' [265] The price of farm goods fell year on year, a saving that is being passed on to consumers in food prices. According to the British Household Survey spending on food and clothing fell from around a third of income in 1950 to a tenth in 1998. According to Northern Food's Chris Haskins '...if we wanted to recreate the countryside of 40 years ago, either the consumer or the taxpayer would have to pay at least twice as much (an extra £50bn) for food.' [266] Food and drink manufacturing is now Britain's largest manufacturing sector, incidentally buying £11bn worth of raw materials from British farmers.

As long as the CAP was intact, small farmers were protected against the consequences of falling food prices, as the Intervention Board boosted those prices with artificial demand. But the reformed CAP no longer subsidises prices, but subsidises production. The small farmers were suddenly exposed to the full impact of their failure to keep pace with new techniques.

The problems in agriculture are without doubt a tragedy for the small farmers who are on the receiving end of these policy failures. Their feeling, that there is an urban elite misunderstanding their plight, is no doubt true. But there cannot be a return to the past. Perpetuating less efficient farming as a hobby, or decoration on the English countryside is not an option – it is a recipe for turning the disadvantages and hardships of the farmers into a permanent institution. Today, UK agriculture accounts for less than one per cent of GDP, while the CAP costs the average family of four, £16 a week. [267] Public opinion will no longer tolerate the permanent subsidy of a way of life that is no longer viable. Yet farmers are not free to sell their land to developers as they might have done pre-1947.

Understandably, small farmers are unwilling to accept defeat, and dedicate considerable ingenuity to rescuing the family farm. The flurry of innovative attempts at diversification are impressive, but in the long run, probably not viable. The best known is the increase in organic farming promoted by the Soil Association in Britain. Since 1994, the government has spent millions subsidising farmers who switch to organic farms, though these still only account for less than one per cent of farm produce in the developed countries. One farmer says that '...I'm lucky to get half as much yield from my organic acres'. [268]

Government policy is dressed-up as a policy to re-purpose agricultural communities as 'market towns' and centres of tourism. But one questionable motivation underlying the policy is the desire to retain the monopoly over land, in the guise of maintaining the 'landscape'. According to the Hill Farms Task Force:

'Should land be abandoned it will profoundly alter the landscape which people expect to see when they visit the uplands. We think there is an urgent need for action to sustain the landscape and wildlife which is now as valuable a product as the stock hill farmers traditionally produce.' [269]

It should be noted that the Task Force's anxiety about land being abandoned comes before any concern about the farmers. Sealing the landscape in amber actually means fossilising the division between town and country, and its current proportions.

The problem is not hard to fathom. As farming produces more on less land, land is 'abandoned', or ceases to be farmland. Naturally enough, the land released by farmers, is potentially land for housing development. Here is a solution to the housing shortage: land is available. But the authorities take a different view. Indeed they are positively alarmed by the growing availability of land due to more efficient agriculture. Instead of grasping the nettle, and releasing the land for development,

267] Felicity Lawrence, 'Greening the farms', Guardian, 28 January 2002

268] R Bate and J Morris, Fearing Food: Risk, Health and Environment (Oxford, Butterworth-Heinemann, 1999) p 6

269] DEFRA, Task Force For The Hills (London, HMSO, 2001) p 4, posted on www.defra.gov.uk

they have instinctively expanded the limitations on development. As land passes from agriculture, the government has stopped it going to development by swallowing it up in national parks, national trust land, green belt and all the other artificial land monopolies that it has at its disposal.

The expansion of the National Trust Nature Reserve at Wicken Fen in Norfolk in the late 1990s is an example. The fen was first allotted to the Trust in 1899, as peat and read cutting declined. During the Second World War, when farmland was needed, Wicken Fen was drained and farmed again. Today, with agriculture once again retreating, Wicken Fen has been enlarged by the Trust's purchase of adjacent farms, thanks to £1 million from the Heritage Lottery Fund, and is planned to grow by 3,700 hectares overall, taking in nearby Swaffham and Burwell, north east of Cambridge. Elsewhere, conservationists propose to turn the South Downs, the former sheep pastures just north of the southern coast of England, running form Southampton to Eastbourne, into a national park. They are opposed by the farmers who want to sell off their land, now that their sheep herds have shrunk, and developers who want to buy it up to house the overspill of the expanding population. Thanks to this sort of land-retirement scheme, the new land that is released from decades of farming is withheld from people wanting homes, and handed over, instead, to areas of scientific interest, landscapes of natural

TOTAL AGRICULTURAL AREA, UK

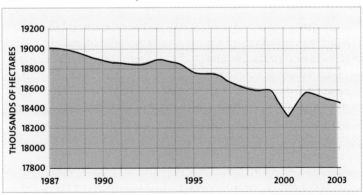

Source: Department for Environment, Food and Rural Affairs, posted on www.defra.gov.uk

NET ANNUAL AVERAGE CHANGE IN LAND USE 1996-98

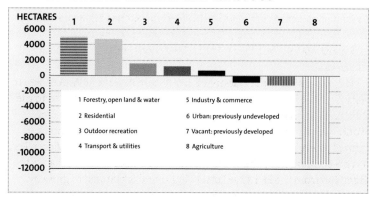

Source: Office of the Deputy Prime Minister, now Department of Communities and Local Government, posted on www.communities.gov.uk

beauty and other tendentious excuses for keeping people off the land. Martin Pawley has rightly commented:

> *'Nowhere is there any acknowledgement that the predicted need for more building land is more than matched by a tremendous superfluity of agricultural produce, which has left a huge surplus of unused agricultural land. So striking and so irreversible is this situation that – were they allowed to – impoverished farmers, land-strapped greenfield house builders and would-be home owners could solve one another's problems at a stroke.'* [270]

Environmentalism provided a rationale for the extensive retirement of land from agricultural production on conservationist grounds. With increased yields, less land produces more grain, so agribusiness needs land taken out of production to avoid a glut. By taking land off the market, the government and the European Union have succeeded in stopping a collapse in farm rents and land prices, but these are now beginning to show a decline, as one would expect with the closure of farms. [271] Conservation provides a convenient justification for governments to exclude land from farm use.

The same is true internationally. In the United States forestland is growing 588,600 hectares on average every year, adding to the one-third of the US already covered by forests, or just over 300 million hectares. [272]

270] Martin Pawley, 'So, Lord Rogers, why shouldn't we build on surplus rural land?', Architects' Journal, 24 February 2000, p 20

271] John Walsh, Valuation Office Agency, 'Agricultural land prices statistics and indicators', MAFF, posted on www.maff.gov.uk

272] United States Department of Agriculture, Foreign Agricultural Service, statistics, posted on www.fas.usda.gov

273] EU Forest Action
Plan, posted on
http://ec.europa.eu/agric
ulture/fore/action_plan/

274] www.forestry.gov.uk

275] Mischa Balen, Land
Economy: How a rethink
of our planning policy will
benefit Britain (London,
Adam Smith Institute,
2006) posted on
www.adamsmith.org

276] Guardian, 6 August
1997

In the European Union forests are growing 486 million cubic metres every year. [273] Since 1919 there has been a sustained expansion of forest cover in many areas of Britain. As a result, at the beginning of the twenty-first century, forests cover nearly 12 per cent of Britain, with the figure in parts of Scotland nearing 25 per cent. It is officially recognised that Britain has moved from being 'forest poor' to becoming 'forest rich'. [274] So it seems unnecessary for Mischa Balen, writing for the Adam Smith Institute, to want most redundant farmland to be turned into still more British woodland, with only a minimal 5 per cent of any of that land to be retired from agriculture into housing. [275]

The growth of national parks and wildlife reserves is the modern equivalent of the great estates. They are created to withhold productive land from labourers, and to limit the unchecked spread of land-squatting subsistence farmers. Professor Bernhard Grzimek, Hitler's curator of Frankfurt Zoo and the champion of the Serengeti nature reserve, claimed: 'A National Park must remain a primordial wilderness to be effective. No men, not even native ones, should live within its borders.' [276] Like the traditional stewardship of the land, the modern nature reserve serves to police the boundaries of economic growth.

CHAPTER SEVEN

THE PHANTOM HOUSING BOOM

WHEN THE AMERICAN RADICAL ECONOMIST DOUG HENWOOD MET *TIMES* EDITOR Robert Thomson in 2003 he wanted to know what it was that kept the UK economy so buoyant in the face of its industrial downsizing. Henwood, author of After the New Economy, was bemused by Thomson's answer: the housing market.[277] To any independent observer it seemed obvious that the housing sector was in very bad shape. After all, house building is at an historic low, compared to the boom years at the end of the 1960s. Yet on the narrow definition, the boom was a success: rising house prices meant an improvement in assets for home-owners. How could so sluggish a sector produce such extraordinary growth? The answer is simple. The housing boom is not a housing boom at all; at least it is not a boom in new house production. Rather it is a boom in house prices. And the boom is taking place almost entirely in the **second-hand** housing market. As Shaun Spiers of the CPRE rightly says, the housing market is '... dominated by transactions involving existing, not new homes'.[278] In the inverted world of housing, most houses and flats are bought second-hand. It is as though Sotheby's shifted more units than Ikea.

The simple explanation for the rise in house prices is that it is caused by the shortfall in house and flat completions. The supply of new homes is not enough to meet the demand, so the prices of the smaller pool of homes rise, dampening demand. But increased prices do not seem to have dampened the demand, and the market continues to boom. And worse still, developers have not responded to the higher prices by increasing house building, all of which seems to add up to a bubble in prices.

277] Doug Henwood, After the New Economy (London, The New Press, 2003)

278] Guardian, letters, 7 September 2004

89

279] Mira Bar-Hillel,
'Young elite go east for
good-value housing',
Evening Standard, 7 July
2004

280] Patrick Collinson,
'Housing Boom Profits
the South', Guardian, 27
February 2002

281] Helen Carter, 'City
living – Manchester goes
mad for it', Guardian, 10
May 2004

In fact, house prices rose year on year from 1997 right through to 2003, by five, ten, 15 and even 20 per cent, only seeming to stop in August of 2004, responding, perhaps to the interest rate rises made by the Bank of England, and to the difficulties facing first time buyers trying to enter the market. The housing boom seemed at first to be restricted to London. Living in central London had become an over-expensive dream for many. 'Forget Notting Hill, Chelsea and Hampstead', wrote Mira Bar-Hillel in the Evening Standard; 'Today's highly-paid and well-connected young professionals are heading east'. A study for Barclays Financial Planning identified a market they called 'affluentials', young professionals, singles and couples, with earnings above £60,000, who have still '...been priced out of London's smartest postcodes and are looking for period properties in more unlikely locations'. The up and coming areas identified were Bethnal Green and Bow, which saw a 60 per cent increase in new residents with an income above £60,000 in 2003, Holborn and St Pancras (57 per cent), North Southwark and Bermondsey (56 per cent), Chingford and Woodford Green (55 per cent) and Ilford North (53 per cent).[279] As wealth washed outwards the sub-urbs saw big rises, too. The London suburbs of Thames Ditton and Teddington showing three-fold price rises between 1991 and 2001, while Ayrshire, Blackpool and Redcar stagnated. Tim Keywood, of Thames Ditton and Esher Estates, was pleased with the new business, though he himself has had to move out, because he cannot afford to live there anymore.[280] But the price rises were not restricted to London's immediate suburbs, but spread throughout the South of England. Over 2004, Bristol and Southampton's prices both rose by 9.1 per cent on average, pushing the price of a semi-detached house up to £174,106 in the former and £166,572 in the latter. Oxfordshire's by 6.3 per cent, pushing a semi up to £212,465. The wealth effect was beginning to slip beyond the South East. In central Manchester most of the 200 flats in the new 47-storey Beetham Tower, with prices starting at £100,000, were '...sold before planning permission was granted'.[281] Estate agents report that investors are buying properties in Manchester and Liverpool, with an eye to letting them.

The causes of the boom are debatable. On the most optimistic reading it is just the effect of rising incomes – a reading that is not without justification. 'Over the long term', wrote the Chairman of the Nationwide Building Society Sir Herbert Ashworth 20 years ago, '...there is a fairly stable relationship between house prices and average earnings'. In fact house prices ran ahead of earnings post war, when there was a housing shortage, with wages only catching up in the 1950s; then Harold Wilson's Labour government imposed wage controls from 1966, but when the Statutory Incomes Policy was overturned three years later, wages rose ahead only to see house prices shoot up in turn in the early seventies.[282] Only the recession of the early eighties dampened both. Between 1985 and 2001 the UK workforce grew by a fifth, from 24 to 28 million. Each of these new incomes potentially represents an ambition to own. Pointedly the regional pattern of house prices closely mirrors economic developments. It is not just that rising prices and new jobs are weighted towards the South-East, which they are. Among the top ten regions for price rises in the decade to 2001 are Lisburn, Newry and Bangor in Northern Ireland, with Belfast coming eleventh.[283] This happy appearance of the peace dividend is mirrored by falling unemployment – 'the economic and social revival of Northern Ireland', say the authors of a geographical analysis of the 2001 Census, is a '... persistent theme', alongside the '... dominance of London and the South East of England'.[284] Financial journalist Heather Stewart calls this the 'crowded island' thesis:

> *The number of households in Britain is rising; since the financial liberalisation of the "greed is good" 1980s, everyone wants to own their own home – and not enough houses are being built to accommodate them all.'*[285]

It is important to put the housing shortage in perspective – at least in its impact upon house prices. Houses are in short supply relative to the increasing number of incomes chasing them. And as Stewart says, the shortfall is in relation to growing expectations of home ownership that were fuelled in the 1980s. Put another way, social housing, and to some extent the private rented sector, have been stigmatised. Homelessness, which was a re-occurring problem in the 1980s, has not become the problem it was. It is true that by the summer of 2004, the numbers in Local Authority temporary accommodation were set to exceed 100,000, having grown by 7,870 over the previous year.[286] This problem was felt most acutely amongst black and Asian families.[287] The Centre for Housing Research at York University found that there were around 44,000 rough sleepers in England between the ages of 16 and 24.[288] Difficult as these circumstances are, they are not characteristic of the

282] Herbert Ashworth, The Building Society Story (London, Franey and Co., 1980) p 206

283] Patrick Collinson, 'Housing Boom Profits the South', Guardian, 27 February 2002

284] Daniel Dorling and Bethan Thomas, People and Places: A 2001 Census atlas of the UK (Bristol, Policy Press, 2004) p 1 and 89

285] Heather Stewart, 'In search of a soft landing', Guardian, 6 August 2002

286] 'Number in TA set to exceed 100,000', Property People, 16 September 2004

287] 'Homelessness soaring among ethnic minorities', Shelter, Press Release, 20 September 2004

288] John Carvel, '52 000 youths have nowhere to live, study finds', Guardian, 11 October 2004

289] Daniel Dorling and Bethan Thomas, People and Places: A 2001 Census atlas of the UK (Bristol, Policy Press, 2004) p 169 and 168

290] Alan W. Evans, Economics and Land Use Planning (Oxford, Blackwell, 2004) p 61 to 62

291] Kate Barker, Barker review of housing supply – delivering stability: securing our future housing needs – Final Report and Recommendations (London, HMSO, 2004), posted on www.barkerreview.org.uk

292] Kate Barker, Barker Review of Land Use Planning: Interim Report – Executive Summary (London, HMSO, 2006) posted on www.hm-treasury.gov.uk

293] Ferdinand Mount, Mind the Gap: The New Class Divide in Britain (London, Short Books, 2005)

greater part of the population's experience of housing. 14 million of us own our own homes outright (up by four million on 1991), and a further 27 million have a mortgage, with about 70 per cent of households being owner-occupiers. At the same time, rising prices have slowed the increase in mortgage lending, and the private rented sector is growing to take up the slack, from 4.7 million people in 1991 to 6.1 million in 2001. 'Private renting is the dominant tenure in much of London' and compared to the rest of the UK '...people are least likely to be buying their homes in inner London'. [289]

The shortcoming of the explanation for the boom from incomes alone is straightforward enough: while average earnings are growing at around four per cent a year, house prices are growing at 20 per cent, pricing many out of the market altogether, as we can see from the rise in the rented sector. One might expect some lag between the rise in prices and producers reacting to increase supply, but in fact the lag has turned into a straight refusal. Now the difficulty is to understand why the sector has proved so unresponsive to the price signals that orthodox economics say ought to engender more output.

Embarrassed at the growing problem, the government has tended to blame the developers, accusing them of sitting on land-banks, speculating on future profits instead of meeting demand today. But the developers in turn have a more straightforward explanation for the non-appearance of new homes; the regulatory framework that holds back new growth. The planning laws, the green belt, the onus on greenfield developments and so on. Alan Evans sets out the economics of the green belt and other controls on development in his *Economics and Land Use Planning*: 'The supply restriction means that prices will rise faster than they otherwise would'. [290] This is the conclusion, too, to Kate Barker's a *Review of Housing Supply*: that the procedure for getting planning permission has to be streamlined to facilitate more development, so meeting the demand for new homes. [291]. Consequently she is now engaged with her Review of Land Use Planning, currently at Interim Report stage. [292] It is also the thinking behind Ferdinand Mount's proposals for freeing up land for development as a way of addressing inequality, in his recent book *Mind the Gap*. [293] Mount pointed to the vast swathes of land in the South East that were vacant, but without planning permission. The idea to lift planning restrictions was earlier proposed as a resolution to the current housing crisis by Ian Abley, in his chapter in

Sustaining Architecture in the Anti-Machine Age – 'Development rights for the hydrogen-fuelled future'. [294] Abley called for the abolition of the Town and Country Planning Acts stemming from 1947, and for land to be treated like any other commodity. It would be '...better to leave people free to decide exactly what the parameters of social responsibility in local development should be'. 'Trust landowners to use their development rights wisely', said Abley in 2001.

It is not just that the Town and Country Planning Act makes it difficult to begin building, though that is problem enough. When investors decide where to put their money, the prospect of a delay of years is good reason to put it elsewhere. In tying up capital, those delays increase costs, often prohibitively. But on top of that, the planning regime imposes additional costs. Section 52 of the 1971 Town and Country Planning Act allowed local authorities to trade planning permission against agreements on the part of the developers to make improvements to the site that might normally have been a public responsibility. These can include road improvements, the provision of parks, capital improvements to local schools, hospital or recreational facilities. Section 52 agreements – renamed section 106 agreements under the 1990 Town and Country Planning Act – turn planning permission into a tradeable commodity. That enables planning authorities to wring resources, or 'Planning Gain', from developers, over and above their commitments to local and national tax. With Section 106 being replaced, it will soon be more familiar for planners to ask for 'Planning Gain Supplement'. But it is the same game.

As Alan Evans says, authorities '...came to realise they had something of value, which others wanted, and the result was, as an economist might expect, that local authorities tried to appropriate some of the profits for themselves'. Champions of civic responsibility will no doubt applaud the attempts to make the developers pay for the upkeep of the social fabric – but they ought to consider how this windfall tax can act as a disincentive to build. Not just local authorities, but any interested local group can turn their right to be consulted on planning permission into a commodity. Evans reports a case where '...it was put to the party applying for planning permission for residential development of a site, by at least two neighbourhood groups, that although they had no objection in principle to the proposal they felt they were not getting enough out of it and would therefore object' [295]

294] Ian Abley, 'Development Rights for the Hydrogen-Fuelled Future', in Ian Abley and James Heartfield, editors, Sustaining Architecture in the Anti-Machine Age (Chichester, Wiley-Academy, 2001) chapter 18, p 210 to 227

295] Alan W. Evans, Economics and Land Use Planning (Oxford, Blackwell, 2004) p 96 and 98

296] David Smith, 'Putting balance back into the housing market', Sunday Times, 23 November 2003

297] Ben Hunt, The Timid Corporation: Why business is terrified of taking risk (Chichester, Wiley, 2003)

298] Department of Trade and Industry, UK Competitiveness Indicators (London, HMSO, 2001) p 37, 68, and 69

The implication being that their objections would be withdrawn if more benefits accrued to them. Again, one might be tempted to applaud the canny locals, rooking the wicked developer, but this is a dampening effect on development, which is stopping new homes being built. London's mayor Ken Livingstone has been aggressive in the use of Section 106 to achieve goals, like the provision of social housing from developers, and most recently, from supermarkets.

According to economic writer David Smith, the building industry '...argues that the government has loaded so many extra costs onto builders, including the requirement in many cases to provide social housing in new developments, that this has become a serious constraint'. There should be no doubt that the restrictive regime of planning has limited development, and that this is a major cause of the housing price boom. However, we cannot be confident that even if the Town and Country Planning Act were abolished tomorrow, that developers would meet the new demand. David Smith acknowledges developers are tied down by the obligations arising out of planning constraints, but insists that '...the problem is that private developers haven't filled the gap left by the public sector'. When annual house completions numbered just over 400,000 in the late 1960s, says Smith, half were completed by local councils. 'That's not a plea for a return to large-scale council housing', says Smith, [296] but it does raise the important question of whether the private sector is in the right frame of mind to meet the shortfall.

Economic journalist Benjamin Hunt examined in detail the 'risk aversion' that he found endemic amongst corporate bosses, in his book *The Timid Corporation*. [297] Hunt identified shareholder activism and its demands to unlock value as one of the main constraints on longer-term investments, and argued that, against expectations, corporations were greatly influenced by the anti-growth mood promoted by environmentalists. 'Greed is good' meets 'the Good Life' in a mutual antipathy to long-term investments in development. Certainly in 2001 the Department of Trade and Industry's investigation into competitiveness found that '...evidence does not suggest that the UK is over-investing'. In fact '...the UK remains relatively risk averse', and '...the UK's relatively more risk-averse approach contributes to lower levels of entrepreneurial activity'. [298] In the construction industry, the problem of risk aversion is evident in the low level of building. After all, they make as much, if not more money selling a few over-priced homes as they do selling lots of realistically priced ones. No doubt they are pleased that the planning regulations make it possible for them to make money without having to take any risks, or put in any effort. In some quarters, developers are under fire for hanging onto land without building. Suspicions of gentlemen's agreements to moderate competition might seem like paranoia, but developers have agreed not to compete for labour – as was revealed when Laing O'Rourke outraged rivals by offering far better pay to recruit labourers to build terminal five at Heathrow. The government might find that it is not enough to lift the planning restraints on development, but will also need to direct investment, with subsidies, to persuade timid investors that their risks are worthwhile. In other words, there will have to be a revolution in attitudes to development on both sides.

THE SPECULATIVE BOOM

Even after identifying the income-driven growth in demand, the regulatory limits on supply and the problem of risk-averse investors, we have not wholly explained the reasons for the house price boom. Economist Sabina Kalyan of the consultants Capital Economics Ltd argues that '…although the number of housebuilding completions has stagnated in the 1990s, the situation has not worsened dramatically – at least not enough to explain the current soaring house price inflation'. [299] Indeed. At least a part of the boom in house prices is part of a pattern that is nothing to do with houses. Instead of buying houses to live in, many people are now buying houses as a way to invest their spare cash. Of course, most of us generally talk about our homes as 'an investment', enjoying their climb in value, and despairing if they fall. But that is not the same thing as the growth of the housing investment market. The Office of the Deputy Prime Minister notes the growth in '…the influx of new landlords due to the introduction of buy-to-let mortgages', and that the number of second homes owned principally as an investment more than doubled between 1994 and 2001. [300] Perhaps the most high profile purchase was that of the Prime Minister's wife, Cherie Booth/Blair, who bought two flats in Bristol in 2002 as an investment – a case fluffed up by the press into **Cheriegate**. Overall, the Blairs did badly in the property market, giving up their ideally located Islington home for Number Ten just at the start of the property boom. Nonetheless, Cherie Booth's Bristol investment drew the public's attention to this new species of

299] Sabina Kalyan, quoted in Heather Stewart, 'In search of a soft landing', Guardian, 6 August 2002

300] National Centre for Social Research, Housing in England 2001/2; A report of the 2001/2 Survey of English Housing, carried out by the on behalf of the Office of the Deputy Prime Minister (London, HMSO, 2003) p 21 and 51

301] Larry Elliott, 'Message no self-respecting pigeon would carry', Guardian, 9 December 2002

302] Phil Mullan in correspondence with the author

303] John Cassidy, Dot.con – The Greatest Story Ever Sold (London, Allen Lane, 2002)

speculation. The *Guardian*'s perspicacious economics editor Larry Elliott hung an assessment of the speculative bubble of the housing market ('what the case of the two Bristol flats has to tell us about the political economy of modern Britain') on the unfortunate Cherie: 'Sadly the trend over many decades means that Britain's economy is now much better suited to buying and selling houses than making things'. Elliott continued to argue that '...the buy-to-let craze has helped stoke up house price inflation and contributed to the current precarious state of the economy'. [301]

Elliott is right to put the housing boom into the wider context of speculative investments. For the last 15 years or so there has been a free-floating speculative bubble that is largely indifferent to the sectors that it inhabits, taking a hold of them, not for the purpose of creating new products, but for realising profits on alienation; buying cheap to sell dear. The speculative bubble has wandered the globe searching for high returns, stoking boom and bust as far a field as Moscow's banks and Hong Kong's real estate – after passing through East European and Thai economies, without apparently adding any positive improvements in the 'real' economy of material production. In time the East Asian asset prices reached unsustainable levels, and investors withdrew their capital – just in time for the Dot.com boom. As economist Phil Mullan explains: 'Surplus capital attaches itself to certain phenomena at different times, such as shares, bonds, commercial property, mortgages, or gold.' [302]

New technology start-ups raised extraordinary funds in flotations by trading on the general ignorance of the Internet, and the consequent anxiety that investors would 'miss out' – just as investment in East Asia and Eastern Europe was pushed forward by a fear of missing out on investment opportunities in emerging markets. As *Sunday Times* and *New Yorker* economics writer John Cassidy explains in his excellent account *Dot.con – The Greatest Story Ever Sold*, financial advisors tore up the rules governing investments on the grounds that the 'new economy' worked differently: asset prices were going in one direction only, upwards, and it no longer made any sense to worry about how the investments would generate the earnings to pay for themselves. [303] Of course, this was a self-fulfilling prophecy. As long as new investors kept joining in the frenzy, then asset prices would continue to rise, as increased demand for Internet shares pushed up the price. The gains came about not by the earning power of the companies being launched – which often proved to be negligible – but in the increase in the price of the shares. Just by buying cheap and selling dear, fortunes were to be made. The boom lasted seven years, from 1993 right through to 2001, reinforcing the belief that the old cycle of boom and bust had been abolished. In April 1996, the search engine Yahoo! was floated, pushing the company price up to $850 million, though it only had 68 people working for it. But eventually shares did fall, and the readjustment was spectacular. Shares in Netscape fell from $88 on October 2000 to $21 in August 2001, Yahoo's from $178 to $11.86. Robert Barbera, Chief Economist at Hoenig & Co. pointed out that the loss in share prices was equal to the aggregate profits between 1995 and 2000, saying '...what it means is that, with the benefit of hindsight, the late 90's never happened'. [304]

But Robert Barbera is exaggerating. The late nineties did happen, and for many years many people made a lot of money on Dot.com shares. Who lost? There is always a case to be made that the bigger, institutional investors were ahead of the curve, so that the smaller investors paid the price: 'Wall Street milks Main Street'. Certainly some people were ruined. But for the most part, the investment bubble just moved on.

Speculative bubbles, according to their celebrated historian, John Kenneth Galbraith, are driven principally by psychological factors, such as the herd instinct, and the usual deference to those with money. [305] No doubt there is a lot of truth in that. But it is also the case that speculative bubbles can only take place where there is surplus capital hunting for a place to go. In the boom years of the post-war growth, from 1950 to1970, speculative episodes were rarer because capital was being directed towards re-building war-damaged Europe. But as Europe moved from underdeveloped ruin to a once-again mature economy, its industries showed signs of saturation and inertia. Though they generated considerable surpluses, they seemed too gargantuan to receive any more investment input, and increasingly pushed their cash reserves into financial speculation instead. As the author of *Cowardly Capitalism*,[306] financial journalist Daniel Ben-Ami explains: 'Surplus liquidity arises spontaneously from the atrophied productive sector. With falling stock markets this has created an added impetus for the house price boom as liquidity has shifted from shares to houses.' [307] So, too, the growing numbers of small investors with cash

304] Robert Barbera, interviewed by Steve Liesman, Arkansas Democratic Gazette, 19 August 2001

305] J. K. Galbraith, A Short History Of Financial Euphoria (Harmondsworth, Penguin, 1993)

306] Daniel Ben-Ami, Cowardly capitalism: the myth of the global financial casino (Chichester, John Wiley & Sons, 2001)

307] Daniel Ben-Ami in correspondence with the author

308] Guardian, 16 April 2004

309] Guardian, 6 August 2002

310] Evening Standard, 23 August 2004

to spare tend to seek out short-term gain, rather than the secure, dependable, but low-performing shares that once made up most portfolios. It is the greater amount of surplus capital in circulation that gives rise to the squalls and twisters of the contemporary speculative bubble. These investment stampedes arise out of needs – the need to put your spare capital somewhere – that come **before** the particular sector that gets selected as the target of the excitement: be it Dot.coms, junk bonds, emerging markets, fine art, South Sea Companies, tulip-mania or houses. The only characteristic that the particular asset has to exhibit is that it is not so plentiful that the price falls, but instead keeps on rising as more people enter the market. The novelty of the Dot.coms made sure that the demand always exceeded the supply, but the low level of housing completions makes house prices a sure bet – at least until the market gets saturated.

The house-price boom gives rise to a lot of moralistic finger-wagging, and commentators follow Galbraith in anticipating a terrible crash – the hangover after the party. In fact most stories about the market are about the coming collapse, hoping that it can be averted by a soft landing. Headlines read 'Can the crash be averted?', [308] 'Will there be a housing crash?', [309] and 'In search of a soft landing'. [310] From the summer of 2004 the market did falter, calling forth a great welter of **I told you so's**. But in fact the 'crash' was just a slower rate of growth in prices.

HOUSE PRICE INFLATION

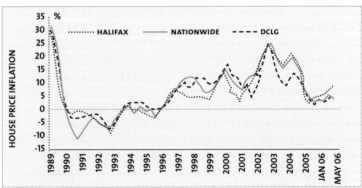

Source: Housing Markets and Planning Analysis Division, Department for Communities and Local Government, 'Housing Market Report – June 2006', comparing Halifax Building Society, Nationwide Building Society, and DCLG house price inflation indices, www.communities.gov.uk

Of course, it is true that prices cannot climb for ever, but like the Dot.com boom, predictions of its end can be expected to go on all the way through the boom. Perhaps by the time you are reading this the market will be in ruins, but that will not take away from the fact that it did boom quietly away for a good few years, before really taking off in 2001, and is still going strong in 2006. For investors, this is has been good news, so far. But investment is only one reason houses are bought and sold; another, arguably more important, is to live in them. When the 'Robber Barons' boosted railway stock in the US in the 1890s many fortunes were made and some people were ruined – but in the process, a great deal of track was laid. Even in the much maligned Dot.com boom of the late nineties, real investments in cable, 3G and other telecom innovations were left after the dust had settled. The potential disaster for the housing market is that phenomenal amounts of capital could pass through the sector without ever engendering any new growth at all. While the housing market is pre-eminently a second-hand goods market, investment will only be speculative, ramping up the prices of existing houses, giving rise to no new production. It really would be a hard-landing if the price boom evaporated, and the only thing that we were left with at the end is the same old dilapidated housing stock we had at the outset.

DESTRUCTIVE SYMPTOMS OF THE BOOM

There is a lot of moralising about the housing boom, so some of the complaints about its negative consequences are prone to being exaggerated. For home-owners the experience of a steady growth in their investment is no doubt a welcome windfall, but unearned income is always a little troubling to the puritanical streak in Cromwell's Island, so we can expect some guilty preoccupation with the potential downside.

So spare a thought for the thirty-something 'cross-shifters' and 'new authentics', who are on the back of the money made on their appreciating houses. Sorry, is that unclear? Blame the researchers at the Future Laboratory, who researched this niche category for Standard Life. They decided that '...too young for a midlife crisis, but too old for a youthful rebellion', the New Authentics are '...bucking the system, using the property boom to build new lives well away from the rat race': [311]

311] Kirsty Scott, 'Solvent thirty-somethings turn backs on rat-race', Guardian, 26 June 2004

99

312] Greg Easterbook, Future Laboratory, The Shape of Dreams to Come: Living, working and changing lifestyles in Britain today (London, Standard Life, 2004) p 10, posted on www.thefuture laboratory.com

313] 'The lifestyle makeover', Times, 7 August 2004

314] Jim Moore, Inside Track, posted on www.jimmoorewealth. co.uk

315] 'House price boom fuels social divide', Guardian, 26 November 2004

316] Kirsty Scott, 'Solvent thirty-somethings turn backs on rat-race', Guardian, 26 June 2004

317] Emily Barr, Plan B (London, Headline Review, 2006) pages 191 and 243

318] Greg Easterbook, Future Laboratory, The Shape of Dreams to Come: Living, working and changing lifestyles in Britain today (London, Standard Life, 2004) p 11, posted on www.thefuture laboratory.com

319] Kirsty Scott, 'Solvent thirty-somethings turn backs on rat-race', Guardian, 26 June 2004

'Rising house equities is one of the tools they use to opt out of the rat race, by moving to the countryside or abroad and choosing a lifestyle or career path that places a greater emphasis on the 'life' side of the life/work balance shift.' [312]

Future Laboratory think that '... one million people in their thirties and forties plan to take advantage of flexible mortgages and the money they have made though rising property prices to start new businesses, downshift to a less stressful way of life or go on extensive travels'. [313] Prospectuses for property investors appeal to similar dreams. 'How you can give up work and become a property millionaire instead', reads the invitation from Inside Track. Rather like the Dot.com boosters, Inside Track shows a graph of property prices – 'it just keeps going up and up'. Inside Track's Jim Moore boasts '...its hard to believe that just a few short years ago I was a humble wage slave with zero prospects', inviting investors to '...free yourself from the grind'. [314] Attractive as these appeals are from an individual point of view, can it really be wise for a society to have got to the point where 42 per cent of the national wealth is invested in houses, twice what it was 30 years ago? [315]

One 'New Authentic' is novelist Emily Barr, who met her husband James on a flight to Tibet after working as a film extra on *The Beach*. Just as the idyll was threatened by approaching prostitution to the corporate world 'we realised that our house was worth an absurd amount of money', so they sold up and moved to the South of France. [316] In her novel *Plan B*, the moral growth of heroine Emma is shown by her renovating the house in the South of France (or rather, telling builders to do it for her, Emma's is a labour of superintendence, she no more builds than did Pharoahs the pyramids), while her partner Hugh's moral shortcomings are uncovered in his 'scummy bedsit', '...sharing a bathroom with three invisible strangers'. [317] An odd theme of the Future Lab's classification is that the New Authentics seem to feel very guilty about their good fortune, looking for a 'more meaningful life': 'The thread linking all the new authentics is a realisation that a focus on money, material possessions and status does not create happiness', according to author Greg Easterbook. [318] 'They often moved to the country or did voluntary work abroad, many retraining as teachers or landscape gardeners' [319] – luxury consumption re-modelled as altruism. These New Authentics bear many of the characteristics of the 'back-to-the-landers' of the 1920s. They were mostly people of independent means investing small bequests in farm businesses. Robertson Scott, the editor of *The Countryman* complained that '...they have no relationship to the hamlet' and '...go neither to church nor the parish'. [320] Even allowing for the gloomy pessimism that greets most good fortune in Britain today, there are destructive symptoms in the current house price boom, primarily because it is a price boom, not a housing boom.

The most obvious problem is that the rise in prices, while good for older people, is pricing first time buyers out of the market. According to Nationwide, the share of first time buyers in mortgage-funded house moves in the first quarter of 2004 were at their lowest since 1973.[321] Alan Evans argues that the restriction on development is regressive in its impact upon house prices and incomes:

> *'Higher- and middle-income families are more likely to own houses and property, while lower-income households are more likely to rent. The former therefore gain from the increase in property values which occurs throughout the urban area, while the latter are made worse off by the increase in the rents that have to be paid.'*

Evans, taking the main cause of the climb in house prices to be government restrictions on new building, sees a diverging interest in the maintenance of planning constraints:

> *'These distributional consequences have political consequences. Middle- and higher-income groups will tend to be strong defenders of the green belt and to resist any change through political pressure groups.'* [322]

Evans is right to say that the climb in house prices aggravates social inequality. This was the finding of Sheffield University's Geography department, in a report prepared for the homelessness campaign Shelter. They found that ten years ago, the sale of the average house in Kensington, central London would have bought two houses in Leven, Fife; today the Kensington property would raise enough for 24 houses in Leven. The income divide can be seen most straight-forwardly in the way that rising prices force lower income families out of inner London. According to Shelter's Adam Sampson, house price inequalities are '...leading to a society increasingly divided by where people live'. [323] In 2004 the Office of the Deputy Prime Minister re-vamped the

320] J. W. Robertson Scott, England's Green and Pleasant Land (Harmondsworth, Penguin, 1947) p 38

321] 'First Time Buyers close the door to the house market', Evening Standard, 5 July 2004

322] Alan W. Evans, (Oxford, Blackwell, 2004) p 64

323] 'House price boom fuels social divide', Guardian, 26 November 2004

324] 'Key workers shun Prescott's low-cost homes', Sunday Times, 9 April 2006

325] 'Prescott's housing scheme ditched', Telegraph, 20 May 2006

'Key Worker Living Programme' to address the '...serious recruitment and retention problems' local authorities were facing. Teachers, policemen and nurses (but not initially firefighters) were offered grants of £50,000, or even £100,000 in the case of 'leadership role' teachers in inner London, to address the problem. The scheme of course was limited, because, as the OPDM says '...resources are finite, so must be targeted'. And, worse still, as must be expected of any kind of welfare assistance, the schemes presume to tell teachers what kind of home they should live in to qualify. Though initially generous the OPDM's scheme, like that promoted by Ken Livingstone's Greater London Authority, has a lingering stench of the gamekeeper's tied cottage, or the medieval almshouse. There is a false flattery in the identification of 'key workers', as nurses have long known; being identified as 'angels' in the public imagination has only helped their employers getting away with paying them less, as the altruistic motivations of their work are emphasized over their wages. Creating the category 'key worker' also sets off one trade against another. London's army of African and East European service sector workers are excluded, though they are much poorer, because they are mostly in informal employment, not working for the government. Most importantly, the existence of the schemes is only symptomatic of the problem. The boom is putting houses out of reach. Schemes seem worthy enough, but actually they only take a hold of the inequality that is emphasized by the housing boom, and turn it into bricks and mortar. As we have already seen, with "Planning Gain" agreements, local authorities have learned the trick of making developers provide the social housing – without understanding that it is the disincentives to development that are helping push prices up and forcing the lower paid out of the market.

The most eloquent judgement on the Key Workers' Living Programme, though, came from the 'key workers' themselves.[324] In April 2006 it was announced that half the homes were unsold, and in May that the occupational restrictions would be lifted.[325]

As well as aggravating social inequality there are other inequalities that are emphasized by the increased cost of housing. Younger people find it harder to get on the property ladder, just as their parents gain. Between the town and the countryside, where incomes are already lower, house prices only exacerbate the difference, making it harder for rural dwellers to buy, just as their villages are being turned into dormitories.

HOUSEHOLD SPENDING MORE THAN 33% OF THEIR INCOME ON MORTGAGE REPAYMENTS

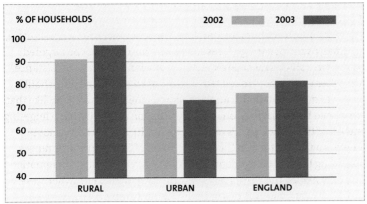

Source: CACI, H.M Land Registry and Mid-Year Population Estimates

HOUSING EQUITY AND EQUITY WITHDRAWAL 1970–2000

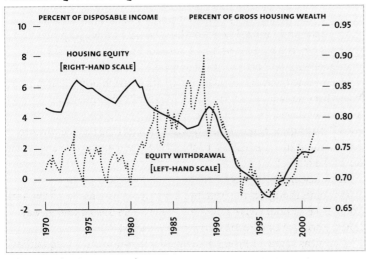

Source: www.hm-treasury.gov.uk

Rising house prices add to indebtedness, just as low interest rates in turn encourage people to spend more, and that helps force up house prices. Eddie George, governor of the Bank of England until June 2003,

326] Heather Stewart, 'Sir Eddie unmoved on house prices', Guardian, 11 December 2002

327] Kosuke Aoki, James Proudman and Gertjan Vlieghe of the Bank of England Monetary Assessment and Strategy Division, 'Why house prices matter', Bank of England Quarterly Bulletin, Winter 2001

328] Nigel Lawson, The view from Number 11 (London, Corgi, 1992) p 630

329] Herbert Ashworth, The Building Society Story (London, Franey and Co, 1980) p 207

kept interest rates low at the beginning of the decade because of the downturn in the world economy – boosting credit helped boost consumer spending, which certainly appears to be the reason the UK weathered those storms rather better than their European counterparts. 'We have taken the view that unbalanced growth is better than no growth at all', Sir Eddie told the cross-party House of Lords economic committee in December 2002, adding that '...the house price issue is a border issue'. [326] In fact credit raised on homes is now relatively easily recycled back into consumer spending, as the Bank of England's economists explained in their paper *Why Prices Matter*.[327] With flexible mortgages people can simply withdraw money to increase their spending. It used to be that people took less money out as they put more in, but nowadays they take more money out for spending at the same time as they are increasing their mortgages, recycling the borrowing on their homes into consumer spending.

Years ago when building societies enjoyed a monopoly over mortgage lending, their rates were set through agreement amongst the Building Societies Association, but under pressure from institutional lenders, the cartel was broken and mortgages became much more responsive to general credit rate movements. According to the Conservative chancellor Nigel Lawson the house price boom of the 1980s was caused by irresponsible lending by banks, competing for the first time for the Building Societies' trade: 'The combination of artificially stimulated demand for housing and some of the tightest planning controls on land use in Europe puts a long-run upward pressure on house prices.' [328] But it had all happened before that, too. In the three years to 1973, house prices nearly doubled. Herbert Ashworth explained that then, too, it was cheap credit extended by a Conservative government hoping to avoid a recession that persuaded people to apply for mortgages. But '...at the same time that demand was growing, the rate of new building was falling'. Housing completions fell from 364,000 in 1971 to 304,000 in 1973; building societies raised their lending from £2,705 million in 1970 to £3,310 million in 1973.[329] Workers' hard earned wage rises were being gobbled up by increasing rents and mortgage repayments, just as fewer of them had jobs to go to.

In the nineties, average house prices rose to 6.5 times the average salary. No doubt it was memories of the end of the Lawson boom, when heavily indebted families found they owed more than their houses were worth, the dread 'negative equity' that became such a cliché of Tory 'boom and bust', that persuaded the new governor of the Bank of England, Mervyn King, to move to dampen the housing boom. King raised the interest rate five times between November 2003 and September 2004 to 4.75 per cent, adding a third to the monthly cost of a variable rate mortgage.[330] At last, the gloom-mongerers' prophecies came true – house prices came down, but not because the supply of new homes had been increased, but because the credit had dried up. The phantom housing boom was dampened.

If the problem were restricted to the speculative bubble alone, it would be problematic enough. But in dampening house prices across the board, the Bank of England has succeeded in **reducing** the number of new homes being built as well. The interest rate rises affect all mortgages, those on second hand homes as well as new ones. Consequently, the financial disincentive to borrow is also a disincentive on new house production. In October of 2004, builders Taylor Woodrow announced that it was cutting its sales target for new homes by six per cent.[331] Choking off the phantom housing boom, the Bank of England is also de-railing the Deputy Prime Minister's target for new house building – as if it was not in enough trouble.

In 2004 the expectation was that there would be what is euphemistically known as 'market correction'. Capital Economics Ltd. said '...we continue to assume that the peak in housing prices will be reached in Q4 and that prices will fall by a cumulative 20 per cent over the subsequent three years'. However, the report concedes that this could be an optimistic prognosis, as prices could easily plunge below their real values, as happened in the late 1980s.[332] In fact the spiral has recommenced, so that in the decade to 2006 the value of the housing stock had tripled, with funds of **£3.4 trillion** walled into Britain's homes.[333]

If prices do fall dramatically, that will have a knock-on effect on the rest of the economy. Worse still, if prices fall solely because of a loss of confidence, the underlying problem of undersupply of houses will persist. The difference will be the form that the problem assumes. Where there is no surplus credit stoking the market, undersupply will give rise to homelessness and overcrowding, instead of inflated prices. Anyone who remembers the 'negative equity' bankruptcies and evictions of the late eighties, or the youth homelessness of the early 1980s, will understand that there are even worse problems than spiralling prices.

330] Ashley Seager, 'House prices fall for the first time in two years', Guardian, 4 September 2004

331] Terry Macalister, 'Taylor Woodrow cuts sales forecast', Guardian, 21 October 2004

332] Capital Economics Ltd., The Housing Market Analyst, Vol. 3, 2004

333] Halifax, 'Value of UK housing stock trebles over 10 years', 18 February 2006, posted on www.hbosplc.com

334] Franklin Delano Roosevelt, quoted in Kenneth Jackson, Crabgrass Frontier: The Suburbanization of the United States (Oxford and New York Oxford University Press, 1985) p 190

335] www.audacity.org/Dilapi dated Dwelling.htm

336] James Woudhuysen and Ian Abley Why is Construction So Backward? (Chichester, Wiley-Academy, 2004)

337] Ian Abley, 'Improving the Efficiency of the Masonry Construction Sector', 2006 to 2010, an Engineering Doctorate at the Centre for Innovative and Collaborative Engineering at Loughborough University, posted on www.lboro.ac.uk/cice/

As the value of houses appreciate, the relationship that people have to them changes. Politicians from Franklin Delano Roosevelt to Margaret Thatcher have understood the essentially conservative effect that home-ownership has on people. Roosevelt said: 'A Nation of homeowners, of people who won a real share in their own land, is unconquerable.'[334] Thatcher aimed to win over council tenants with 'the right to buy' their homes. The recent house price boom is a windfall, but like most property, it can also be something of a burden.

As prices rise people's relationship to their home changes; instead of a place to sleep and eat, it becomes an investment, needing constant attention. Home improvements preoccupy a nation watching *House Doctor*, *Changing Rooms* and *The Block*, reading Wallpaper, spending their money on DIY. No wonder their homes demand constant attention: they have to stand so much longer than their grandparents' homes did. More than likely, they are their grandparents' homes. Film-maker Patrick Keiller looked at the peculiar relationship the British have to their homes in his film-essay *The Dilapidated Dwelling*:

'In the UK, most consumer items – food, domestic appliances, cars and so on – had become cheaper, either as a result of new technology, or of shifting production to lower-wage economies, or both, but the cost of housing went on increasing. The housing stock was ageing and not generally in very good condition. New houses were comparatively few, and were mostly reduced versions of the houses of 50 or 100 years ago.'[335]

It is not hard to understand why people keep on repairing their homes. The value of them is so great that the most practical solution, to knock it down and rebuild it, would send the most courageous into a nervous breakdown. So much value is locked up in the Englishman's Castle that he is a prisoner in it. In an audacious proposal James Woudhuysen and Ian Abley suggest going in the opposite direction, and mass-producing homes that are designed to be a pleasure to use, upgraded where possible, but disposable and replaceable, like all other modern products.[336] Abley is now investigating just this potential in sectors like house building for the masonry side of the construction industry.[337] While the practical aspects of the housing problem are important, addressing them also depends on a revolution in attitudes to the home.

CHAPTER EIGHT

URBAN RENAISSANCE?

'In England we are starting to see people moving back into the city centres, drawn by a lifestyle where home, work and leisure are interwoven within a single neighbourhood.' Lord Richard Rogers, chairman, Urban Task Force, Towards an Urban Renaissance [338]

THROUGHOUT THE 1980S, INNER CITIES WERE SYNONYMOUS WITH DECAY. 'The inner city' wrote Paul Harrison in 1983, is '...a universe apart, an alien world devoid of almost every feature of an ideal environment'. [339] 'Urban' was a word most commonly linked to 'problem', or just as often, 'race problem'. Cities were associated with poverty and racial conflict. But since the mid-nineties, there have been strong claims made for the recognition of an 'urban renaissance'. Perhaps the most dramatic city turnaround was New York's. Under Mayor Koch and his successor David Dinkins New York teetered on bankruptcy, as well as earning an unenviable reputation for inter-racial conflict. In 1993 Rudy Giuliani's controversial 'zero-tolerance' policy towards street crime coincided with an economic upturn that helped to revive, and even gentrify the inner city areas that had been blighted. In the 1980s New Yorkers looked on their city with a kind of gallows humour, and titillated themselves with morbid tales of muggings and vigilantes. But in the 1990s security was restored so that New Yorkers could again take pleasure from the dynamism of their city.

The template of urban renaissance was repeated in London: An emerging 'café society' on the 'City Fringe' (the areas north of the financial district), the development of Bankside and Westminster on the

338] Urban Task Force, Towards an Urban Renaissance – Final Report of the Urban Task Force (London, HMSO, Spon, 1999) p 27

339] Paul Harrison, Inside the Inner City (Harmondsworth, Penguin, 1983) p 21

340] Peter Hall, The World Cities (London, Weidenfeld and Nicolson, 1966)

341] George Barlow, Foreword, Draft Economic Development Strategy, (London, London Development Agency, 2000)

342] Patrick Wright, A Journey Through the Ruins: The Last Days of London (London, Radius, 1992)

343] Richard Rogers, Cities for a Small Planet (London, Faber and Faber, 1997), p 19 to 20

344] Stryker McGuire and Michelle Chan, 'The NY-LON life', Newsweek, 13 November 2000

345] Theodor Zeldin, speaking at Demos seminar, London, 1997, chaired by Geoff Mulgan

south of the river, and a gentrification of Notting Hill in the West, and southern Islington in the North all added to the picture of the 24-hour city; the 'world city', [340] capital of 'Cool Britannia'. 'The creativity and dynamism of a world city comes', says the London Development Agency's George Barlow '...from the chance and unplanned interaction of culture and commerce'. [341] But as late as 1992, author Patrick Wright took Dalston in the East End as an experiment in cataclysmic deprivation being generalised across London, in his book *A Journey Through the Ruins: The Last Days of London*.[342] Wright's jeremiad was forgotten in the uplift of London, swinging once again. British architect Richard Rogers chose the example of Barcelona as an illustration of what an urban renaissance could be. Rogers credits 'Mayor Pascal Maragal, and his Minister of Culture, the architect Oriel Bohigas' for using '...the hosting of the 1992 Olympics as a catalyst for visionary reform'. 'Barcelona has been transformed into a world class city where people long to visit, work and live'. [343]

It seemed that the reproduction of the Urban Renaissance could create a new platform for world citizens. In 2000 Newsweek investigated NY-LON, a hybrid city: 'Throngs of transatlantic commuters are reconfiguring old New York and London into the new bicontinental megalopolis of NY-LON.' [344] Oxford University professor of sociology Theodor Zeldin proposed that European Unity would be achieved not at the level of national diplomacy, but through the emergence of a 'Europe of the Cities', where urban Amsterdam might have more fellow feeling for London or Paris than it would for the rest of the *patrie*.[345]

The *New Statesman* finds evidence of an urban renaissance in the most unexpected places: 'We are witnessing something of a renaissance in the creation and use of public space in (sharp intake of breath) Birmingham' [345]. The gulp is due to Birmingham's reputation for its new brutalist concrete 'Bull Ring' shopping centre, which, though remarkable in its own right, failed to attract people to the centre, becoming a refuge for charity shops and teenagers loitering in gloomy underpasses. But Birmingham's car-dominated array of junctions is finally giving way to a more pedestrian-oriented city.

Historian Tristram Hunt thinks that '...across the Victorian cities, a similar tale of design-led renewal is apparent'. He cites the 'vibrant public space' in Leeds' Millennium Square, 'an array of civic improvements' in Manchester, and perceives 'a new confidence' in Liverpool and Sheffield.[357] These are striking judgements, not least because each of these cities was emblematic of economic decay in the 1980s, such that one Conservative politician could complain that '...the anti-entrepreneurial culture of the North has kept capital at bay'.[348] Economist Charles Leadbeater and think-tanker Kate Oakley find that 'the centre of Glasgow has a palpable buzz', seeing the once depressed shipbuilding town as a model of the new 'creative city'.[349]

The urban renaissance itself might be put down to the general upturn of Western economies in the nineties, except that with cities contributing so great a proportion of national wealth, it is an explanation that borders on tautology. Still it is undeniable that this rising tide really has lifted all (or at least most) ships. Neighbourhoods and districts that exemplify everything depressed in a recession turn out to have hidden charms when spirits rise. There is also a rhythm of regeneration, where economic collapse lays the basis for rejuvenation – what Joseph Schumpeter called 'creative destruction'.[350] In inner cities, the downward spiral of the 1980s reduced property prices, making districts attractive to bohemian middle classes – people who would make the area attractive, later on, to wealthier parts of the population. Rock musician Mick Farren describes the shift of London's culturati from the West to the East End:

'Artists inspired this migration east... The influx of a few visual artists, and the freaks like us who followed hardly constituted a mass migration. I doubt our numbers could have topped a hundred even at the peak of the trend, but in a small way we added our own measure of spice to the exotic stew.'[351]

Accounts of urban renaissance stress different factors – notably the creative sector, secure neighbourhoods, consumer-driven growth, cultural diversity and so on. But in Britain Urban Renaissance has been bound together with the strictures of the Urban Task Force formed by the New Labour government in 1998 under Richard Rogers, Lord Rogers of Riverside. They reported in *Towards an Urban Renaissance* in 1999. The Urban Taskforce has had a significant influence upon the debate about regeneration – perhaps too much influence.[352] Richard Rogers' views were expressed with such confidence that they dominated thinking on building, though the government later backtracked on its commitments to the task force's conclusions. 'I know at first hand the reaction of ministers and officials to the Urban Task Force's Report', writes economic journalist Will Hutton. 'They consider it as largely

346] 'Loitering with intent', New Statesman, 4 September 2002

347] Tristram Hunt, Building Jerusalem: The Rise and Fall of the Victorian City (London, Weidenfeld and Nicholson, 2004) p 335

348] Robin Wright, quoted in David Smith, North and South: Britain's Growing Divide (Harmondsworth, Penguin, 1989) p 45

349] Charles Leadbeater and Kate Oakley, The Independents: Britain's New Cultural Entrepreneurs (London, Demos, 1999) p 31

350] Joseph Schumpeter, Capitalism, Socialism and Democracy (New York Harper, 1975) first published 1942

351] Mick Farren, Give the Anarchist a Cigarette (London, Pimlico, 2002) p 48 and 50

352] Lord Rogers takes issue with the author, Guardian, letters, 28 February 2005

353] Will Hutton, 'Foreword', Richard Rogers and Anne Power, Cities for a Small Country (London, Faber and Faber, 2000) p. vi

354] James Heartfield, 'Who's New', LM, Junius Publications, November 1999, issue 125

355] Sir Crispin Tickell, foreword, Richard Rogers, Cities for a Small Planet (London, Faber and Faber, 1997) p vi

356] Richard Rogers, Cities for a Small Planet (London, Faber and Faber, 1997) p 4, 7 and 38

misconceived', he claimed. [353] If they do feel that the Urban Taskforce's report is misconceived, the government only has itself to blame. Coming to office in 1997, the administration was attempting to break away from the conventional lines of policy-formulation of the Labour Party in the country. Rather than be hostage to the ostentatious expectations of the party faithful, this government contracted out policy-making to 'experts', drawn from the City of London and elsewhere. Within two years of coming to power, the Labour government had '...created more than 300 different taskforces and panels to advise government on different aspects of policy'. [354] The task forces were headed by the great and the good, by New Labour 'luvvies', the literati who were thought to be more in tune with the government's ambitions than the more staid party members. But Deputy Prime Minister John Prescott soon found out that he had a different kind of problem with Lord Rogers of Riverside.

As an architect, Rogers was associated with many of the more adventurous, imaginative and modernist buildings of his generation. From the Pompidou Centre in Paris (1977), Lloyds of London (1986) to the Millennium Dome (2000), the Richard Rogers Partnership has been putting its futuristic designs in the public eye. But Rogers' views on cities turned out to be more conservative than his buildings.

It should be remembered that, for the government, the context of the task force was first the policy goal of creating four million new homes, and second, to take full advantage of the economic recovery in British cities. But Richard Rogers' view was at odds with the government's. As he had made abundantly clear in his 1995 Reith lectures, Rogers' overwhelming preoccupation was with limiting growth. Though framed in terms of a programme for cities, Rogers' views are, to say the least, ambiguous towards cities. Cities, he writes, are '...the major destroyer of the ecosystem and the greatest threat to mankind's survival on the planet'. 'Cities are producing disastrous social instability that is further driving environmental decline'. Rogers' collaborator on the Urban Task Force, Sir Crispin Tickell adds in a foreword to Cities for a Small Planet, that cities '... are like organisms, sucking in resources and emitting wastes'. [355] Welcome to the Urban Renaissance!

In the Reith lectures, and their longer, published version, Cities for a Small Planet, the architect argues that the environment cannot sustain extensive urban growth, favouring instead 'Compact Cities'. [356]

By an economy of movement and other resource use, Compact Cities will reduce the 'environmental footprint' of the city. This is a theme that continues into the Urban Task Force report, where Rogers argues that '...the compact, many-centred city of mixed uses which favour walking cycling and public transport is the most sustainable urban form'. 'The compact urban form', says the report, '...highlights the value placed upon proximity and ease of contact between people'. For that reason the pedestrian must be put first and '...use of the car reduced significantly'.

Though posed in terms of an urban policy, this is in fact a policy for restricting the growth of cities, and especially for restricting the expansion of suburbs. 'Large tracts of our countryside have been eroded', complains the Urban Task Force, repeating the anti-suburban clamour of the Nimbys. Rogers supports cities only insofar as their regeneration works to contain urban sprawl. So he takes comfort from the fact that '...in the last few decades population growth in urban centres has picked up', but worries about how to persuade '...people to re-consider urban living'. 'Many people will continue to move to the suburbs', the Taskforce concedes, but '...we must look to persuade more families to stay'. [357] When Rogers came to re-work the task force report as *Cities for a Small Country*, with Social Policy lecturer Anne Power, the imperative mode was more strident: 'Many argue that we cannot and should not make people's choices for them', they write, only to add ominously: 'We take a different view'. [358] The coercive cast of Lord Rogers' thinking springs from his belief that city-dwellers and suburbanites are a threat to the country-side, which must be contained by designing in limits to their expansion.

URBAN DENSITY

'We must change the way we respond to urban density'. Urban Task Force.

The central proposal of the Urban Task Force is for more densely populated cities. The task force is aware that this is an argument that has not been won: ' 'Intensity' and 'density' carry connotations of urban cramming: too many buildings and cramped living conditions.' [359] You might think that increasing density means cramming, but the Task Force thinks that this is just an unfortunate over-reaction to the Victorian slum. Nonetheless, Rogers' case for the Compact City is typically translated into urban policy in the slogan: 'build up, not out'. The Urban Task Force draws on ideas developed by the respected urban theorist

357] Urban Task Force, Towards an Urban Renaissance – Final Report of the Urban Task Force (London, HMSO, Spon, 1999) p 26, 35, 40 and 41

358] Richard Rogers and Anne Power, Cities for a Small Country (London, Faber and Faber, 2000)

359] Urban Task Force, Towards an Urban Renaissance – Final Report of the Urban Task Force (London, HMSO, Spon, 1999) p 59 and 60

360] Jane Jacobs, Death and Life of Great American Cities (New York, Random House, 1961)

361] Harley Sherlock, Cities are good for us; The case for close-knit communities, local shops and public transport (London, Paladin, 1991)

362] Ian Katz, Guardian, 29 October 2002

363] Urban Task Force, Towards an Urban Renaissance – Final Report of the Urban Task Force (London, HMSO, Spon, 1999) p 59 and 63

Jane Jacobs, whose *Death and Life of Great American Cities* of 1961 was very influential.[360] Jacobs died in 2006 And on the British architect Harley Sherlock, who published *Cities are Good for Us* in 1991.[361]

It is of course worth asking the question whether the Urban Task Force itself is willing to adopt the 'compact living' that they recommend for others. We have already seen that Task Force member Sir Crispin Tickell advocates an end to new homes in the countryside, while living himself in a Somerset farmhouse. Lord Rogers of Riverside's home was briefly described by Ian Katz in the *Guardian*:

> 'He leans back in one of the boxy leather chairs that occupy a corner of the vast living space in the Chelsea home he shares with his wife, Ruth Rogers, co-founder of the River Cafe. (Space because, two stories high and running the full width of the two Georgian terrace houses Rogers knocked through, it has more in common with Tate Modern than most living rooms.)'[362]

It is 'Do as I say, not as I do', for the Urban Task Force, then. But are their prescriptions on density plausible? Rogers' argument is that **design** can square the circle of greater density without cramming: 'It is possible through good design, to create liveable urban neighbourhoods designed to higher densities than tends to be allowed by existing planning rules and regulations.' Though the Task Force presents many interesting examples, overall it is not entirely convincing.

Framing a general rule on density is a bit like trying to hit a moving target. 'There can be no hard and fast rule for establishing ideal density levels', says the Task Force – but that has not stopped it from making such pronouncements.[363] But a quick look at both urban densities in fact, and the variety of standards declared, illustrates the difficulty.

The first thing to note, much bemoaned by the Urban Task Force, is that densities decline markedly over time. As dense as inner London Bloomsbury and Islington are today, they are still much less so than the LCC in 1938. In fact the re-concentration of inner London has been overstated, only moderating the underlying trend for people to conquer more space for themselves. (So, for example, the conversions of office and warehouse space into flats in fashionable Hoxton generally results in larger, not smaller dwellings.)

The second thing to note is that cities considered as a whole have markedly less density than specific neighbourhoods, or estates. This is not hard to work out. Cities include lots of space that cannot be lived in – like rivers and roads at one extreme, but also industrial and office space, shops, parks and parking space, and so on. Proponents of greater densities bridle at these various other uses. Jane Jacobs and Harley Sherlock dismiss the view that parks are the 'lungs of the city' as science fiction. Particularly irritating to them is the perennial presence of vacant land and empty dwellings. Sherlock has high hopes for the utilisation of '…London's twenty-five square miles of derelict land',[364] while the Task Force has designs on the 'land-banks' of Public Utilities, and worries about spare pockets left over after planning.[365] But the truth is that, even though there might be some better use for surplus land in cities, there will always be some vacant lots, and many empty dwellings. To think otherwise is like imagining a perfect equilibrium, or a system without friction. But most importantly the density of a city cannot be set by extrapolating upwards from the density of given estates or neighbourhoods. However compact the Popham Street and Frederica Street estates are, nearby Upper Street's broad pavements and the largely decorative Islington Green will tend to cancel them out. More than that the failure to find a profitable use for the 6,000 square metres of the Agricultural Hall in the decades preceding its re-opening as the Islington Business Design Centre were not administrative oversight, but a reality that could not be designed out of existence – not until economic conditions had improved again.

The difference between city-wide calculations and those on given estates makes a nonsense of the densities proposed by the Urban Task Force, and other champions of the compact. Looking at the blueprints of estate designs it seems reasonable to think that you can squeeze scores of people into each acre. But those numbers cannot be extrapolated up to whole districts, because towns are so much more than houses. Richard Rogers' proposal for 80 dwellings per hectare in the Thames Gateway is higher than the Ur-density, the density of the first city, Ur, in the year 2000 B.C., where, according to the archaeologist Henri Frankfort was 20 dwellings to the acre, or 49 to the hectare.[366] Is this progress? It would mean a population density of 180 people per hectare in the Thames Gateway, assuming the national average of 2.3 persons per household. But 180 people per hectare is a density higher than London's, **even when we exclude parks, lawns, rivers and woods** from the calculation of London's acreage. It is ironic that Richard Rogers charges suburbia

364] Harley Sherlock, Cities are good for us; The case for close-knit communities, local shops and public transport (London, Paladin, 1991) p 150

365] Urban Task Force, Towards an Urban Renaissance – Final Report of the Urban Task Force (London, HMSO, Spon, 1999) p 57 and 220

366] Henri Frankfort, cited in Lewis Mumford, The City in History (Harmondsworth, Penguin, 1991) p 78

DENSITIES, PROPOSED AND ACTUAL

Table of Assessments of Population Densities per Hectare or Acre

Site	People per hectare	People per acre	Source	Source's assessment
Greater London in 1973 (actual)	55	22	Sherlock 215	Disapproves
London County Council in 1938 (actual)	135	55	Sherlock 215	
London (inner and outer) 2000	41	16	Focus on London, 2.1, 3.1	
London (inner and outer) excluding non-urban	70	28		
Ebenezer Howards Garden Cities (proposed)		80	Sherlock 84	Disapproves as too low
LCC's optimum in 1938	336	136	Sherlock, 216	approves
1980s local authorities maximum	247	100	Sherlock, 216	Disapproves as too low
Popham Street estate (LBI)	390	158	Sherlock, 223	Approves
Frederica Street estate (LBI)	310	125	Sherlock, 223	Approves
Corbusier's vertical city planned		1200	Jacobs, 21	'fantastically high'

Table of Assessments of Population Densities per Hectare or Acre

Site	Dwellings per acre	Source	Source's assessment
Brooklyn Heights (heart)	125-174	Jacobs, 203	vital and popular
Brooklyn Heights (majority)	75-124	Jacobs, 203	Less so
Brooklyn Heights (fringe)	45-74	Jacobs, 203	Vitality and popularity drop off'
New York City average	55	Jacobs, 204	
East Bronx	Well below 55	Jacobs, 204	Typical of grey belts that have become the despair of cities
Suburbs	Six	Jacobs, 209	Can work out well
'semi-suburb'	10-20 dwellings per acre	Jacobs, 209	'will not generate city liveliness or public life'
In cities	20 dwellings to the acre and above	Jacobs, 210	'many people who live near each other geographically are strangers to one another'
In cities	100	Jacobs, 211-212	'vitality falls of ... too low'
In cities	275	Jacobs, 216	Not possible to go higher
Barcelona	160	Towards an Urban Renaissance, 59	'the most compact and vibrant European City'
Bloomsbury and Islington	40-80	Towards an Urban Renaissance, 59	'Some of the most lively inner city areas'
Standard densities today	8-12	Towards an Urban Renaissance, 60	'Car dependent monocultures'
Moderate density	16-24	Towards an Urban Renaissance, 60	'vitality... energy efficiency'
Thames Gateway (proposed)	32	R. Rogers' Thurrock presentation	Ideal
Ur, 2000 B.C.	20	Mumford, The City in History, 78	Approves

with monotonous uniformity, when he proposes to pack people in so tight that they will have room for nothing but continuous estates.

The third thing to note is that even the proponents of greater density have conceded ground over the years, arguing successively for less extreme densities. The leading modernist architect of the twentieth century, Le Corbusier, thought nothing of packing 3,000 people into a hectare of his vertical city; in 1961 Jane Jacobs thought one could go no higher than 679 dwellings per hectare (say 1,561 people per hectare); Harley Sherlock cites the 390 per hectare of the Popham Street Estate as optimum; Richard Rogers proposes 180 people per hectare in the development of the Thames Gateway.

All of these proposals are far denser than most people would choose for themselves. But even if, like me, you think that Richard Rogers' figure of 180 is too high, we can still ask him, why not 390, or 1,561 or 3,000? The answer is that there is no matter of principle being defended in the actual numbers – only that the trend to greater dispersal should be arrested. The case for higher density has had to moderate its claims in response to the predominant, secular and popular trend towards lower density. It is remarkable that among professionals the case for limiting urban sprawl is taken for granted, whilst in their living choices the great mass of people seem to make no reference to it at all. The gap between the attitudes of the planners and the public are so singularly at odds that we ought to ask just what is it that makes people resist the compact city.

Champions of compact cities tend to see the move towards dispersed dwelling as an error, either on the part of the planners, or on the part of those choosing the suburbs. Jane Jacobs thinks that suburb pioneer Ebenezer Howard '...looked at the living conditions of the poor in late nineteenth century London, and justifiably did not like what he saw' – but made an error in extrapolating that all cities were bad. [367] Sherlock too thought that '...in getting rid of bug-infested slums, we unwittingly threw the baby out with the bathwater', since many were not 'over-crowded', just in need of repair. He also thought that local authorities over-reacted to the unpopularity of tower blocks, setting optimum densities too low.[368] The Urban Task Force generally blames public policy for 'outward migration', but also thinks that the suburban flight has failed to notice that urban areas can offer the qualities that the task force thinks they are looking for elsewhere: low crime rates, good transport, health facilities, good schools and so on.[369]

367] Jane Jacobs, Death and Life of Great American Cities (New York, Random House, 1961) p 17

368] Harley Sherlock, Cities are good for us; The case for close-knit communities, local shops and public transport (London, Paladin, 1991) p 13, 14, and 216

369] Urban Task Force, Towards an Urban Renaissance – Final Report of the Urban Task Force (London, HMSO, Spon, 1999) p 34 to 35

115

Though all of these factors have contributed, none really account for the shift in living patterns in the twentieth century. The dispersal of human habitation cannot be reduced to mistaken policies, or individual confusions about resources. It operates at a more elemental level. The principal factor has been the generalisation of the productivity gains of industrialisation. With the broadening base of industry, new technologies penetrated all areas of life, being slowly, but inexorably generalised throughout the population, unevenly at first, but over time more broadly. The important changes are:

> The generalised cheapening of consumer goods, which has broadened the basis of domestic consumption over time – more things, corresponding to more income.
> Technological developments in building and building materials: tarmacadam, concrete, high rise construction.
> The increase in life expectancy, in time spent in education, in time in retirement; and the reduction in working time, leading to greater leisure; which is offset by the increase in employment spreading incomes across the sexes.
> The transport revolution; the railway suburbs of the late nineteenth/ early twentieth century; followed by the Underground Railway suburbs of the first half of the twentieth century; and finally by the motor suburbs of the post war period. Central to these has been the 'trickle down' effect whereby first rail tickets, then cars got cheaper, until they were almost universally affordable.
> The enlargement of public utilities: water, waste disposal, gas, electricity, followed by radios, telephones, televisions, cable and the internet.
> Factory farming, and the revolution in food preparation, convenience foods, distribution and retailing; which in turn leads to higher yields and in consequence more farm produce from less land: a surplus of land for new development.

Though many of these changes are taken out of their context and deplored, they are in fact woven into each other in a way that makes it difficult to separate them out. A pick and mix approach will not work. You cannot un-invent, electric generators, say, and keep the telephones – though electricity generation might change its energy source, as from coal to gas.

Put another way, the changes that have taken place are not just changes in technology – they change us. To demonstrate: in 1900 the population of Britain was 29 million, today it is 60 million, which is to say that, numerically, half of us owe even the fact of our physical existence to the increased output in food and basic necessities. In our domestic lives we are almost as different from our great grandparents as from another species – covered sewers, indoor toilets, gas ovens, electric lights, carpets (and vacuum cleaners), fridges, washing machines, central heating, and emulsion paint have made living immeasurably more comfortable and less arduous; over and above biological reproduction, all of us owe our cultural heritage to the developments in print, newsprint, education, telecommunications, media and science. In 1900, only a small minority were educated to today's GCSE level, newspaper readership was only beginning to climb under the influence of the 1870 Education Act, computer literacy was non-existent. Popular familiarity with genetics, black holes, Freud's theory of the unconscious, the social sciences, the sensibility of camp, are all due in part to modern mass media.

It is simply inconceivable that the kind of alteration that has taken place in the human species over the last century would have no impact upon its living conditions. Of course people's expectations of available living space have risen. Homes with bathrooms are necessarily larger than those without. And homes with electric light, central heating and television are places where one might voluntarily spend waking hours. The ambition to colonise a greater area of physical space is inseparable from the general raising of the population's cultural level.

And new technologies change the city directly. Social scientist John Adams makes an interesting point about mobility, when he writes '...the amount of time that the average person spends in motion has ...changed very little since 1950.' He explains that '...people make their travel decisions within the constraints of time and money budgets.' [370] But though the time spent travelling is the same, the distance travelled in that time has increased six-fold from five to 30 miles a day. [371] The reason for the greater distance travelled is the increase in the availability of transportation – railways, with new lines, more cars, belonging to a greater proportion of the population (due to falling costs), and more roads. Between 1991 and 2001 the percentage of the population with no access to a car fell from 20 per cent to just 12 per cent. [372] It is not hard to see the effect on dwelling space. People make choices about where they can live within the constraints of their obligations to get to work, to get

370] John Adams, 'Social consequences of Hypermobility', reproduced as an annex to Project On Environmentally Sustainable Transport; Proceedings From The Ottawa Workshop (London, OECD 1999) p 118, posted on www.oecd.org

371] John Adams, 'Hypermobility', Royal Society of Arts lecture, 21 November 2001

372] Daniel Dorling, Bethan Thomas, People and Places: A 2001 Census Atlas of the UK (Bristol, The Policy Press, 2004) p 157

373] James Heartfield, 'Nowhere near enough homes', Blueprint, September 2002

374] Marcial Echenique and Rob Homewood, The Future Of Suburbs And Exurbs; Report for The Independent Transport Commission (Cambridge, The Martin Centre for Architectural and Urban Studies, 2003) p 6

375] Paul Barker, 'Edge City', in Anthony Barnett and Roger Scruton, Town and Country (London, Jonathan Cape, 1998) p 209

children to schools, to shop, and to keep contact with friends and family. If, over 50 years, the distance you can travel expands six times, then the distances at which urban populations disperse can expand by the same factor – assuming no other restraints on their movement, which of course is not strictly the case, and assuming that they want to disperse.

SUBURBAN BRITAIN

Do people want to disperse? The Commission for Architecture and the Built Environment polled the public to ask them where they want to live. Fifty nine per cent would prefer to live in a bungalow or village house.[373] These findings were not what CABE wanted to hear, so they did not publish them, arguing that the question was in any event flawed (since it asked where would they like to live apart from where they live now). But there is no need to take an opinion poll, since Britons have already voted with their feet. Marcial Echenique and Rob Homewood of the Martin Centre for Architectural and Urban Studies analysed government census population to find out where people live. The results are remarkable. The Department of Environment, Transport and the Regions divides Britain into wards, classified as Rural, Suburban /Rural, Suburban, Suburban/Urban, Urban.

> 'The 'Suburban/Rural' wards are distributed in agricultural areas that include isolated villages. 'Suburban' wards are concentrated on the fringes of towns. 'Suburban/Urban' wards are in the suburbs of the metropolitan areas and larger towns. Finally 'Urban' wards are generally located in inner London Boroughs and the city cores of the Metropolitan areas.'[374]

On this classification fully 84 per cent of all people live in suburban-type wards. Of course that might be a definitional rather than an actual expansion of the suburbs. So we could exclude the inner suburbs ('urban/suburban'), though these are unlikely to meet the standards of compactness demanded by the Urban Task Force. But even without the inner suburbs 63 per cent of the population are 'suburban'. Even the rural wards are not necessarily peopled by farmers and their labourers, since '...hardly anyone in the countryside any longer has any functional economic link with the land', according to Paul Barker.[375] Echenique and Homewood note that though 8 per cent of the population lives in rural wards, agriculture employs only 1.31 per cent of the population: 'A large percentage of the people living in Rural areas must commute to towns offering non-agricultural employment.'[376] These figures are corroborated by government, with marginal variations:

PERCENT OF POPULATION BY URBAN, SUBURBAN AND RURAL AREAS

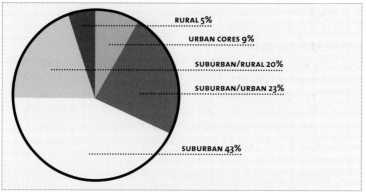

RURAL 5%

URBAN CORES 9%

SUBURBAN/RURAL 20%

SUBURBAN/URBAN 23%

SUBURBAN 43%

Source: Based on analysis from Living in Urban England: Attitudes and Asperations, DETR; 2000

376] Marcial Echenique and Rob Homewood, The Future Of Suburbs And Exurbs; Report for The Independent Transport Commission (Cambridge, The Martin Centre for Architectural and Urban Studies, 2003) p 6

377] Peter Hetherington, 'Tories shift focus from inner cities to "forgotten" suburbs', Guardian, 26 August 2004

378] Urban Task Force, Towards an Urban Renaissance – Final Report of the Urban Task Force (London, HMSO, Spon, 1999)

Despite all talk of an urban renaissance, Britain has become a predominantly suburban country – largely due to the influence of greater incomes and declining travel costs. This fact should at least give pause for thought about the value of a public policy oriented primarily to the cities. In Echenique and Homewood's figures, wholly urban wards house just eight per cent of the population – the same share as wholly rural wards. Of course everyone understands that the cities are vital to the productive life of the country, and that they tend to house society's leaders, entrepreneurs and opinion-formers. But Conservative Party Chair Theresa May had a point when she questioned the government's '...outdated obsession with their solutions for the inner city at the expense of the suburbs and towns'.[377]

HOW DID LONDON EXPAND?

The backdrop to the case for an Urban Renaissance is the perception that, over the long-term, cities are being abandoned, through the process of suburban flight.[378] In London, the evidence seems to be compelling. From 1901 to 1950 the County of London's population fell. In the 1930s the annual rate of decline was quite steady at around eight per cent, but between 1938 and 1947 that climbed to 40 per cent, reducing the County to a population of 3,245,000; By 1961 that had reduced to 3,200,000. But these numbers do not show an absolute decline in London's population: 'Many Londoners had simply moved to the suburbs, the green belt or the Outer Country Ring', notes Stephen Inwood. Within that broader area, the population had climbed to 10.6 million.

London's population changes continued to present a confusing picture. In 1965, Greater London incorporated parts of Essex and Middlesex to take account of the popular movement. But then between 1961 and 1981 the population of this new, Greater London began to fall, by 15 per cent, representing a loss of 1,186,000 people. Then in 1984, against everyone's expectations, the direction of population movement changed again with the outer suburbs stabilising, and inner London once again growing, albeit modestly, by 100,000 between 1981 and 1993.

YEAR	GREATER LONDON POPULATION
1939	8,615,000
1951	8,197,000
1961	7,992,000
1971	7,452,000
1981	6,806,000
1991	6,890,000
1993	6,933,000

Source: Stephen Inwood, A History of London

Not only did London's population move unexpectedly, it moved, roughly speaking, in the opposite direction from that planned for. In Patrick Abercrombie 1944 plan for Greater London, new towns were created to absorb London's surplus population – but in fact the new towns grew, without substantially reducing London. When at the end of the 1950s London's population did start to fall again, planners had a change of heart, seeing this less as the creation of an airier city through slum clearance, and more as a sign of inner-city decay. In 1976, the South East Joint Planning Team concluded that

> 'The present problem of London is basically one of population and employment decline coupled with declining resources and sustained pressures to provide, for example, additional housing and to

*cater for the rapid movement of vast daily flows of the people,
goods, and services essential to a major world capital.'*

379] Stephen Inwood, A
History of London,
London, Macmillan, 1998,
p 572, 812, 837, 893, and
894

380] A.N. Wilson, The
Victorians (London,
Hutchinson, 2002) p 262

This was, as Stephen Inwood says '... a renunciation of the Abercrombie-
Barlow principles that had guided the planning system for the previous
thirty years'. Long before Lord Rogers sought to promote the city against
sprawl, planners were trying to reverse the flow of people from London.
What is it about London's expansion that is so confusing?

In fairness, London's growth is a little confusing, because it combines
two distinct trends. The underlying trend is towards expansion and dis-
persion, for the reasons outlined above of economic growth and technological change; the second, which confuses the issue, is the more cyclical
movement of the economy, which combines contraction and expansion,
meaning that it can seem to work against the underlying trend at one
point in the cycle, but accelerate it in others. This is Schumpeter's
'creative destruction'. Policy makers probably ought to see the broader
trend, but then, as John Maynard Keynes said, in the long run, we are all
dead, and it is understandable that they react to the immediate problems presented by economic cycles. Still, a lot of the confusion comes
from taking cyclical for underlying developments.

The first trend, the secular expansion and dispersal of London's population can be seen in the fact that the thinning out of inner London's
population is roughly proportional to the expansion of outer London.
From 1940, the same trend is expressed in the decline of Greater
London's population relative to the expansion of the outer suburbs,
in Surrey, Essex, Middlesex and Hertfordshire.
'In each decade, the centres of growth moved a little farther out.' [379]
Transportation is the most important factor in dispersal. A.N. Wilson
notes that even in the mid-nineteenth century the breakthrough of
elliptic springs led to the '... age of the "carriage folk"', and that this was
in turn spurring a movement out of the centre: even '... the Marxes
abandoned their cramped flat in Soho and moved to a variety of new-built
family houses in Kentish Town on the edges of Hampstead Heath'. [380]
So too did William Morris, in his Pre-Raphaelite phase, move from
lodgings in the then run-down Red Lion Square, to Bexleyheath in Kent,
where he built his celebrated Red House with Philip Webb in 1859.
'He continued to curse the iniquities of railways', writes his biographer
Fiona MacCarthy, '... but he was to make good use of Abbey Wood,

381] Fiona MacCarthy, William Morris: A life for our time (London, Faber and Faber, 1994) p 154

382] H.J. Dyos, 'Railways and Housing in Victorian London', Journal of Transport History, 2, 1955, p 15

383] Christian Wolmar's The Subterranean Railway: How the underground was built and how it changed the city forever (London, Atlantic Books, 2004)

384] Lewis Mumford, The City in History (Harmondsworth, Penguin, 1991) p 573

385] Asa Briggs, Victorian Cities (Harmondsworth, Penguin, 1968) p 16

his local station, only three miles away on the newly opened North Kent line'. [381] Edward Burne-Jones and Gabriel Dante Rossetti were just some of the medieval revivalists collected from the station in Morris's specially built carriage.

DECADE[S]	TOWN	PERCENTAGE GROWTH	
1881-90	Leyton	133	Outer London
	Willesden	122	Outer London
	Tottenham	95	Outer London
	West Ham	59	Outer London
1891-1900	Acton	278	Outer London
	Edmonton	278	Outer London
	Ilford	278	Outer London
	East Ham	194	Outer London
	Wimbledon	137	Outer London
1901-10	Ealing	137	Outer London
	Southall	137	Outer London
	Wembley	137	Outer London
	Chingford	128	Outer London
	Coulsdon	128	Surrey
	Purley	128	Surrey

According to Stephen Inwood, '...the growth of the late-Victorian suburbs was fuelled by the arrival of the lower middle-class commuter.' Workmen's tickets helped clerks to establish themselves in Hackney, Wood Green, Hornsey, Hendon, Willesden, Balham and Camberwell. However, these same railway terminals were also adding to the over-crowding of inner London, as land was found for stations by knocking down working-class slums, or 'rookeries' – with the surplus population generally moving to the adjacent neighbourhood.[382] In the early century it was electric trams and underground extensions. 'The bold initiative of Frank Pick, as head of the London Underground,[383] played no small part in London's twentieth century suburban development', thought Lewis Mumford.[384] Historian Asa Briggs says that the slogan of the North Metropolitan Railway (extended from Baker Street to Harrow in 1880) *Live in Metroland!*, 'showed that it was not so much satisfying existing needs as creating new residential districts'.[385] The railway company published an annual, *Metroland*, between 1915 and 1932 that '...featured

DECADE[S]	TOWN	PERCENTAGE GROWTH	
1921-1939	Dagenham	1076	Essex
	Hornchurch	335	Essex
	Chingford	295	Essex
	Billericay	179	Essex
	Romford	163	Essex
	Barking	116	Essex
	Ilford	96	Essex
	Rickmansworth	100	Herts
	Elstree	100	Herts
	East Barnet	100	Herts
	Crayford	264	Kent
	Beckenham	264	Kent
	Orpington	264	Kent
	Chislehurst	264	Kent
	Sidcup	264	Kent
	Bexley	264	Kent
	Merton & Morden	300	Surrey
	Carshalton	300	Surrey
	Banstead	100	Surrey
	Coulson	100	Surrey
	Purley	100	Surrey
	Surbiton	100	Surrey
	Sutton & Cheam	100	Surrey
	Egham	100	Surrey
	Malden	100	Surrey
	Wembley	552	Middlesex
	Hayes & Harlington	386	Middlesex
	Ruislip-Northwood	348	Middlesex
	Harrow	275	Middlesex
	Potters Bar	273	Middlesex
	Uxbridge	100	Middlesex
	Heston	100	Middlesex
	Hendon	100	Middlesex
	Feltham	100	Middlesex

386] 'Metro-Land: British Empire Exhibition', 1924 Edition, republished (London, Southbank Publishing, 2004)

evocative descriptions and photographs of historic villages and rural vistas' in the region served by the line.[386] Stephen Inwood notes that '...between 1921 and 1939 the pace of growth in many of the suburbs

387] Stephen Inwood, A History of London (London, Macmillan, 1998) p 717

388] Iain Sinclair, London Orbital – a walk round the M25 (London, Penguin, 2003) p 10

served by new underground or Southern Electric Trams was spectacular'. 'Middlesex', says Inwood, '...became an almost entirely suburban and industrial county, with a population of over two million in 1938'.[387]

In the postwar period the South-East went through another expansion, one that was driven by the car, rather than the train, which was losing out to its more versatile rival. In 1951 the M1 to Birmingham opened, and then in 1958 the Beeching Report led to the closure of many suburban branch lines, just as car ownership spread among the middle classes. In 1970 the Westway took the M40 right into central London, and in 1986 the London orbital outer ring-road, the M25 was opened by the Prime Minister Margaret Thatcher. 'The original Thatcherite pitch (civil engineering plus photogenic road-building programme being part of the Great Leader package) was anti-metropolitan; it was about protecting the suburbs,' writes a rather paranoid Iain Sinclair.[388] Greater car ownership was helping to accelerate the process of suburbanisation, coupled with the policies pursued in the 1980s of promoting home ownership (at the expense of public housing). Tories took pride in winning over 'Essex Man' – the psephological construct of the aspirant working class voter. Though between 1981 and 1991 it was Cornwall, Cambridgeshire, Buckinghamshire whose population grew fastest, while those of London, Liverpool and Belfast were all stagnant or falling.

Alongside the steady advance of technologies, especially transport technologies, there was another influence on London's population that was less linear, and that was the cycle of boom and bust in the economy.

The stock market crash of the 1930s is known to have impoverished working people, millions of whom were made unemployed. But the Depression mainly affected employment in the older heavy industries, such as steel and cloth manufacture, which were based predominantly in the North of England. In the south east the newer industries of aeronautical engineering, light engineering and electrical manufacture continued to expand, albeit at a slower rate than in the 1920s. The new factories, such as the iconic Hoover factory in what is now the outskirts of North West London were powered by electricity and so could locate in green field sites close to the larger roads. These factories facilitated the first large scale migration of working people into the suburbs. The migration of skilled workers out of the inner cities continues to the present day.

If the skilled working classes of the South East did not suffer so severely from the depression then their middle class neighbours may actually have benefited. Indeed one consequence was that capital migrated from the older heavy industries, and looking for a safe outlet, moved into mortgage companies. According to researchers Simon Gunn and Rachel Bell, '...building societies such as the Halifax and the Woolwich, [had] their coffers swelled from the capital market, following the Wall Street Crash of 1929 [as] financial investors saw building societies as a safer haven for their funds than the stock market'. [389] Across the country, the annual loans of the building societies increased from £32 million in 1923 to £140 million in 1936, encouraged by a fall in rates from 6.5 to 4.5 per cent.[390] The inter-war suburban growth owed much to the cheap credit that followed the 1929 stock market crash – a shift echoed perhaps in the housing boom of 2002-04. The new suburban growth had already been encouraged by Acts in 1923 and 1925 which permitted local authorities to lend to house buyers.

Cheap mortgages in the inter-war period accentuated the dispersal of London's population. Following the Second World War it was envisaged by Sir Patrick Abercrombie and the London County Council that the process would be accelerated even more by the planned relocation of the surplus population to the new towns, and the clearance of inner London's slums. But the slum houses were not demolished; they just lost more value as people moved out. Shirley Green describes what happened next: 'The central clearing houses for residential rubbish, the London Auction Mart in Queen Victoria Street, became a hive of activity for what were known in the property world's brash jargon as Stamford Hill Cowboys.' Houses were sold for as little as £5 or £10, and many fortunes made. As many houses were at the end of their leases, there was little incentive to repair dilapidated houses. As Green says, these were '...landlords who specialised in sweating the tail-end leases'.

The Abercrombie plan, on top of the exodus to the suburbs in the interwar years, had the unintended effect of depressing the value of London estates. Some of the large aristocratic and institutional landlords sold off their London estates immediately after the war: the Duke of Westminster sold the 42-acre St George's Estate, Pimlico, in 1952; the Church Commissioners disposed of most of their Paddington Estate during two sales in 1955 and 1958, reducing their residential holdings in London from 40,000 to 4,000 properties. The Colville Estate in West London had been in the hands of the families of Mark Strutt and

389] Gunn, Simon, and Rachel Bell, Middle Classes: Their rise and sprawl (London, Phoenix, 2003) p 62

390] Alan A Jackson, Semi-Detached London (London, Allen and Unwin, 1973) p192 to 194

391] Shirley Green,
Rachman (London,
Michael Joseph, 1979) p
34, 39, 50, 51, and 57

392] Evening Standard, 9
July 1963

393] 'New Light on
Rachmanism', Twentieth
Century British History,
Vol 12, No 1, 2001, p 86

Sir Edmund Bacon for two generations, but they sold it off in 1948:
'This is not an estate that our sort of families can be associated with',
they decided. 'If we can find a buyer, we must sell.' Ironically, the estates
were auctioned off just as the demand for inner London housing was
about to rocket. Demobbed servicemen were joined by immigrants –
recruited to solve Britain's labour shortages as the economy began to
grow again. When Mark Strutt and Sir Edmund Bacon toured the
Colville Estate in the 1930s it was 27 per cent underlet, but by 1947 it was
130 per cent over-let, as tenants – illegally but unavoidably – sub-let
rooms to pay the rent.

Slum landlords were hate figures in 1960s Britain. But they were,
in a sense, only scapegoats for the failure of the post-war government
to take the chance to clear the slums and rebuild. Peter Rachman, a Jew
who had escaped the concentration camps to fight in the Polish Army
before coming to England, lent his name to slum landlordism. The word
'Rachmanism', was made up by Ben Parkin, the Labour MP for
Paddington North, an ex-public school teacher. Rachman was no
worse than many of the landlords operating in London, and much of
the hostility he drew was due to his willingness to house West Indian
immigrants (most of whom remembered him quite fondly, according to
Shirley Green).[391] The case against Rachman was spear-headed by the
Tommy Farr and Stuart Douglass. Their Stephens Gardens Tenants
Association was inundated with support from white residents when
it launched a protest against the West Indians' illegal drinking clubs.
Themselves disturbed by the racial overtones of that campaign,
Farr and Douglass shifted their sights onto Rachman instead, making
a perfect bogeyman for the press. The *Evening Standard* gleefully
reported Mrs Ian Fleming's reaction to seeing Rachman: 'It's one of Ian's
villains – straight out of Bond'.[392] In one respect at least he was like
a Bond villain, being foreign. Historian John Davis downplays the racial
undertones of the anti-Rachman campaign, writing that '...the extent of
latent anti-Semitism in this crusade remains difficult to discern, but it is
clear that the attacks on the 'never-had-it-so-good' society had little to
do with the black community.' However, the strength of the campaign
was surely that it dressed up anti-black and anti-Semitic sentiments in
respectably left-wing clothes.[393] As it turned out, Rachman's empire
was chronically overmortgaged, and he had already sold off most of his
properties when he died of a heart attack on 29 November 1962 leaving

an estate worth just £8008. In death, though, the bogey of Rachmanism came into its own. 'I know he's dead', Ben Parkin told Stephen Douglass: 'But don't tell anyone, and keep the rumours going – because if Rachman is dead, our case is dead too.'[394] In July the following year, Labour leader blamed the 'disease of Rachmanism' on the Tory govern-ment – but the truth is that all the political parties had failed to clear the slums when they had the chance. Where they should have met the housing shortage by re-building they turned instead to landlords like Peter Rachman, Peter Davis and Nicholas van Hoogstraten to wring the last drops of cash out of dilapidated estates.

'Rachmanism' in the private sector was a blight on London's housing stock in the 1960s. But by the 1980s it was also apparent that the large post-war council estates and high-rises were proving to be a disaster. Paul Harrison records that '...out of Hackney's 46,000 houses and flats some 4,000 (nine per cent) were unfit for human habitation in 1979 and a further 8,900 (19 per cent) needed substantial renovation or repairs'.[395] Much of the blame was put on the architects and developers, though in fact many of the post-war high rises were great buildings poorly maintained. Attitudes to high rise flats often depended on the degree of optimism or pessimism that people felt about their lives. The Dockers' leader Jack Dash moved into a 16-storey skyscraper, as a result of slum-clearing and road-widening under the Greater London Plan – 'I chose a flat on the sixteenth floor which has a panoramic view of east London and the Thames'. Dash looked over East London and dreamed of a socialist Britain: 'I get a feeling of confidence'.[396]

But Jack Dash's optimism was out of step with the anxieties of the day, and planners were derided for imposing monumental scale and inhuman designs on people. But the problems that emerged were not in the architecture, but in society. Council estates, like the worse end of the private rented sector, had become a trap for communities who were too poor to improve their surrounds. It was the persistence of unemployment and low incomes that was turning the high rises into 'vertical slums'. It is a useful reminder that architecture cannot design social inequality out of existence – the remedy is elsewhere. It was the tragedy of modernist architecture that the only client for large residential blocks were the local authorities, who were, by the 1970s, providing 'social housing' – a welfare provision that had the effect of concentrating all those families on low incomes in the same place.

394] Shirley Green, Rachman (London, Michael Joseph, 1979) p 213

395] Paul Harrison, Inside the Inner City (Harmondsworth, Penguin, 1983) p 205

396] Jack Dash, Good Morning Brothers! (London, London Borough of Tower Hamlets, 1995) p 124

397] www.myhampstead.
co.uk/hampstead/arts-
Goldfinger.htm

398] 'Trellick Tower',
posted on
www.open2.net

399] Peter Ackroyd,
London; the Biography
(London, Vintage, 2001)
p 757

400] Ros Weaver, 'Sky flats
hell can be heaven',
Observer property,
16 March 2003

Erno Goldfinger's Trellick Tower, a 32-storey block in West London illustrates the point. Completed in 1972, Trellick Tower was the focus of tabloid scare stories: 'Women raped in elevators, children attacked by heroin addicts in the basement, and homeless squatters setting fire to flats were among the more lurid'. Here was another Bond Villain in the world of London property; Ian Fleming called his master criminal Auric Goldfinger, having failed to stop Erno Goldfinger's Willow Road Estate in Hampstead. [397] An unrepentant Goldfinger blamed the tenants for the problems in Trellick Tower: 'I built skyscrapers for people to live in there and now they messed them up – disgusting.' Goldfinger's comments might sound harsh, but it was true that local authorities had used the tower blocks to house the poorest and most vulnerable families, adding to the social problems. *[398] Today, Trellick Tower is a Grade II listed building, inhabited by the over-spilling aspirants to the life of adjacent Notting Hill, and is recognised as a landmark of British modernism.

Demonstration that the problems of London's housing were not implicit in the brick and mortar – or concrete and glass – came with the eventual reversal of inner London's association with economic decline. A short economic boom in the years 1985-88 seemed to be crushed by a slump in the early nineties, but then the economy slowly recovered from around 1993 thereafter notching up a decade of steady growth. The recovery of inner London's population started right at the beginning of the first 'Lawson boom'. With the financial sector leading the recovery, while the industrial north continued to flounder, London addresses enjoyed a premium they had not for some time. But such were the restraints imposed on London's expansion by the green belt that competition for homes in central London rose and with it property prices. Peter Ackroyd describes the trend:

'The resurgence of interest in restoring old dwellings, the process of "gentrification", the growth of "loft" living, the whole emphasis upon renewal, are the direct consequences of the green belt which forced London and all Londoners to look inwards rather than outwards.' [399]

London's property prices shot up like tomatoes in a greenhouse under the summer sun. The few flats in Trellick Tower that are up for sale go for as much as £350,000, [400] now marketed as 'urban cool', not urban decay. Even Peter Rachman's old 'slum' properties fetch prices that would have seemed astronomical only a couple of years ago. In April 2004 Bruten & Co advertised a two bedroom flat in St Stephen's

Gardens, 'a period terraced property' for £389,950, while Marsh & Parsons wanted £365,000 for the same in Powis Gardens, '...a lovely flat situated on the raised ground floor of this converted end-of terrace'. And Rachman was branded a profiteer for asking £6 a week.

This is the process that is now called an urban renaissance, the gentrification of the inner city. There is no doubt that the gentrification of inner London is a boon. It raises the standard of housing in the capital. But equally the gentrification that has taken place is not a model that can be made into a template for all housing as the Urban Task Force implies. The urban renaissance is not an alternative to suburbanisation; it is a cause of suburbanisation. Indeed taking account of the larger living spaces created by 'gentrification' the urban renaissance can be seen as a sort of suburbanisation of the inner city. According to the government's policy wonks on the Performance and Innovation Unit, the important trend is the 'counter-urbanisation cascade' of population flows '... from the most urban areas to the suburbs; from the suburbs to the fringes; and from the fringes to rural areas.'[401] They list the main reasons for moving as job-related, due to a change in family circumstances (having another child) and a response to rising prices. Though the Urban Task Force sees suburbanites gripped in crime panics and other kinds of hysteria, a simpler explanation for many moves is that most people simply cannot afford to live on Lord Rogers' Riverside.

It should be understood that the real meaning of Lord Rogers' prescriptions on density, the preference for brownfield over greenfield development, sustainability and mixed housing is to **limit** the number of homes built. While playing lip-service to the target for new homes, Rogers set such restrictions on what kind of homes ought to be built that the net effect of would be, and has been, to limit the number of new homes. This is not such a surprise. The real meaning of Rogers original Reith lecture is a distaste for new development. The city is only praised to the extent that it is compact, or leaves a small footprint, which is to say that it is contained, limited and constrained.

That the Urban Task Force should have set the parameters for housing policy is a disaster. It is also a reversal of the Labour Party's historic commitment to providing new homes to meet people's needs. Twenty years ago, Labour's shadow housing minister Eric Heffer made the party's stance plain:

401] Nick Donovan, Tony Pilch, and Tracy Rubenstein, Geographic Mobility (London, Performance and Innovation Unit, 2002) p 13

402] Eric Heffer, Never a Yes Man (London, Verso, 1991) p 105, 169, 170, 206

403] Time for Decision, Labour Party Manifesto, 1966

404] Ian Abley, 'A lack of commitment in the Labour "commitment" of a decent home for all', 12 October 2003, posted on www.audacity.org

405] Margaret Thatcher, The Downing Street Years (London, Harper Collins, 1995) p 279

'It is intolerable in a caring society that tens of thousands of people are sleeping rough, and are denied adequate help, and are denied adequate help because of the meanness of this government. It is intolerable, too, that half a million building workers should be on the dole while half a million new homes are needed.'

Trained as a carpenter, Heffer had been a councillor in Liverpool, where the group leader Jack Braddock put him in charge of the new Direct Works department. 'We built houses, flats and all kinds of municipal buildings', Heffer recalled proudly. When the Labour government proposed to cut back subsidies to council housing, Heffer rallied the party faithful against them at the 1977 conference. [402] Labour members remembered the party's historic commitment in election after election to building new homes. In 1966 Harold Wilson had renewed that commitment with a promise of half a million homes in three years:

'Our first priority is houses...We have announced – and we intend to achieve – a Government target of 500,000 houses by 1969/70. After that we shall go on to higher levels still. It can be done – as other nations have shown. It must be done - for bad and inadequate housing is the greatest social evil in Britain today.' [403]

The contrast with the present-day commitments is remarkable. As Ian Abley has explained, in the Deputy Prime Minister's Sustainable Communities announcement of Spring 2003 the headline figure of an additional 200,000 new 'affordable homes' were to be built up to 2016. And '...that meant only 16,000 additional homes every year'. [404] The influence of the Urban Task Force outlook on Labour's ambitions is lamentable.

As the limits of Labour's strategy of public housing became apparent at the end of the 1970s, their Conservative rivals appeared to have an answer, privatisation. Prime Minister Margaret Thatcher was right that legislation extending council tenants a 'Right to Buy' their homes had been a great success. [405] This was after all the party of Stanley Baldwin, whose government oversaw the greatest expansion of home-owning suburbanites ever. But though the party gained support in the suburbs of the South-East, relating to the upwardly mobile aspirations of Essex Man, the statistical short-fall in new house starts from the public sector was never made up by the private sector. Without new stock coming on the market, easier credit only fuelled a price boom, leading many first-time Tory voters into severe debt. Soon the Tories were retreating from any optimism about housing. Minister John Patten worried that over-crowding in South-East England was jeopardising support, bearing in mind that '...the countryside...has always been the place to go in order to collect Tory voters by the trailer load'. Though Patten was militant in preferring free market solutions to every question, the exception was development, where, like Richard Rogers, Patten thought that '...any twenty-first century planning legislation must have community as its touchstone'. [406] Though their reputation for bulldozing the countryside preceded them, the Conservatives were already committed to reining in growth by the mid-nineties, when Margaret Thatcher's successor John Major appointed Sir Crispin Tickell head of the government's Sustainability Panel, and John Gummer, a '...fully paid up member of the green welly brigade', environment secretary. [407]

Between Labour's austerity of the 1970s and the Tories conversion to sustainability in the 1990s, the stage was set for the Urban Task Force's case for restraining growth.

406] John Patten, Things to Come: The Tories in the Twenty-first Century (London, Sinclair Stevenson, 1995) p 215 and 241

407] John Major, The Autobiography (London, Harper Collins, 1999) p 511

CHAPTER NINE

LET'S DRIVE

THREE AND A HALF HOURS FROM EIGHTY FIVE PER CENT OF THE COUNTRY
is the unsung town of Dirft. Nobody spells out the acronym, Daventry
International Rail Freight and Transport, though they might, as
explanation expand to Dirft Logistics Park. Three and a half hours
is important because that is the maximum that a long-distance lorry
driver can travel before he has, by law, to stop for a break. Off Junction
18 of the M1, Dirft is within four miles of the major M1/M6/A14 interchange at the heart of the UK. It connects with the M6 going westwards
to Birmingham, Manchester and Liverpool, the M1 going north to Leeds
and south to London, and the A14 going east to Felixstowe.

Dirft is a town like no other. Nobody lives there (though 700 000
live within 30 minutes drive-time, in Daventry and Rugby). It is two
million square feet, with as much again earmarked for further
development. The only traffic is made up of great container lorries
elegantly gliding from roundabout to roundabout, before backing into
the loading bays of vast white oblong warehouses, picking up another
load, then setting off to another destination, three and a half hours
from Dirft.

As economic growth has shifted from heavy industry to consumer
goods, from the mill towns to the high street, distribution looms much
larger. In your fridge, in your home, through your letterbox, goods from
all over the country, from all over Europe will have passed through Dirft.
Seeing the elegant economy of effort in planning the lorries' routes it is
not hard to see why 82 per cent of all freight goes on roads, while just
eight per cent goes by rail. But for all those who dream of an enhanced

408] Balanyá et al, Europe Inc (London, Pluto, 2000) p 70

409] Highways Agency, M1 J19 Roads Based Study, Final Report (London, HMSO, 2002) p 5

role for rail in a more rational transport network, Dirft is helping to put retail goods on trains.

Dirft's location and infrastructure help Tesco's '…to distribute frozen foods to 70 per cent of the UK, and distribute 6,500 different clothing product lines to more than 770 outlets', according to their IT and logistics director, Philip Clarke. In Dirft, and nearby, Tesco has one million square feet of warehousing, including freezer space equivalent to 23 million domestic freezers. The Royal Mail built a 262,500 ft2 cross dock processing centre there to rationalise their national transport network. Asda Wal Mart runs six trains to Grangemouth in Scotland – just some of the 120 trains out of Dirft each week.

In 1991 the European Union wrote a plan for ten Trans European Networks,[408] integrating rail, road and waterways to be created to cut across the nationally-oriented networks: The A14/M6 corridor forms part of the Ireland/UK/Benelux Trans European Network.[409] In 1997 Princess Anne opened the Dirft Logistics Park.

Andrew Cross is the man to record the quiet poetry of Dirft. Though graduating in Fine Art from Bath, he has moved, without quite meaning to, into photography and now film. *English Journey* takes its title from J. B. Priestley's book subtitled *A Rambling but Truthful Account of What One Man Saw and Heard and Felt and Thought During a Journey Through England During the Autumn of the Year 1933*. Like Priestley's, Cross's journey runs from Southampton up to Manchester but by way of Dirft, and on the latest model articulated truck – thanks to Scania trucks. 'It is the antidote to [Stephen Spielberg's film] Duel' says Andrew, proudly, as he shows me sequences on his monitor, at his home in Bethnal Green. 'It is England,' says Andrew emphatically, '…look how green it is'. And it is true. What Stanley Baldwin called 'Deep England', the 'green and pleasant land' is undeniably there, speeding past the windscreen. Though the captions tell us we are going past Newbury, these roads do not seem to scar the landscape, but open it to view.

Arriving at Dirft, always end and beginning of a journey, the Trumpton-like round of little roundabouts and slip roads unroll queasily. Traffic, without pedestrians, it turns out, is less Mad Max, than what Henri Lefebvre called the quotidian, 'everdayness', with all the lurching friction of older trucking subdued by hydraulics and computerisation. At its heart though, Cross's project is democratic. He is interested in the working processes that make life possible, even though they are mostly invisible to us. There are echoes of the GPO Film Unit movies, most obviously of Grierson and Auden's Night Mail, recording the rail journey from London to Glasgow. But more generally, there is an interest in the litany of jobs and professions that make the reproduction of human life possible. 'I don't understand the objection to wind farms,' he tells me. 'Where do people think that things come from?' Dirft, it seems, is the most likely answer.

Andrew Cross's affection for motorways and lorries is exceptional. Nowadays the internal combustion engine is more likely to be seen as the enemy, than a means of betterment.

The Reclaim the Streets network manifesto AntiCaR makes an alarming case:

1] 'Cars consume vast amounts of raw materials. Mining ores carves great open cast scars in the landscape.'

2] 'The petrol car's need pollutes at its point of production and consumption and every point in between: the super tanker, the filling station and the engine. Cars use a third of world's oil. In OECD countries 40 per cent in 1973, 60 per cent in 1989. Two thirds of cars are in G7 countries.'

3] 'Cars create so much waste. Thousands of used tyres are dumped at sea, the rest accumulate in massive dumps. Millions of used batteries leak in toxic waste dumps.'

4] 'Cars are the biggest cause of atmospheric pollution and global warming. Exhaust fumes make us ill from the nitrous oxides, the carbon monoxide and the hydrocarbons.'

5] 'Lead in exhaust fumes brain damages children. But unleaded petrol is higher in cancer causing agents and requires more crude oil to be made.'

6] 'Millions of animals are squashed each year by cars.'

7] 'New roads carve up the countryside.' [410]

410] Reclaim the Streets, AntiCaR, posted on http://rts.gn.apc.org

411] Alan McKinnon
'Life without lorries,
The impact of a
temporary disruption to
road freight transport in
the UK', Commercial
Motor, November 2004,
p 3, 20 and 21

412] '40pc of road projects
face axe in Budget',
Telegraph, 26 November
1996

The militant campaigners of Reclaim the Streets have highlighted their cause with protests, from jamming the M42 in 1991, to stopping mothers in 4x4s on the school run in Belsize Park in 2005.

But the thinking behind the hostility to the internal combustion engine is confused. Motor vehicles are not primarily a means of killing people, but on the contrary, of creating the conditions for human existence. That is why building new homes depends on building the transport infrastructure to support them.

In November 2004 Alan McKinnon of Heriot-Watt University's Logistics Research Centre analysed '... what would happen if no lorries operated on Britain's roads for a week'. Professor McKinnon's calculations are based on extensive research, into a distribution system, in which '...lorries deliver 4.5 million tonnes of freight each day, approximately 80 kgs per person' which is '...more that the average body weight'. Those 4.5 million tonnes are 82 per cent of all freight transport in the UK. According to McKinnon supermarkets, industry, petrol stations, hospitals and schools would be out of action within one week. (See Box: Probable effects of the lorry stoppage over five days)

No doubt, to some, professor McKinnon's calculations only demonstrate our dangerous dependence on the internal combustion engine. But more usefully they show that – just considered as a component of the production cycle – motor vehicles are what make contemporary living possible. As McKinnon says, the public might dislike lorries, but that is because they '...often fail to see the connection between the lorry traffic on the road and the availability of goods and services they take for granted.'[411] Almost everything you own, the very means of life itself, was transported by road. While anti-road protesters brand the car a killer, 3.8 million emergency responses are made by ambulance each year and half a million fires are attended by the fire services.

The debt we owe to motor transport is for the most part never taken into account. Instead the road system has become a focal point of unhappiness with contemporary life. At a crucial moment in the mid-1990s, roads became the target of radical protesters against modernity, just as they were also identified as a costly drain on the public purse. For John Major's government the Conservative instinct to face down the road protesters was muted by the need to fill a budgetary black hole. In 1996 the Department of Transport cut 40 per cent of new road building schemes under pressure to meet spending cuts from the treasury.[412]

PROBABLE EFFECTS OF THE LORRY STOPPAGE OVER FIVE DAYS

DAY 1	DAY 2	DAY 3	DAY 4	DAY 5
All movements of lorries over 3.5 tonnes cease at 12 am	Supermarket stocks of many perishable/short shelf-life product run out, including bread, milk and eggs	Most petrol stations run out of fuel	Petrol stations run dry	Half of the car fleet without fuel
Most mail and parcel deliveries stop		Around 15 per cent of the car fleet without fuel	Most of the manufacturing sector shutdown	Large proportion of the labour force laid-off or unable to travel to work
No newspapers Manufacturers operating on a just-in-time basis suspend operations	Milk disposal on farms More manufacturing in low-inventory sectors closes down Shortage of cash in banks and ATMs	Supermarket stocks of fast-moving grocery lines exhausted	Most non-electrified rail services suspended	Retail stocks of most grocery products exhausted
No supplies of fresh produce in grocery outlets		Introduction of rationing for fuel and some food products	Serious cash shortages	
			Bus companies reduce off-peak frequencies, esp. in rural areas	Almost all manufacturing closed down
		Fast food outlets close		Severe disruption of the health service
	Construction work ceases on most building sites	Widespread lay-offs from manufacturing sector	Gas and water utilities disrupted by lack of fuel and spare parts	Serious problems from the accumulation of waste
	Growth of farmers' markets	Busier pubs run out of beer		
			Congestion at ports stops off-loading vessels	Range of non-food products in shops substantially depleted

413] 'Escape from the killer car?', New Statesman, 5 November 1995

414] Nick Mathiason, 'British Waterways', Observer Business, 12 December 2004

415] British Waterways, Annual Report and Accounts, 2003/4, p 16

416] Telegraph, 1 August 1998

417] Claire Fox, 'A new cycle of transport', The Municipal Journal, 30 January 2003

418] Department of the Environment, Transport and the Regions, Transport Trends (London, HMSO, 2004) p 13

The previous year the Royal Commission on Environmental Pollution report *Transport and the Environment* had argued the need to reduce reliance on road use. The *New Scientist* embraced the proposition, editorialising:

> '*More and faster public transport, buses that run on time, freight travelling by canal instead of along crowded roads, fewer cars...It sounds like paradise. And it might even be possible in our lifetime.*'[413]

Possible in the abstract, perhaps, but the *New Scientist* was not being very scientific about what would need to happen to make such changes. Was it really likely that freight would move by canal, rather than by road, for example? Far from expanding its canal freight trade, British Waterways has been closing it down. Today there is just one working wharf left in London, while British Waterways earns money not from freight, but providing leisure services, and by selling off land for property development.[414] In 2003, canals moved 1,600,000 tonnes,[415] while three times as much went by lorry every day. To even make a dent in road freight, canals would have to increase their capacity by several hundred-fold. The *New Scientist*'s changes would envisage either a vast canal-building programme, or a savage reduction in consumption, and population.

If government failed to move freight transport off the roads, it was also interested in reducing private car use – but was that any more plausible? The new Labour government of 1997 thought so. They dropped one hundred more road schemes, announcing the end of the 'predict and provide' approach to road building, which, argued John Reid, only led to ever-increasing traffic.[416]

In 1997 the Road Traffic Reduction Act was passed empowering local authorities to force traffic off the streets by extending pedestrianisation, cycle lanes, congestion charges and other 'traffic calming' (sic) measures. The rationale behind the policy is the proposition – taken from neo-classical economics – that as long as supply (of roads) increases, so will road use. This might make sense in the rarefied mathematical formulas of 'rational choice theory', but it bears little relationship to the real world. Over the past fifty years road space has increased by just one quarter, while the number of vehicles on the road has increased seven times.[417] In fact '...the number of licensed vehicles increased by 63 per cent between 1980 and 2003, from 19.2 to 31.2 million'.[418] To anti-road

protesters, this increase is seen as a disaster. But it is the opposite –
a great victory for democracy. Today just 26 per cent of the population
have no access to a car. Though green critics often attack the car as
a sign of privilege, it is only at the point that car ownership has become
generalised that it has provoked hostility. Today's anti-car sentiments
are no doubt sincerely felt. But then so were the anti-cycling sentiments
of a century ago, as described by the sociologist Geoffrey Pearson:

> 'Undoubtedly the most extraordinary aspect of this grumbling
> against the tendency of the working class to assert its noisome pres-
> ence in places where it clearly had no right to go, was to be found in
> the magnified excitements which surrounded the bicycle craze of
> the 1890s. Cycling was at the centre of a number of social panics.
> It was feared that the push- bike was a health hazard, for example
> causing 'bicycle face', 'bicycle hand', and 'bicycle foot', as well as the
> dreaded kyphosis bicyclistratum, or 'cyclist hump', which resulted
> when the handlebars were set too low. Evidence placed before the
> Physical Deterioration Committee even suggested that bicycling
> was a threat to the nations' manliness, inducing varicocele of the
> testicles 'from the pressure of the saddle'.'

> 'More grievous allegations were brought against the bicycling
> 'scorchers' who went to fast or, to strike another note of discontent,
> who went too far and barged into middle-class leisure haunts. There
> were editorial fumings in The Times (15 August 1898) about the
> 'East-End or suburban "scorcher", dashing along quiet country roads
> through peaceful villages with loud shouts and sulphurous language,
> and reckless of life and limb', and the Lancet (6 August 1898) saw fit
> to have a medical entry on 'The Fool on the Cycle'. Accounts of
> youths whizzing about madly on their bikes, causing pandemonium
> among the traffic, frightening horses, and knocking over pedestrians
> were as commonplace as the headlines which repeatedly sensation-
> alised 'The Cyclist Terror', 'The Risks of the Cycle', 'The Perils of the
> Wheel', 'Moloch of the Wheel', 'The Dangers of City Cycling' and
> 'Cyclomania'.'[419]

Today's anti-car sentiments are comparable. Scapegoated for our lack of
exercise, asthma and other illnesses, the car is also blamed for anti-social
behaviour. But like the bicycle before it the car has opened up this green

419] Geoffrey Pearson,
Hooligan: A History of
Respectable Fears
(London, Macmillan, 1983)
p 66 to 67

420] Transport Studies, University of East London, 'Public transport gender audit evidence base', Mobility Unit of the Department of the Environment, Transport and the Regions, p 6

and pleasant land for hundreds of thousands of people. The National Parks, museums and heritage sites as well as the myriad of privately owned and run leisure amenities, not to mention the seaside, are visited and enjoyed for the most part by car. Disparate families can see each other regularly, old friends can be reunited, and new friends met. While more can always be done to reduce the loss of life through car accidents it must also be remembered that the car enriches and varies the lives of most people. The potential for civilised living has been almost universalised by the car. It is disingenuous to blame the car if the babbling classes have failed to persuade people to visit the gallery rather than the shopping centre.

Furthermore '...virtually all the recent increase in car-use is attributable to women.'[420] It is not hard to understand the changes that have brought about the increase in car use. Principally, they are the reduction in the price of cars, and the increase in those in work, especially women. Pointedly, the school run has been a target of anti-car protesters, but few people appreciate that this overwhelmingly an attack on women. The critics wonder why mothers prefer to run their children to school than to walk, failing to understand that this is a way of organising the trade off between child-care and commuting to work. The reality of transporting files from work, PE kits, book-bags and homework. The fresh quota of 'five a day' – fruit and veg. The inevitable and frequently fragile cardboard masterpiece, as well as the actual, usually tired, children on public transport, and in British weather. All this, experience tells, us is often avoided by even the most fervent guardians of the climate – if they have a car at their disposal. The green proscription assumes that parents have such minimal working commitments that the mother, or less probably the house-dad, has nothing better to do than amble along the road. The working day is for most people eight hours long. To facilitate what should rightly be called the home-nursery-school-work-shops-school-nursery-edifying or healthy after school club-home run all on bike or foot (not forgetting tea, homework, bath and into bed before eight) then the city will have to be very compact indeed. The social change that the anti-car types are targeting is the recent increase in women's employment.

Perhaps people should live closer to work? Putting aside the difficulty of each partner being able to find work in one locale, one partner changing jobs, moving house and changing schools to change jobs and the spectre of parochial living, there is an underlying assumption that all work is located in the city. But the suburbs are not exclusively domestic; cement works, regional and national business HQs, call centres and factories as well as the shopping and leisure centres so loathed by critics provide jobs for large numbers of people in the suburbs. In 2004 Terence Bendixson of the Independent Transport Commission published a report, *Suburban Future*, which reported:

> '*Suburbs and exurbs are not predominantly dormitories for city centre office and shop workers. Most of their residents live, work and play in the suburbs and visit city centres only from time to time.*'[421]

As *Suburban Future* makes plain, commuting is quicker in the suburbs than in cities. It takes residents within the suburbs and exurbs 24/25 minutes, 34 minutes for residents within cities like Bristol and Birmingham and 43 minutes for those living and working in Greater London. This is backed up in research by the Transport Research Group since their *Transport in the New Millennium* conference in 1999,[422] which Austin Williams quotes when he says:

> '*Even though Britain has the longest commute times in Europe, commuting still takes up just a measly 46 minutes of our day... that's 23 minutes each way. Surely we should be getting this so-called problem into perspective.*'[423]

Many people, usually the less well off, already work near home, but they still need a car to get there.

> *Having failed to restrict the absolute increase in mobility, what about shifting transport from the roads? By the number of trips taken, cars accounted for 64 per cent in 2002/3 compared to 57 per cent 1989/90. Walking, bus journeys and bicycle journeys are all down. But realistically, other modes of transport could hardly have made any impact at all on the distance travelled by car. Each year Britons travel on average 5,600 miles by car, and just 200 miles by train. Rail capacity would have to increase five times just to reduce car transport by one fifth. It is time to wake up to the fact that transport policy for the last ten years has been working against the grain of social change. Like King Canute holding back the tide, "traffic calming" is a pointless (and ultimately destructive) measure. All it has succeeded in doing is wasting people's time.*[424]

421] Independent Transport Commission, Suburban Future, (London, ITC, 2004) posted on www.trg.soton.ac.uk

422] Austin Williams, editor, Transport in the New Millennium (Newcastle, Transport Research Publications, 2000)

423] www.futurecities.org.uk/reviews.htm

424] Barrie Clement, 'The 45-minute commute', Independent, 22 July 2003

141

425] Austin Williams, 'No U-turns for transport', Daily Telegraph, 21 December 2002

Like the bias towards high-density living promoted by the Urban Task Force, persuading people off the roads was a policy foisted onto the Labour Party by a single-issue lobby that is out of touch with real people's behaviour. In 2002 transport secretary Alistair Darling seemed to respond to the problem by promising a £5.5 billion road-building programme. But on closer inspection it turned out that the £5.5 billion was only the first three years of the £180 billion ten-year plan already announced in 2000. Furthermore, it was not earmarked for road-building, but all transport spending. Even the road spending is mostly just motorway widening and the provision of crawler lanes. Useful no doubt, but not really a road-building programme. [425]

LABOUR'S MANIFESTO PROMISES

[1959] 'With half a million new cars coming on the roads each year, the Government's road programme is entirely inadequate. But, to solve the problem, road-building must be related to a national plan which covers all the transport needs of an expanding economy.'

[1970] 'The road programme will be further extended as we embark upon the recently announced inter-urban road programme which will double the capacity of the trunk road system by the end of the 1980s.'

[1983] 'Give a high priority to building by-passes.'

Even in 1997 the government's decision to continue the Tory government's moratorium on new motorways was not included in the manifesto, except obliquely as a 'review'.

The provision of a transport system appropriate to the needs of the hyper-mobile British public is intimately bound up with the building of new homes. Transport has been key to the transformation of the way that people live. Marcial Echenique argues the case for taking greater mobility into account in planning new settlements:

'The introduction of the railway system in London led to the suburbanisation of housing and popularisation of the semi-detached house; and, at the same time, to the concentration of offices and retail outlets around central communication nodes (in this case railway stations) as well as to the development of the department store'. Echenique continues:

'Likewise, the introduction of the motor car and the corresponding growth in highways have led to further suburbanisation (and the near-universal development of detached housing). Simultaneously, offices and retail outlets have concentrated around the new communication nodes – motorway junctions – and new forms of building have appeared such as the shopping mall and the business park'. [426]

No doubt at some point in the future the car will give way to some other kind of transport. Already researchers are working on hydrogen-fuelled cars as a potential replacement for petrol and diesel ones, just as leaded petrol has been replaced in our lifetimes. No doubt oil is finite – but all the evidence is that exhaustion is hundreds of years in the future, not around the corner. [427] As Jane Jacobs observed recently,'...all my life I have been hearing that the oil was going to run out. It never happens. They keep discovering new oil fields.' [428] Innovation, rather than scarcity is a more likely reason that the car might be replaced. As the former Saudi oil minister Sheikh Yamani said, 'The Stone Age did not come to an end because we had a lack of stones, and the oil age will not come to an end because we have a lack of oil'. [429] Realism demands that any plans today to move away from car-use should demonstrate what is to replace our 5,600 miles a head of journeying, or how we could organise a democratic and complex economy with less travel. Anything less is just posturing, intended to demonstrate the moral superiority of its exponent, rather than a serious proposition.

As we consider the development of the Thames Gateway, the M4 corridor or Milton Keynes, everyone understands that these new homes depend upon an increase in transport, rather than a reduction. New building means more transportation, and more driving. But instead of looking at transport as a problem, we need to understand it as part of the solution – the means by which wealth is created for people to live.

426] 'Mobility and space in metropolitan areas', in Echenique and Andrew Saint editors, Cities for the New Millennium (London, Spon, 2001) p 33

427] James Heartfield, 'The economics of sustainable development', in Ian Abley and James Heartfield, editors, Sustaining Architecture in the Ant-Machine Age (Chichester, Wiley-Academy, 2001) chapter 7, p 94 to 103

428] Jane Jacobs, Metropolis Magazine, March 2001

429] Mary Fagan, 'Sheikh Yamani predicts price crash as age of oil ends', Telegraph, 25 June 2000

THE UTOPIANS

William Morris

(1834-96) *A Dream of John Ball* (1887)

Karl Marx

(1818-1883) *Capital: A Critical Analysis of Capitalist Production* (1867)

Ford Madox Ford, nee Huefer

(1873-1939)

THE REFORMERS

Edward Bellamy

(1850–1898) *Looking Backward* (1888)

Ebenezer Howard

Tomorrow (1898), republished as *Garden Cities of Tomorrow* (1902)

Patrick Geddes

Cities in Evolution, (1915, republished 1949)

Lewis Mumford

(1895-1990) *The Culture of Cities* (1938), *The City in History* (1961)

THE MODERNISTS

Le Corbusier, nee Charles-Edouard Jeanneret-Gris

(1887-1965) *Towards a New Architecture* (as *Vers Une Architecture*, 1923)

Frank Lloyd Wright

(1867-1959)

Robert Moses

(1888-1981)

THE URBANISTS

Jane Jacobs

(1916-2006) *The Death and Life of Great American Cities* (1961)

Harley Sherlock

Cities are Good for Us (1991)

Richard Rogers

(b.1933) Cities for a Small Planet (1997)

NEW THINKERS

Peter Calthorpe

The Pedestrian Pocket Book (1989)

Herbert Girardet

The Gaia Atlas of Cities (1992)

CHAPTER TEN

THE CANON OF URBAN THEORY

THE PRESUPPOSITIONS AND CONCLUSIONS OF THE URBAN TASK FORCE DO NOT
fall from the sky, nor are they the self-evident result of observing circumstances on the ground. Like all critical reflection they are informed,
whether consciously or not, by those who thought about the issues
before. As a pre-eminently practical matter, urban development is not
guided by theory, though that has sometimes been tried, rather the
theories tend to reflect the development of urban settlements.
Practitioners, architects and planners have dealt with issue as they
have arisen. All the same there is what we might loosely call a canon
of urban theory that develops from the first utopian reflections on the
question of town and country; through Ebenezer Howard's plans to
develop 'Garden Cities' – which inspired the New Yorker's architecture
critic Lewis Mumford's theoretical account, the *City in History*; the
Modernist architects Le Corbusier, the Bauhaus School, and Frank Lloyd
Wright brought industrial methods to building, realising some of the
utopian vision as well as its shortcomings; subsequently, Jane Jacobs
reacted against the visionaries, emphasizing the 'social capital' of city
neighbourhoods. To understand the intellectual framework of contemporary urban policy, I will look at the key theoretical exponents starting
with the more recent and working backwards. There is, of course, some
danger of confusing the issue with that running order, especially since
many of these writers were reacting against the excesses of those that
preceded them. Such is the nature of debate that often the arguments
ended up in false counter-positions – of town against country,
city against suburb, of planners against spontaneous development.

430] Herbert Girardet takes issue with the author, Rising East Online, posted on http://www.uel.ac.uk/risingeast/

431] James Heartfield, 'The economics of sustainable development', in Ian Abley and James Heartfield, editors, Sustaining Architecture in the Ant-Machine Age (Chichester, Wiley-Academy, 2001) chapter 7, p 94

432] Herbert Girardet, Creating Sustainable Citie; Schumacher Briefing 2 (Fox Hole, Green Books, 19990 p 19

On the other hand, just as they were polemicising against their predecessors, often the underlying themes were just as striking – the themes of the continuity and change, of the dangers of automobility, and a pointed fear of the future.

HERBERT GIRARDET'S SUSTAINABLE CITIES

Cultural anthropologist and ecological advocate Herbert Girardet's influence on urban theory – and on Urban Task Force chief Richard Rogers – is profound.[430] Born in Germany, Girardet has lived in Britain since he went there to study in 1963. He helped put environmentalism on the map with the television series *Far From Paradise*, made with John Seymour for the BBC in 1985. After working with the United Nations on the environment, he was awarded a UN *Global 500 Award for Outstanding Environmental Achievements* at the Rio Earth Summit of 1992. Girardet's growing interest in urban planning was reflected in the 1994 television programme *Metropolis*, about London's metabolism, for Channel Four. The following year he wrote the report *Getting London into Shape for 2000*, for London First, and in 2000 he was co-curator of the Royal Institute of British Architects' exhibition *London Living City*. Girardet's many books include *Blueprint for a Green Planet*, 1987, *The Gaia Atlas of Cities*, 1992, and *Creating Sustainable Cities* 1999. He was a contributor to the Urban Task Force report.

The core concept running through Girardet's work has been **sustainability**, both in its original sense of a sustainable relationship with the environment, and in its enlarged sense of a sustainable society – an idea that he helped to formulate. The concept of sustainability is itself something of a compromise between the (deep green) ideal of a no-growth, or 'steady-state' economy, first mooted in the 1970s and the practical difficulties of getting that idea heard. Realising that an absolute brake on development was too extreme for most people, environmentalists moderated the message to emphasize 'sustainability' instead.[431] The idea could be defined as meaning an aspiration to leave the world in no worse a state than this generation finds it. It puts the onus on renewable resources, over non-renewable, and, insofar as it elevates a far-greater sense of caution about development, is difficult to reconcile with the aspiration to build millions more homes. So Girardet worries '...can modern cities reduce their impact on the biosphere by processes of enlightened self regulation and self limitation'.[432]

Girardet's special contribution to ecological thinking was to some extent to humanise it. Where deep green ideas like the concept of 'Gaia' (from the Goddess of nature), imputed purpose to nature, in a desire for equilibrium, regardless of human design. 'The theory states that earth acts as a living thing, a super-organism served by it constituents – living and nonliving – in the same way that the organs of the body serve the person.'[433] This is to anthropomorphise nature, and correspondingly to diminish man. Failure to serve nature's greater purpose threatens the equilibrium, which might forcefully reassert itself, in the form of famine or disease. Girardet's reintroduced human settlement into the Gaia concept, proposing a metabolism between cities and their hinterlands.[434]

Girardet's concept of 'metabolism' draws on the Japanese architect Kisho Kurokawa, who capitalised it to mean the symbiosis between man and nature. 'In contrast to Japanese architecture, which merges with nature and favors continuity with the natural surroundings', Kurokawa thought '...European architecture stands in opposition to nature and emphasizes its own independence and separateness.'[435] Girardet may also have been interested in the concept of 'social metabolism', which features in Karl Marx's early works, meaning man's exchange with nature through labour, as contrasted with the metamorphosis of goods in exchange.[436, 437] In Samuel Moore and Edward Aveling's translation of Capital, the term was changed to the less loaded '...social circulation of matter'.[438] But even the original anti-capitalist had a more optimistic view of agri-business than Girardet: 'Agriculture, e.g., becomes merely the application of the science of material metabolism, its regulation for the greatest advantage of the entire body of society.'[439]

Highlighted in the television programme Metropolis and in books such as Sustainable Cities is the relationship between the City and its hinterland, or what Girardet calls its ecological footprint – which is to say the area of land that the city draws upon for its sustenance, in food, water, fossil fuels, metals and so on, as well as the land that it uses for the disposal of waste, human and man-made, including greenhouse gas emissions. Girardet adopts an estimate of Londoners' ecological footprint of 6.63 hectares per habitant. As he points out, this means that Londoners effectively need an area twice the size of the United Kingdom to sustain them. If all people in the world lived at this rate of

433] Laurence Levine, 'Gaia: Goddess and Idea', Humanism Today, Volume 6, 1991, p 166

434] Herbert Giradet, The Gaia Atlas of Cities: New Directions for sustainable urban living (London, Gaia books, 1996

435] Kisho Kurokawa, 'The West, Conqueror and Domesticator of Nature', in The Symbiosis of Man and Nature, of Philosophy of Symbiosis, posted on www.kisho.co.jp

436] Karl Marx, Grundrisse (Harmondsworth, Penguin, 1973) p 489 and 705

437] Karl Marx, Contribution to the Critique of Political Economy (London, Lawrence and Wishart, 1981) p 86 and 95

438] Samuel Moore and Edward Aveling, translators, Karl Marx, Capital (Moscow, Progress, 1974) p 106.

439] Karl Marx, Grundrisse (Harmondsworth, Penguin, 1973) p 705

440] Lester Brown, 'Feeding Nine Billion', in Lester Brown and Chriistopher Flavin, editors, State of the World Atlas (London, Earthscan, 1999) p 120 to 121

441] Herbert Girardet, The Gaia Atlas of Cities (London, Gaia Books, 1996) p 86

442] Herbert Girardet, Creating Sustainable Cities; Schumacher Briefing 2 (Fox Hole, Green Books, 1999) p 33

443] I. Rubin, A History of Economic Thought (London, Pluto Press, 1989

consumption, Girardet argues, we would need three planets to sustain us (around 40 billion hectares, rather than the 14 billion hectares of landmass on our earth).

Girardet's calculations, though, have some weaknesses. First, he adopts a value of 6.63 hectares from the *City Limits* report, rejecting his own earlier estimate of three hectares – suggesting that this is a far from an exact science, or worse, that it is prone to exaggerate problems to make its case. Second, the 'ecological footprint' calculation suggests that with both population and consumption per head rising, the ecological footprint ought to be increasing. But in plainly measurable dimensions, it is not. Since reaching its record high of 732 million hectares in 1981, the grain harvested area of the world shrunk back to 690 million hectares in 1998. How is that possible? The element missing from Girardet's ecological footprint estimates is the increasing productivity of the land. Between 1950 and 1998 the grain harvested area per person halved from 0.23 hectares to 0.12 hectares, while actual consumption increased. [440]

Behind these blind-spots in the theory lies a problem of method. Though Girardet's reading of ecology seems to include humanity in nature, it does so in a way that reduces man-kind one-sidedly to consuming (and polluting man) ignoring man's creative and productive side. So the estimation of 'the city as parasite' [441] is a curious inversion of reality. Far from being parasitical, cities are creators of wealth. How is it that Girardet can see the city as net consumer? The answer is that he accounts for all resources, but one, labour. Everything but man is precious to Girardet, but man himself is not precious, at least not in his productive aspect, and not to be accounted for. His analysis of 'the Metabolism of London' registers 'Inputs' under heading one as oxygen, water, food and so on, but heading two is not 'Outputs', but 'Wastes', including CO_2, SO_2 and Nitrous Oxide. [442] The only city product that counts is pollution. Successive schools of economic thought have often privileged one kind of labour as truly productive over another. In eighteenth century France, the school known as the physiocrats thought that only agricultural labour yielded a net-product, while town-based crafts only reordered the materials that the countryside supplied – a view that persisted until Adam Smith showed that industry yielded a net-product in 1776. [443] Now Girardet and the school of the 'ecological footprint' aims to reverse that advance, dismissing all city activity as a waste of natural resources. No doubt Herbert Girardet would dismiss the inference as unfair, but it is pointed that aspects of city living that he does cherish are those of conviviality and interaction, rather than production, which is absent.

Girardet's ethos of 'sustainability' whilst seeming humane, aims to put limits on humanity. He wants to see cities '... improving their metabolism' with nature, by which he means 'reducing their ecological footprints'. [444] It is the thinking behind the 'carbon neutral' houses of Beddington Zero Energy Development – BedZed – in Sutton. Carbon neutrality is achieved by a mix of recycling materials, planting trees, photo-voltaic cells and limited parking spaces. [445] Sadly, BedZed's Biomass-fuelled heating and electricity system packed up early in 2005, leaving the block dependent upon the national grid. The failure of the heating system was followed by the reed-bed sewage filter that was to have recycled water for toilet-flushing and gardens in October of the same year. The live-work idea behind planning workshops and housing together proved illusory, since most residents work a distance from home like everyone else living in suburbia. Even the car club failed to take off, leaving carbon neutrality a distant dream.

Resource neutrality, or a light ecological footprint is a chimera. People's lives are secured by enlarging their ecological footprint, not reducing it. The greater the metabolism between man and nature, the larger are human possibilities, and therefore security. Resource efficiency does not come from limiting industry, but expanding it. 'Sustainability' is just another word for austerity. The easiest way to build a 'carbon neutral' house is not to build one at all. None of this would matter if it were only the prejudice of a handful of eco-warriors, but in 2001, RIBA President Paul Hyett made it clear that he would campaign for a 'moral imperative' upon architects to design with sustainability in mind. [446] The knowledge that architects could be held liable for damaging future generations would be a considerable constraint on new building.

Girardet's cheerful presentation of the material belies an underlying pessimism about the planet, which has not always proved to be justified. In 1976 he warned that '...Britain now produces just over 50 per cent of the food it consumes'. [447] Dependency on food imports put Britain dangerously at risk, he argued, though not specifying the foreign menace alluded to. In 1998 Britain produced more than 100 per cent of its sheep, pork, milk, wheat, barley and oats; more than ninety per cent of poultry,

444] Herbert Girardet, Creating Sustainable Cities; Schumacher Briefing 2 (Fox Hole, Green Books, 1999) p 12 and 14

445] www.peabody.org.uk/bed ZED

446] Paul Hyett, 'If sustainable design isn't a moral imperative, what is?', in Ian Abley and James Heartfield, editors, Sustaining Architecture in the Ant-Machine Age (Chichester, Wiley-Academy, 2001) chapter 7, p 22 to 31

447] 'New Towns or New Villages', in Herbert Girardet, editor, Land for the People (London, Crescent Books, 1976) p 99

448] Office for National Statistics, Britain 2000 (London, HMSO, 2000) p 446

449] Herbert Girardet and John Seymour, Far from Paradise – the story of human impact on the environment (Marshall Pickering, Green Print, 1988) p 149 and 152

450] Herbert Girardet, 'A Quarter Century', Resurgence, Issue 201, July/August 2000, posted on www.resurgence.org

451] P'eng Shu-tse, The Chinese Communist Party in Power (New York, Monad, 1980) p 290

452] 'New Towns or New Villages', in Herbert Girardet, editor, Land for the People (London, Crescent Books, 1976) p 105

and eggs, more than 80 per cent of beef and veal, and potatoes. Only butter (77 per cent) cheese (65 per cent) and sugar (64 per cent) were lower. [448] And though the Ministry of Agriculture did estimate self-sufficiency in food at just 55 per cent in 1976, the figure was lower by ten points because of the inclusion of non-indigenous food-types, and had been in any event improving year on year. Furthermore, the method of calculating food was changed in 1998, after it was discovered to systematically over-estimate the value of imported foods in processed goods. More important than the bad estimate is the underlying paranoia: so what if we import food? The European Union as a whole has been plagued by the over-production of food. Far from indicating a reliance on foreigners, the EU was properly understood as a net subsidy from Britain to European farmers. In 1986, researching the influential television series *Far from Paradise*, Girardet was once again inflating problems. He went with the film-makers to West Germany where he discovered that the forests were 'dying'. The problem was a consequence of industry: 'West Germany' was after all '...the most intensively industrialised country in Europe, perhaps in the world'. The problem was not restricted to Germany, he thought. Rather '...symptoms of serious forest decline are being experienced all over Europe'. [449] But as we have already seen, forests in the European Union are growing at a phenomenal rate.

Girardet's persistent pessimism needs explaining. The doom-laden estimations do not arise out of empirical findings alone, but are shaped by his own situation in relation to economic growth. In a memoir, Girardet recalls being a part of a back-to-earth movement in the 1970s when '...tens of thousands of people abandoned large cities such as London and Birmingham for the countryside' [450] – not long after intellectuals in China had been sent to work in the fields as part of Mao's 'cultural revolution'. [451] Their spur, in this account was '...a world of rampant materialism and the ever-present fear of nuclear annihilation'. It was around this time that Girardet advocated 'new villages', in '...an expansion of agricultural production with the aim of food self-sufficiency'. [452] In retrospect, Girardet described his ambition to '...build houses that were largely self-sufficient in energy with built-in solar greenhouses, surrounded by vegetable gardens and orchards, and set in new villages where we could bring up children in peace and tranquillity'. Though dressed up in the language of Tom and Barbara Good in the 1975 BBC comedy, *The Good Life*, all that Girardet is really describing is the push to suburbanisation: 'Finding an escape hatch from cities whose dependence on fossil fuels and long-distance transport systems seemed increasingly ominous and unsustainable'.

Unfortunately, the good life turned out to be a bit too rustic for Girardet and his comrades. 'Many rural resettlers found it hard to make a living on a few acres, beyond the most basic subsistence', he recalls, and that '...many were also made less than welcome by the locals in their adopted areas, who were bewildered by newcomers who had little understanding of the traditions and realities of rural living'. Conveniently for them, the green activists were excused the responsibility of realising their dream by the more pressing ecological disasters in the wider world – 'Reports about burning rainforests, oil spills killing millions of birds and sea mammals, squalid squatter settlements on the periphery of the new megacities of Africa, Latin America and Asia'. And ironically '...in between escapist programming of all kinds, television helped give birth to a new global consciousness'. So it was that '... in the late seventies, many new rural resettlers were beginning to question whether getting away from it all was a realistic option'. Moving back to the cities, these ecologists were not chastened by the failure of their utopia, but on the contrary, determined to impose their ideals but now on the city itself. This is the origin of Girardet's concept of the 'urban village', now neatly dovetailing with the embourgeoisement of pockets of inner London. Even in 1976, he kept his options open: 'As new settlements grow in the rural areas, as people move from urban employment to rural co-operative villages, the big cities will continue to shrink – as they have done for a generation – to a more realistic size, a more sustainable size'. [453] What this turned out to mean, though, was, the sooner all you oiks move out of Islington to Hertfordshire, the sooner we media types can colonise it.

Re-introduced into urban planning, Girardet's concept of 'sustainable cities' proved to be a useful one for all kinds of political goals. That is not surprising given its elasticity. Girardet was careful to include a social dimension to sustainability. Considered as 'sustainable communities' cities would have to meet standards of social equity and inclusion, as well as standards of environmental protection. [454] However, these were always sketched so vaguely as to constitute no literal promise to citizens, and at the same time, almost any ambition imaginable for policy makers. Girardet poses the question 'Can cities be sustainable?' [455] It is a complex question, since cities, by which Girardet means all human settlements

453] Herbert Girardet, 'A Quarter Century', Resurgence, Issue 201, July/August 2000, posted on www.resurgence.org

454] Herbert Girardet, Cities People Planet (London, John Wiley, 2004) p 7

455] Herbert Girardet, The Gaia Atlas of Cities (London, Gaia Books, 1996) p 13

456] Herbert Girardet, Cities People Planet (London, John Wiley, 2004) p 11

457] Tristram Hunt, Building Jerusalem: The Rise and Fall of the Victorian City (London, Weidenfeld and Nicholson, 2004) p 353

above the village, plainly exhibit all the signs of unsustainability according to the theory. Girardet comes close to proving that human life is impossible. The combined populations of the urbanised countries, the USA, the EU 15, Japan, Korea, Singapore, Hong Kong are 859 million. If each of these people had an ecological footprint of 6.63 hectares, that would amount to 5.7 billion hectares. The world's total land mass is 13 billion hectares, of which more than a third is desert, leaving only 8.35 billion hectares. The remaining five billion of the world's population, according to Girardet's method, ought to be living on the remaining 2.65 billion hectares, or half a hectare each. And yet cities do sustain themselves. In fact they more than sustain themselves, they sustain pretty much everything else as well. According to Girardet, this is only because '...we are able to maintain this global overdraft on a temporary basis by eating into the earth's capital stocks of fish, forest and fertile soils'.[456] Beyond empirical verification, sustainability becomes something like a religious belief in man's limitations, which can be turned up when the need to restrain arises, or down, when the urban villagers need their creature comforts.

JANE JACOBS AND SOCIAL CAPITAL

Tristram Hunt is surely right when he says that Richard Rogers is '...heavily indebted to the work of Jane Jacobs'.[457] Born in Scranton, Pennsylvania in 1916, Jane Jacobs moved to New York in 1934 and started writing for *Vogue*, *Harpers*, the *Herald Tribune* and *Q Magazine* about the Greenwich Village she had made her own, eventually getting a staff job at the *Architectural Forum* in 1952. It was there that she wrote the articles that would form the basis of *The Death and Life of Great American Cities* in 1961. Jacobs represented community action against the big developers, like Robert Moses, the city planner who blighted New York neighbourhoods with the cross-Bronx expressway. She moved to Canada, sickened by the Vietnam war, and published further books *The Economy of Cities* (1969), *Cities and the Wealth of Nations* (1984) and most recently *Dark Age Ahead* (2004). Jacobs died on April 25, 2005.

Jacobs *Death and Life of Great American Cities* anticipates much of the urbanists' case for compact cities, and against outward expansion. Like the Urban Task Force, Jacobs thought that '...today everyone who values cities is disturbed by automobiles'. She also thought that it was a good thing that '...in the dense diversified city areas people still walk, an activity that is impractical in the suburbs'. And like Lord Rogers of Riverside, she was an early champion of the waterfront: 'The waterfront is the first wasted asset capable of drawing people at leisure.'

Jacobs', like the Task Force, put great value on diversity, resisting the accepted thinking of her day that residential and employment building should be separated. She saw the positive in mixed neighbourhoods, with '...streets livening up with workers at midday when they go dead from the dwellings, livening up in the evening when they go dead from the work'. That was the advantage for a neighbourhood of '...a good healthy mix of work stirred alongside its stretch of dwellings'.

Jacobs was first to question the received view that more space was what cities needed, mocking planners for their dogmatic assault on 'highdensityandovercrowding' Jacobs gave examples of very compact areas that were, nonetheless desirable and thriving: 'In Brooklyn, New York, the most generally admired, popular and upgrading neighbourhood is Brooklyn Heights; it has much the highest density of dwellings in Brooklyn' – so, too, Greenwich Village in Manhattan and Boston's North End. Resisting the temptation to say that there is a strict mathematical correlation between high density and success, Jacobs does say that '...dense concentrations of people are one of the necessary conditions for flourishing city diversity' (and diversity in this argument is taken to equal vitality).

Just as she anticipated the thinking of the Urban Task Force, Jane Jacobs also anticipated one of the key concepts of contemporary sociology, that of social capital. Acknowledging that the city population is exceedingly mobile, Jacobs insists that '...underlying any float of population must be a continuity of people who have forged neighbour-hood networks'. And it is '...these networks' she says, that 'are a city's irreplaceable social capital.' [458] (Robert Putnam, whose seminal essay *Bowling Alone* made 'social capital' a buzzword for policymakers for a while, acknowledged that 'To my knowledge, the first scholar to use the term 'social capital' in its current sense was Jane Jacobs, in *The Death and Life of Great American Cities*.'[459]) This 'problematic oxymoron', [460] 'social capital' tries to parcel up the informal relations that people have as a definite object and put a value on it, as though looking out for one another was an investment, that could be weighed in the balance against other investments, such as the cross-Bronx expressway for

458] Jane Jacobs, Death and Life of Great American Cities (New York, Random House, 1961) p 159, 175, 203, 205, 206, 230, and 338

459] Robert Putnam, 'Bowling Alone: America's Declining Social Capital', Journal of Democracy 6:1, Jan 1995, p 65-78

460] Andy Blunden, 'Social Solidarity vs. Social Capital', posted on http://werple.net.au/~andy/works/

461] Jane Jacobs, Death and Life of Great American Cities (New York, Random House, 1961) p 339

462] Carol Lloyd, 'Urban visionary sees 'Dark Age Ahead' but also holds out hope for the fragile "human contraption"', SF Gate, May 25, 2004

463] James Howard Kunstler New York, Metropolis Magazine Ltd, March 2001

example. It is an argument that tries to translate non-economic imperatives into the acceptable terminology of profit and loss accounts.

But placing a value on community and neighbourhood can end up putting a premium on stability, not change. Development risks squandering the 'social capital' – until now, a rather woolly idea. So Jacobs' fear of the car emphasises the potential for losses that do not show up on the bottom line. Traffic can have the effect that 'Downtowns and other neighbourhoods that are marvels of close-grained intricacy and compact mutual support are casually disembowelled', she writes. 'Landmarks are crumbled or are so sundered from their contexts in city life as to become irrelevant trivialities.'[461] It is pointed that the underlying theme here is the **fragility** of the city neighbourhood. These relationships of neighbours looking out for one another are easily wrecked, like delicate cobwebs.

In a recent interview, promoting the jeremiad Dark Age Ahead, an octogenarian Jacobs told journalist Carol Lloyd: 'It's the human condition. So many things can go wrong. You can see how fragile the whole human contraption is.'[462] But one could make a stronger case about the robustness of human societies, accommodating recessions, wars, epidemics. What is more fragile is a certain kind of community that Jacobs saw in Greenwich Village in the 1950s. This was less a model for all neighbourhoods than a very specific moment that was unlikely to be repeated.

The special condition of Greenwich Village in the 1950s was that of a working class neighbourhood getting more bohemian, eventually becoming gentrified. (Since the publication of *The Death and Life of Great American Cities*, Greenwich Village became too gentrified, and Jacobs' contemporaries moved out, though not as far as Toronto: 'Parts of Brooklyn now are, you might say, the outliers of Greenwich Village', she told James Howard Kunstler in an interview in 2000.[463]) Gentrification of inner-city neighbourhoods would become commonplace, but the experience Jacobs described was indeed a peculiarly democratic moment in US history, after the Second World War, with many second and third generation immigrants, Southern and Eastern Europeans, being integrated into mainstream America through the New Deal, the War and its aftermath, the GI Bill (that put demobbed soldiers through college), breaking down the barriers to White Anglo-Saxon Protestant privileges.

Jacobs does not say 'gentrified' of Greenwich Village, she calls it 'unslumming': 'The unslummed former slum in which I live'. When

Jacobs writes: 'In my neighbourhood, this unslumming drop did not represent a replacement of the old slum population by a new and different middle class-population. It represented much of the old population moving into the middle-class.' [464] Here she puts the trajectory of Greenwich Village firmly in the New Deal paradigm, identifying its rise with the rise of the New Deal's urban constituency. Marshall Berman thinks that '...her inventory of the people in the neighbourhood has the aura of a WPA mural or a Hollywood version of the World War Two bomber crew: every race, creed and colour working together to keep America free for you and me'. [465] But Jacobs' idealisation of the urban New Deal coalition is a fleeting moment. Bringing the southern and eastern European immigrants that swelled American cities at the end of the nineteenth century into the American mainstream did not stop with their supporting Al Smith in 1928 and electing Roosevelt in 1932. [466] Just as the 'hyphenated Americans' [467] were being elevated to all-Americans, they were also moving out of the cities and getting homes in the suburbs – assisted by the Veterans Administration and the Home Owners Loan Corporation. [468, 469] Though Jacobs saw the elevation of Greenwich Village as an extension of the democratisation of New Deal America, it was actually quite a different kind of community. With the gentrification of inner city Greenwich Village the core of the New Deal constituency was already disappearing, leaving an altogether more fractious coalition in charge: upper-class liberals and inner-city blacks, collaborators in City Hall, but socially, utterly divided.

Marshall Berman thinks that the WPA roll-call is missing one: there are '...no blacks on her block'. 'This', he writes '...is what makes her neighbourhood vision seem so pastoral: it is the city before the blacks got there'. [470] Berman's criticism is not entirely fair. Jacobs is interested in black neighbourhoods. 'I see no reason to believe that Negro slums cannot unslum, too', writes an optimistic Jacobs. But that optimism, based on the post-war expansion of the US was running out of steam by the end of the 1960s, and Jacobs' speculates:

> 'If America has now, in the case of the Negroes, reached an effective halt in this process and in general reached a stage of arrested deve opment – a thought I find highly improbable and quite intolerable – then it may be that Negro slums cannot effectively unslum in the fashion demonstrated by slums formed by other ethnic populations.' [471]

464] Jane Jacobs, Death and Life of Great American Cities (New York, Random House, 1961) p 275 and 281

465] Marshall Berman, All that is Solid Melts into Air: The experiences of modernity (London, Verso, 1983) p 324

466] Andersen, Kristi, Creation of a Democratic Majority 1928-36 (Chicago, University of Chicago Press, 1979)

467] Theodore Roosevelt, 'There is no room in this country for hyphenated Americanism', 1915, in Philip Davis, editor, Immigration and Americanization (Boston, Ginn and Company, 1920)

468] Kofi Buenor Hadjor, Another America: the politics of race and blame (Boston, South End Press, 1992)

469] Kevin Phillips, The Emerging Republican Majority (New Rochelle, Arlington House, 1969)

470] Marshall Berman, All that is Solid Melts into Air: The experiences of modernity (London, Verso, 1983) p 324

471] Jane Jacobs, Death and Life of Great American Cities (New York, Random House, 1961) p 284 and 285

472] Douglas Massey, Nancy Denton, American Apartheid: Segregation and the Making of the Underclass (Harvard, Harvard University Press, 1994)

473] Michael N. Danielson, The Politics of Exclusion (New York, Columbia University Press, 1976)

474] Jerald E. Podair The Strike That Changed New York: Blacks, Whites, And The Ocean Hill-Brownsville Crisis (New Haven, Connecticut, Yale University Press, 2002)

475] Richard T. Gates and Frederic Stout, editors, The City Reader (London, Routledge, 1996) p 103

By the 1980s, Jacobs' fears appeared to have been realised. The racial divisions of the era confirmed the division between white suburbs and black inner cities. [472, 473] In New York, the slow breakdown of the coalition was marked by the conflicts between Jews and Blacks, from the 1968 teachers' strike, after a mostly black Ocean Hill-Brownsville school board dismissed white, and often Jewish, teachers, [474] to the rioting in Crown Heights in 1991 – following the deaths of seven-year old Gavin Cato, run over by an orthodox Jew, and Yankel Rosenbaum, stabbed after being rounded on by a group of blacks. Far from being the universal model of neighbourhood relations, New York City, and Greenwich Village in turn seem to have represented a fleeting moment of inter-racial harmony.

But there was a vitality to Jacobs' Greenwich Village – which can still be seen today. It is less popular than she describes, though. It is the experience of the gentrifying inner city. 'The book encouraged and justified gentrification by the middle classes of formerly working class neighbourhoods,' is the stark judgement of the Urban Studies teachers Richard LeGates and Frederic Stout. [475] The Urban Task Force seems to have recognised in Jacobs' account an anticipation of their own 'urban renaissance', though without ever acknowledging the real character of it. Jacobs' emphasis upon the cultural life of the city reveals the actual basis of her 'unslumming' Greenwich Village. 'Do my suggestions for additional uses based on leisure time attraction seem frivolous and expensive?' she asks. Indeed they do. But that is because she is generalising the experience of a leisured intelligentsia, however dressed up as middle class America. Making the case for older buildings Jacobs explains that '...only operations that are well-established, high-turnover, standardized or heavily subsidized can afford, commonly, to carry the costs of new construction'. Her preference, though, is for '...the unformalized feeders of the arts – studios, galleries, stores, for musical instruments and art supplies, backrooms where the low earning power of a seat and table can absorb uneconomic discussions – these go into the old buildings'. Little wonder that the proponents of café society recognise themselves in Jacobs' account. Just as the old shells of warehouses and offices are being renovated for restaurants and flats in Clerkenwell, here is Jane Jacobs describing the same process in New York forty years earlier. 'In Greenwich Village, almost no old building is scorned by middle-class families hunting a bargain in a lively district, or by rehabilitators hunting a golden egg'. And just as the Urban Taskforce embraces the charm of older buildings they find sanction in Jacobs' account: 'In successful districts old buildings 'filter up' ...the last thing we need is new construction.' [476] Here is a picture of the narrowly-based leisured classes, generalised as if it were a model for all society, contrasted favourably to the soulless suburbs.

In the face of the great changes of the post war period Jacobs' urges the case for the city neighbourhood. Marshall Berman's characterisation of 'pastoral' seems strange – usually associated with the countryside. But Berman's meaning is precise. He is saying that Jacobs romanticises the city, as English pastoral romanticised the countryside. The city neighbourhood is a mythical community, the ideal of togetherness in the face of great change and division: in Jacobs' case the migration of whites out of (and blacks into) New York. Gates and Stout found her vision '...oddly reflected in the fantasy-nostalgia of Sesame Street'. [477] Marshall Berman calls this side of Jacobs *Death and Life of Great American Cities* '...an anti-modernist subtext' under 'her modernist text', '...an undertow of nostalgia for family and neighbourhood'. [478] It is the myth of community solidarity in the face of change that recommends Jacobs to the proponents of 'mixed communities', who fear the social divisions that arise from suburbanisation. [479]

It was her critique of the planning enthusiasts that preceded her that found Jacobs at her strongest. Their resentment of the city was, she thought, a reaction against specific conditions, rather than a general rule to be followed for all time: 'Things have changed since the days when Ebenezer Howard looked at the slums of London and concluded that to save the people, city life must be abandoned.' Jacobs' barbs against Howard strike home:

'Ebenezer Howard's vision of the Garden City would seem almost feudal to us. He seems to have thought that members of the industrial working classes would stay neatly in their class, and even at the same job within their class; that agricultural workers would stay in agriculture; that businessmen (the enemy) would hardly exist as a significant force in his Utopia; and that planners could go about their good and lofty work, unhampered by rude nay-saying by the untrained.'

Charging Howard with conservatism Jacobs argues that:
'Howard wanted to freeze power, people, and the uses and increments of money into an easily manageable and static pattern. Indeed

476] Jane Jacobs, Death and Life of Great American Cities (New York, Random House, 1961) p 160, 188, and 193

477] Richard T. Gates and Frederic Stout, editors, The City Reader (London, Routledge, 1996) p 103

478] Marshall Berman, All that is Solid Melts into Air: The experiences of modernity (London, Verso, 1983) p 324

479] Urban Task Force, Towards an Urban Renaissance – Final Report of the Urban Task Force (London, HMSO, Spon, 1999) chapters 8 and 13

480] Jane Jacobs, Death and Life of Great American Cities (New York, Random House, 1961) p 83, 218, and 289

481] Jane Jacobs, quoted by James Howard Kunstler, Metropolis Magazine, March 2001

he happened to want a pattern that was already obsolete. "How to stem the drift from the country is one of the main problems of the day," said he.'

Telling as this criticism is of Howard, it is even more so of Jacobs herself. It is Jacobs that wants to freeze one pattern of living, one derived from her own experiences, and make it into a model for all time. More than that, it was already an obsolete pattern by the time *Death and Life of Great American Cities*, was written. She charges Howard with wanting to stem the drift from the country, a mistake no doubt. But she in turn is left trying to stem the drift from the city to the suburbs, just as it has become the defining feature of American living.

Jacobs' most cutting remarks against Ebenezer Howard, and his American interlocutor Lewis Mumford, were that they did not like cities. Of Ebenezer Howard, she wrote he '...hated the city and thought it an outright evil and an affront to nature that so many people should get themselves into an agglomeration'. 'His proposal for saving the people', she added '...was doing the city in.'[480] In interview with James Howard Kunstler more recently she sneered at Lewis Mumford:

'I had my doubts about him because we rode into the city together in a car. And I watched how he acted as soon as he began to get into the city. And he had been talking and all pleasant but as soon as he began to get into the city he got grim, withdrawn, and distressed. And it was just so clear that he just hated the city and hated being in it.'[481]

And yet it is all too clear that it is Jacobs that hates cities, at least cities as they are, widely dispersed, semi-suburban, car-dominated. Her ideal city it turns out is a rarefied fragment of city life, what David Brooks called 'BoBo' – the bourgeois-bohemians, the culturati, café society, and her ideal of community based upon it just the bad faith of that social grouping's alienation from their fellow man.

THE CITY OUT OF HISTORY:
LEWIS MUMFORD AND EBENEZER HOWARD

Ebenezer Howard, who earned his living as a stenographer, inaugurated urban planning with his essay *To-Morrow: A peaceful path to real reform* (1898), better known by his book title of 1902,

Garden Cities of To-Morrow. [482] Howard was influenced by the debates in England over the 'social question' raised by reformers like Henry Mayhew, Octavia Hill and Seebohm Rowntree. In particular it was Edward Bellamy's *Looking Backward* that inspired him.

Garden Cities of To-Morrow was remarkable for its detailed plan for re-structuring the city, with specialised zones and green belts (as described in chapter three). But Howard's own contribution to the canon of urban theory was to identify the city as a special object of study. Compelling as Howard's blueprint was, it was his influence on the New York architecture critic Lewis Mumford that did most to develop urban theory.

Mumford, a graduate of the New School of Social Research in New York, influenced by Howard's collaborator Patrick Geddes, founded the Regional Planning Association of America in the 1920s, and published *The Culture of Cities* in 1938. *The Culture of Cities* was followed by Mumford's magnum opus *The City in History* in 1961, and a spate of other books until his death in 1990.

The City in History was a book with a grand sweep; too grand a sweep in fact. Over nearly seven hundred pages, Mumford comments on everything from the necropolis to medieval housekeeping, from baroque power to suburbia and beyond. This was a style of big sweep book that was popular in the interwar years, but already looking a bit grandiose by the sixties. Influenced by the leftist anthropologist V. Gordon Childe, Mumford sketched the history of cities across the ages, with a tendency to collapse different eras into one another. 'The modern city itself, for all its steel and glass, is still essentially an earth-bound Stone Age structure', wrote Mumford. 'By the year 2000 B.C., at all events, most of the major physical organs of the city had been created', he went on. For Mumford, it seems, the City was not in history, but outside of it. In fact, the city is older than the human species itself, since '...the social insects ... anticipated urban man'. He pondered that '...one certainly does not find religion or ritual sacrifice in these insect communities': 'But the other institutions that accompanied the rise of the city are all present: the strict division of labour, the creation of a specialized military caste, the technique of collective destruction' etc. etc. [483] But if the city was already present in what Mumford calls, without a hint of irony, **insectopolis**, then it really is outside of human history.

482] Ebenezer Howard, Garden Cities of To-Morrow (London, Swan Sonnenschein, 1902)

483] Lewis Mumford, The City in History, (Harmondsworth, Penguin, 1991) p 26, 59, and 91

484] De Re Edifacatori (1450), cited in Lewis Mumford, The City in History (Harmondsworth, Penguin, 1991) p 552

485] Lewis Mumford, The City in History (Harmondsworth, Penguin, 1991) p 550

486] Eric Hobsbawm, 'Labour in the Great City', New Left Review, issue 166, November 1987, p 39

Big history books, like Arnold Toynbee's *Change and Habit*, H G Wells' *History of the World*, even Fernand Braudel's three volumes of *Civilisation and Capitalism*, tend to collapse different historical eras into underlying patterns in the **longue durée**. Mumford's light trot across the centuries takes in a lot of historical detail, but tends to reduce specific historical moments into mere variations on the eternal theme of the city. So for example, Mumford finds evidence of that typically twentieth-century phenomenon, the suburb, not just as far back as the Italian renaissance, in Leone Battista Alberti's treatise on building, [484] but also '...evidences of suburban development in "Greater Ur"'. [485] At which point, of course, the suburb becomes just a detail in the greater story of the city, dwarfed by 4000 years of history.

The reason it matters that Mumford takes the City out of history is that it has the effect of rendering a specific historical form of human association as if it were eternal. The fact that we commonly use the same word, city, to describe such different settlements as the tribute gathering encampment at Ur, the Athenian polis, Imperial Rome, medieval Bruges, renaissance Florence, industrial Manchester and post-industrial Palo Alto only confuses. The subsumption of radically different kinds of social organisation to one uniform 'city' ends up mystifying what is going on. Far from turning the focus onto historical change, the eternal city abolishes change, or at least reduces it to the surface interference above the still depths.

The effect of the ahistorical method is that it takes for granted precisely what needs to be explained: the city. Without origin or end, the fact of the city is pushed outside of the realm of investigation. Specifically, Mumford fails to understand the one city that he needs to – the city of his own time, the industrial city of the nineteenth- and early twentieth-century. 'The giant city was a new phenomenon in Western capitalism, and a type of human settlement virtually unprecedented in the non-oriental world before the eighteenth century: that is to say, the city whose population was measured in several hundreds of thousands, and very soon in millions' [486] It is this city that establishes the patterns of human community in Mumford's own time, and remains the paradigmatic city in the discussion of town and country to this day. Cities of other eras, courts and ancient cities crowd out the nineteenth-century city in Mumford's history. (In fact these are not truly understood in their own right, but merely as supporting material in the overall thesis of the eternal city.) The one city that Mumford ought to account for is submerged in the dizzying procession. Indeed Mumford shows a marked unhappiness with the city of the nineteenth century, the first truly mass urban settlement that we would recognise as a city like our own.

Allowing that it is only in the nineteenth century that cities – 'Coketowns' – came close to the population levels we know today, Mumford insists on putting the one truly modern city form **outside** of the history of the city: 'Such urban clots could and did expand a hundred times without acquiring more than a shadow of the institutions that characterise a city in the mature sociological sense.' Furthermore '...except in shrunken, residual forms, even the characteristic organs of the Stone-Age city [sic] were lacking.' But this is all upside down. It is not the industrial city that fails to live up the standards of the pre-historic settlements, but rather it is the industrial city that sets the standard from which we can look back on the settlements of previous eras. It seems that Jane Jacobs' assessment is correct. Mumford just did not like the city – which, if true, makes his eternalisation of the City outside of history even more extraordinary. But that is precisely how Mumford's method works – what is truly original, the modern city is subsumed, tamed, reduced to a small footnote in the four millennia of the City, with a capital C.

Mumford does dislike the nineteenth-century city, which he calls 'paleo-technic' (roughly what today's urban theorists would, with the same pejorative intent, call 'carbon-based'). But his substantial criticism is that Coketown is unplanned, with individualism taking precedence over community. 'This myth of untrammelled individualism', he argues eloquently, '...was in fact the democratisation of the baroque concept of the despotic Prince: now every enterprising man sought to be a despot in his own right'. To his dismay, until 1838 neither Manchester nor Birmingham '...even functioned politically as incorporated boroughs: they were man-heaps, machine warrens'. Interestingly, the same case is being made today, except it is made against the suburbs, that they lack civic ties, and are dominated by the spirit of individualism. But then they were anticipated already by Mumford, who wrote of the 'universal suburb' as 'a nightmare' and a '...proliferating non-entity': 'A large scale pattern of expressways and airfields and sprawling car-parks and golf courses envelops a small-scale, increasingly shrunken mode of life'.

487] Lewis Mumford, The City in History (Harmondsworth, Penguin, 1991) p 510, 518, 522, 524, 534, 540, 542 and 565

488] Jenny Uglow The Lunar Men (London, Faber and Faber, 2003)

489] Gareth Stedman Jones, Outcast London (Harmondsworth, Penguin, 1984)

490] Frank Mort, Dangerous Sexualities (London, Routledge, 2000)

491] Gertrude Himmelfarb, The Idea of Poverty (New York, Random House, 1983)

At the core of this argument is the planner's jealousy of the individual's autonomy. Mumford despairs that as regards factories, "Free competition' alone determined location, without thought of the possibility of functional planning'. (Such a terrible prospect: no work for the planners.) 'There were no effective centres in this urban massing', he tutted, '...no institutions capable of uniting its members into an active city life: no political organisations capable of organising its common activities'. Mumford asks, 'How build a coherent city out of a thousand competing individualists who knew no law but their own sweet will?', as if there was nothing worse than people making their own decisions for themselves.

In this way the stage is set for Mumford's hero, Ebenezer Howard. Under the heading 'The counter-attack', he writes, '...perhaps the greatest contribution made by the industrial town was the reaction it produced against its own misdemeanours'. So it was, he argues, that '...despite the theoretic claims of **laissez faire**, the nineteenth century became, as Beatrice and Sidney Webb correctly pointed out, the century of municipal socialism'. Pointing to the advances in municipal water, sewage, gas, Mumford considers that, '...only the public ownership of land for town extension, town protection, or town colonization was lacking'. Predictably, '...that step forward was one of the significant contributions of Ebenezer Howard's garden city'. [487]

Mumford's Manichean view of the nineteenth century divides between (good) gas-and-water socialism and (bad) laissez-faire capitalism. But it was the laissez-faire capitalism – or at least the labour that it put in motion – that created the wealth on which municipal socialism was based. The great advances in productivity of the industrial revolution were the means by which the roads, sewers and town halls were built, just as the forward motion of the society gave rise to the political will that demanded them. No doubt much of this was imposed on individual masters against their narrow interests. Nowadays, the contribution of the industrialists is more favourably reckoned – celebrated in Adam Hart Davis' television show *What the Victorians Did for Us*, or Jenny Uglow's *The Lunar Men*, [488] for example. On the other hand, historians have been less kind to the Victorian moralists. [489, 490, 491] Their reputation for reining in the excesses of the capitalists has been tempered by a more critical assessment of their own petty moralising and conservatism. The Victorian philanthropists' judgemental distinction between deserving and undeserving poor, their predilection for the pseudo-science of eugenics, and their obsession with social purity all add up to a less attractive picture than Mumford paints.

More importantly, Mumford's assessment of the industrial city decries the dynamic side, in favour of the conservative one. This is what he draws out from Ebenezer Howard's garden cities ideal: the attempt to restrain city growth. Mumford's bent towards taking the City out of history is the intellectual accompaniment to Howard's proposal to rein in city growth through the green belt and the public control of land.

Mumford's ahistorical approach tends to eternalise one contrast in particular, and that is the division between the Town and the Country.

THE UTOPIANS: ABOLISHING THE TOWN-COUNTRY DIVIDE

Before there was 'urban theory' people were thinking, writing and talking about cities, the problems and the opportunities they created. In a sense it was easier to see the City in perspective in the nineteenth century. The growth of the nineteenth-century industrial city was such a remarkable phenomenon. One could not help be impressed by the sudden arrival of the modern city. And just as you could see the City rise up before your eyes, so too could you imagine it passing away, too. The early commentators on the City were not so accustomed to its existence that they assumed it would last forever, as 'urban theory' does.

There was a degree of curmudgeonly protest in the initial attitudes to the City – to say the least. Historian G.M. Trevelyan never ceased to lament '...the harsh distinction between rural and urban life'. [492] But there was also an insight that the City was not set in stone, even if actually it was. More than just the bricks and mortar, though, nineteenth-century commentators were interested in the social transformation that had taken place – the division between the town and the country. This was a division that set one part of the kingdom against the other, and it was not one that many people felt that they had to take for granted. Rather, the division between town and country was something which could be overcome. It is this willingness to imagine the alteration of city-countryside relations that made the earlier commentaries on city life, more insightful than the later.

The Christian socialist Charles Kingsley, for example, imagined '...a complete interpenetration of city and country, a complete fusion

492] G.M. Trevelyan, quoted in Keith Thomas, Man and the Natural World: Changing Attitudes in England 1500-1800 (Harmondsworth, Penguin, 1984) p 243

493] Charles Kingsley, quoted in Tristram Hunt, Building Jerusalem: The Rise and Fall of the Victorian City (London, Weidenfeld and Nicholson, 2004) p 331

494] Robert Blatchford, quoted in Tristram Hunt, Building Jerusalem: The Rise and Fall of the Victorian City (London, Weidenfeld and Nicholson, 2004) p 313

495] Karl Marx, German Ideology (London, Electronic Book Company, 1998) p 99

496] Karl Marx and Frederick Engels, The Communist Manifesto (London, Verso, 1998) p 61

497] Lewis Mumford, The City in History (Harmondsworth, Penguin, 1991) p 585

498] Karel Teige, 'The antithesis between town and country – a few citations', The Minimum Dwelling (London, MIT Press, 2002) p 394 to 397, and 394

of their different modes of life, and a combination of the advantages of both'. [493] So too, did the socialist Robert Blatchford, in his *Merrie England* (1895) dream of '...towns rebuilt with wide streets, detached houses, with gardens and fountains and avenues of trees'. [494] These were reactions against the early brutality of city life, but also against the limitations of the countryside.

Among those early utopian protests against the division between town and country were the young Karl Marx and Frederick Engels. A radical from his college days in Germany, Karl Marx was inspired by the industrial age, and pressed his friend, Engels to tell him about England, and Manchester, where he had moved to work in his father's business. Engels' account of *The Condition of the Working Class in England*, published in Germany in 1844 told the truth about Britain's impoverished cities before Henry Mayhew's *London Labour and London Poor* (1851) Charles Booth's *Life and Labour of the People in London* (1889), and Seebohm Rowntree's *Poverty, A Study of Town Life* (1901). Marx, in his manuscript *The German Ideology* (1846), drawing in part on Engels' experience, considered the town-country division, the original division of labour, writing of: a '...subjection of the individual under the division of labour...a subjection which makes one man into a restricted town-animal, the other into a restricted country-animal, and daily creates anew the conflict between their interests'. Following the Utopian socialists, Marx argued that the '...abolition of the antagonism between town and country is one of the first conditions of communal life'. [495] Later, Marx and Engels included this ambition in the *Communist Manifesto of 1848*: 'Combination of agriculture with manufacturing industries; gradual abolition of the distinction between town and country, by a more equitable distribution of the population over the country.' [496] From there on in, the abolition of the distinction between town and country became a tenet of the left. Peter Kropotkin, [497] Paul Lafargue, August Bebel and V. I. Lenin, all committed themselves to the proposition. In 1872, Engels returned to *The Housing Question*: 'Wishing to solve the housing question while at the same time wanting to preserve today's large cities is absurd.' [498]

Underlying the socialist proposal of overcoming the opposition of town and country was a quite different understanding of the character of human societies than that that was found among the later proponents of Urban Studies. For Karl Marx and Frederick Engels in particular, a training in the German philosophy of G.W.F. Hegel prepared them to see human institutions as transitory, and always changing, not just in their proportions, but so as to successively call into question all provisional arrangements, boundaries and definitions. So, Marx's rough manuscript for his later work *Capital* contains this speculation of the actual course of the City in history:

> 'Ancient classical history is the history of cities, but cities based on landownership and agriculture; Asian history is a kind of undifferentiated unity of town and country (the large city must be regarded merely as a princely camp superimposed on the real economic structure); the Middle Ages (Germanic [feudal] period) starts with the countryside as the locus of history, whose further development then proceeds through the opposition of town and country; modern history is the urbanization of the countryside, not, as among the ancients, the ruralization of the city.'[499]

What marks Marx off from the later approach of Urban Studies, from Lewis Mumford, right through to Jane Jacobs and contemporary geographers is his insistence on the historically relative understanding of different eras of human settlement. Though here he is still hostage to the formal term 'city', the unavoidable meaning is that these 'cities' are all quite different in their underlying character.

Within Urban Studies, David Harvey looked again at Marx and Engels' approach to cities and thought that the proposal that the antithesis of town and country should be overcome a 'much too simplistic a recommendation in view of the very complex patterns of surplus circulation in contemporary capitalist and socialist countries'. Whatever Harvey's complication is, the actual course of development shows that events do indeed lead away from the antithesis of town and country.[500]

The socialists' proposal for overcoming the division between town and country differed from the original conservative reaction against the city. They saw the city not as a moral evil, but a stage in human evolution that served its purpose. They acknowledged the accomplishments of urban society, but did not make a fetish out of a given geographical arrangement. So the Russian revolutionary V. I. Lenin wrote that '...even if we admit that the large cities of capitalist society have played a progressive role, this does not prevent us from including the prospect of their elimination in our programme for abolishing the antithesis

499] Karl Marx, quoted in David Harvey, Social Justice and the City (London, Edward Arnold, 1973) p 204

500] David Harvey, Social Justice and the City (London, Edward Arnold, 1973) p 235

501] Karel Teige, 'The antithesis between town and country – a few citations', The Minimum Dwelling (London, MIT Press, 2002) p 396

between town and country'. [501] In England, William Morris is generally cast in the role of romantic hater of the cities. Of course it is true that Morris was a fierce critic of urban dehumanisation. But in later life Morris moved to the left, adopting a more positive attitude to the possible contribution of industry. In 1884 Morris took issue with the middle-class reformer Octavia Hill in the pages of the socialist paper Justice. She had written that there should be no more than one family to a room, a proposal of such parsimony that Morris sketched out a plan for housing working people on a much more generous basis. Pointedly, Morris does not opt for country cottages, but skyscrapers:

> 'It might be advisable, granting the existence of huge towns for the present, that the houses for workers should be built in tall blocks, in what might be called vertical streets, but that need not prevent ample room in each lodging ...also it must not prevent the lodgings having their fair share of air and sunlight.'

Note that Morris' solution is provisional, '...granting the existence of huge towns for the present', not for all time. This is where Morris differentiates himself from '...the pessimistic revolt...led by John Ruskin against the philistinism of the triumphant bourgeois'. Unlike Ruskin, Morris wants to overcome the limitations of city life. Following Marx, Morris saw '...the aggregation of people into towns and the consequent increasing division of labour' as both negative and positive. Negative because it saw men subordinated to capital, positive because it created the conditions for '...an alteration of the machinery of life in such a way that all men shall be allowed to share in the fullness of that life, for the production and upholding of which the machinery was instituted'. In later life, Morris did not romanticise the countryside. In the essay, *Under an elm tree*, he recounts a story of farm labourers idle while hay waits to be cut, because the farmer will not pay enough. Enjoying the scenery, Morris despairs at '...all this country beauty so tragically incongruous with the country misery'. But equally Morris departs himself from his 'socialist friends' who think '...this is all that can come of your country life': 'Turn the page, I say'. Even the countryside can be put on a more cooperative and rational basis.

Unlike Lewis Mumford, Morris deplored the reformers like Octavia Hill and Charles Booth, whom he called 'five per cent philanthropists' and '...workhouse socialists'. That was because he understood their programme to be ameliorative, while he, late in life, had committed himself to revolutionary change. As he saw it, their concern for the poor still '...takes it for granted that the workers must be in the main paupers'. But already, by the 1880s, workhouse socialism was finding an audience among the professional middle classes. In the *Commonweal* Morris reviewed the Boston-based reformer, Edward Bellamy's *Looking Backward*, the inspiration for Ebenezer Howard's *Garden Cities of To-Morrow*. The author of *The Dream of John Ball* and *News from Nowhere* is surprisingly sniffy about the literary form of the Utopia that Bellamy adopts. Morris is particularly sceptical about what he sees as Bellamy's view that '...the change to socialism' is '...taking place without any breakdown of that [modern] life, or indeed any disturbance of it, by means of the final development of the great monopolies'. Bellamy, though, proves more far-sighted than Morris envisaging '...a great reduction in the hours of labour by mere machinery', which the latter sees as just a dream.[502]

Morris also thought that Bellamy was wrong to assume that the city would be the form that future settlements would take. Ebenezer Howard was much closer to Bellamy's ameliorative socialism, than he was to Hill and Booth. But the early socialist goal of overcoming the antithesis of town and country persists, at least in outline, in Ebenezer Howard's Garden Cities. 'Town and country must be married, and out of this joyous union will spring a new hope, a new life, a new civilisation,' Howard wrote. London, thought Howard, provided the opportunity to overcome the division:

> 'Elsewhere, new cities are being built; London then must be transformed. Elsewhere the town is invading the country; here the country must invade the town.'[503]

Between conception and realisation, between Howard's blueprint and Patrick Abercrombie's plan, something happened. The old socialist ideal of abolishing the division between town and country was truncated into the planned creation of new towns, and, ironically, the attempt to institutionalise the boundaries of the city. The ideal of bringing the country into the town was stopped, with the creation of some city parks. And the dissolution of the division between town and country became instead the formalisation of that division in the green belt,

502] William Morris, Political Writings (Bristol, Thoemmes Press, 1994) p 50, 51, 421, 429, 430, 484, 486, and 594

503] Ebenezer Howard, quoted in Tristram Hunt, Building Jerusalem: The Rise and Fall of the Victorian City (London, Weidenfeld and Nicholson, 2004) p 317 and 320

504] William Morris,
Political Writings (Bristol,
Thoemmes Press, 1994)
p 53

505] John Ruskin, quoted
in Lewis Mumford, The
City in History
(Harmondsworth,
Penguin, 1991) p 540

what Mumford called the public control of the land. It was, sadly, as Morris anticipated: 'We cannot be allowed to use the earth to live on, like men'.[504] This was the mockery that 'workhouse socialism' had made of the original dream – not an abolition of the monopoly of the land, but the transfer of the monopoly from the big landowners to the state, which continued to enforce it against spontaneous settlement. Conservatives embraced the formalised distinction between town and country that the green belt represented. So Ruskin demanded that workers' houses be '…walled round, so that there may be no festering suburb anywhere, but clean busy streets within, and the open country without, with a belt of beautiful garden and orchard round the walls'.[505]

If the Utopian dream of overcoming the division between town and country was turned into its opposite by Abercrombie, the underlying dynamic had not gone away. Cities, by virtue of their energetic growth, continued to strain against the boundaries set upon them. The optimistic side of the Utopians continued, albeit in a more narrowly technical way, in the writings and plans of the modernists. Focused on the excitement of cities, they liked the expansionary dynamic rather than fearing it. Architects like Le Corbusier and Mies van der Rohe were too excited at the creative potential of new technologies to pay too much attention to traditional land allocation.

The writer Ford Madox Ford summarised the inventiveness of the early twentieth century in an essay *The Future of London* (1909). Ford lambasted the 'tyranny of the past' in words to goad today's heritage industry: 'The future, on the other hand, wages a ceaseless war against the monuments of the past'. Ford's London is utterly different from Abercrombie's. Instead of depopulating, he dreams of a Great London '…not of seven, but of seventy-million imperially minded people'. Such an increase seems impossible until you get the true measure of his 'Great London'. Presciently, Ford considered the capital in relation to its suburbs – though he refused to call them 'suburbs', which he thought derogatory, from the latin *sub urbe*, meaning less than the town, and preferring instead the more ambitious fore town: 'The fore town of my Great London would be on the one hand, say, Oxford, and on the other, say, Dover.' Ford continued: it takes in, this circle, Winchester, the delightful country around Petersfield, Chichester, all the coast down to Brighton, Hastings, Dover, all Essex and round again by way of Cambridge and Oxford'. Distance would be no barrier, since 'Oxford is

60 miles from London, and in my non-stop monorail express, this should be a matter of half-an-hour'. (Today the fast train to London takes an hour, so we are getting closer to Ford's 1909 plan.).

Ford's plan seems drafted to provoke today's nimbies and greenies, and a lot of other people as well. Anticipating objections he makes a simple argument, it is happening already:

'Yet there is nothing Utopian about the idea...it is coming about every day. The residential portion of the population is more and more abandoning the clayey bottoms of the Thames Valley.'

And, anticipating the actual trajectory of the South-East, Ford continued:

'It is on the road, this change, it has to come. All south-eastern England is just London.'

The damage, he says, is not done by embracing the change, but by ignoring it. That way the change will still happen, but it will descend upon us, without our being prepared for it or able to control it:

'It is only a question of how swiftly these changes shall take place: of whether they shall be conscious or unconscious, enlightened or enforced by the slow-grinding mills of time.'[506]

Neither Utopian, nor Dystopian, Ford's vision proved accurate. Sir Richard Rogers says as much himself, in his *Cities for a Small Planet*:

'While the city population has declined, the population of outer London has increased, sprawling outwards in an ever-widening circle. London, some thirty miles wide in 1945, is now a commuter belt 200 miles wide stretching from Cambridge to Southampton, and is the largest and most complex urban region in Europe.'[507]

In their comprehensive atlas of the 2001 census, *People and Places*, Daniel Dorling and Bethan Thomas observe that '...the metropolis of Greater London...now extends across all of Southern England', '...from Gainsborough in the north to Penzance in the west'.[508] Ford was right, too, that in failing to embrace the change, but attempting to deny it, the foretowns were reduced to the status of suburbs, and many of the opportunities of the expansion lost. The elements of Ford's plan that never got off the drawing board were his proposals for central London,

506] Ford Madox Ford, writing as Madox Huefor, 'The Future of London', an appendix to W.W. Hutchings, London Town: Past and Present, Volume II (London, Cassell, 1909) p 1102 to 1105, and 1099

507] Richard Rogers, Cities for a Small Planet (London, Faber and Faber, 1997) p 112

508] Daniel Dorling and Bethan Thomas, People and Places: A 2001 Census Atlas of the UK (Bristol, The Policy Press, 2004) p 7 and 183

509] Ford Madox Ford,
writing as Madox Huefor,
'The Future of London', an
appendix to W.W.
Hutchings, London Town:
Past and Present, Volume
II, (London, Cassell, 1909)
p 1101 and 1102

and he does not stint on the provocations. 'If we spared St Paul's and the Mansion House', he writes, mischievously, '...could we not afford to pull down all the houses between and around them?' Furthermore '...we might pull down all the dull houses between Westminster Abbey and the Bank of England'. 'This pulling down would have to be ruthless... And then there would be that great plain with a silver Thames flowing between banks of white stone.' [509] Anathema no doubt to the conservationist lobby, but Ford's plan to thin-out central London was the opportunity missed in the post-war reconstruction, eager to hang onto the Duke of Westminster's slum tenements.

In any event, the great advantage of Ford's proposals, is that, unlike the thinkers who came after, he sees the dynamic of growth, and its tendency to overshoot mere administrative boundaries. More remarkable than Ford's anticipated Future of London has been the (ultimately fruitless) attempt to box London into its early industrial boundaries, as if change could be avoided. Ford's essay is closer to the original Utopian ideas because it saw all definitions and boundaries as relative, rather than absolute. He continued the vision of the Utopians, with the verve of the early modernists. The tragedy is that Ford's vision was ignored, and the real day-dream, that of a London contained, has continued to dominate policy.

The remarkable thing is that it was the 'Utopian' proposition to overcome the opposition of town and country that proved the more real, while the apparent realism of the later Urban Studies approach founders as the city itself refuses to stand still. If Engels was wrong, it was only in thinking that the opposition of town and country could not be abolished under capitalism. Today, in the South East, the actual course of human settlement everyday strains against, and, with some distortions, overcomes the narrow attempts to re-impose definitions of urban areas that are nineteenth-century fossils.

CHAPTER ELEVEN

LONDONOSTALGIA

WHEN PEOPLE LEFT THE COUNTRYSIDE TO WORK IN THE TOWNS, THEIR attitudes to nature changed. Landscape was romanticised, viewed with nostalgic longing, once it ceased, for most people, to be a place of work. Nostalgia created a mythical 'countryside' that elbowed aside the real one.

510] Robert Elms,
BBC News Online,
25 May 2004

Nowadays, we take the romance of the countryside with a pinch of salt. But there is another kind of romanticism, trendier but maybe just as bogus, and that is the romanticism of London, *Londonostalgia*. The chief Londonostalgics are Peter Ackroyd, author of the city's 'biography', published in 2000, and poet Iain Sinclair, whose account of circum-navigating the M25 was a surprise hit in 2002. Ackroyd's London anti-quarianism was on display at the London Architecture Biennale in 2006, of which he was president. Both Sinclair and Ackroyd assert a debt to *Mother London* by the prolific science fiction writer Michael Moorcock.

Alongside the literary expressions of London Pride is the growing political power of London, its new Mayor Ken Livingstone, and his ability to get one over the Prime Minister; London's booming economy, and monopoly over financial, publishing and creative industries create one sixth of the entire country's wealth. The 'urban renaissance' celebrated by Lord Rogers of Riverside was pre-eminently a London renaissance, the emergence of 'café society' in Shoreditch, Islington, Fulham and Putney. *Time Out*'s, Robert Elms – Livingstone's 'mini-me' – proposes that '...the People's Republic of London, with the population of about eight million, would be the eighth richest country in the world, with one of the most modern and dynamic economies'. [510] (Though actually it

511] Finian Davern,
'Suburban Sprawl',
Evening Standard, 19
December 2003

512] Michael Moorcock,
Mother London,
(Harmondsworth,
Penguin, 1988) p 386

513] Peter Ackroyd,
London: The biography
(London, Vintage, 2000)
p 11

514] Stephen Inwood, The
History of London
(London, Macmillan,
1998) p 14

would be only 31st richest) What is more London's renaissance marries well with the aspiration to restrain building in the countryside. Mayor Ken Livingstone wants to keep people in, just as the Nimbies want to keep people out. 'With careful and efficient use of the land available, particularly opportunities opening up in East London, I believe we can meet London's housing needs without eating up any of our green spaces,' he told the Evening Standard.[511]

Just as the cockney chest is swelling with pride, however, there are morbid signs in London's self-image. Against the superficial trend towards modernity – millennium Bridges and riverside apartments – the stronger undercurrent is for a gloomy nostalgia.

The London imagined by Ackroyd and Sinclair is above all a backward-looking one. The Londonostalgics adore everything arcane and archaic about the city. They have revived the mythical origins of King Lud, and of Brutus, come from Troy 1000 years before Christ. Moorcock mines the myths to tell his story *Mother London*, closing with the lines: 'By means of our myths and legends we maintain a sense of what we are worth and who we are'[512] Ackroyd on the other hand gives the myths themselves some credence: 'Those of a sceptical mind may be inclined to dismiss such narratives but the legend of a thousand years may contain profound and particular truths'.[513] But how many Londoners have ever heard of King Lud, let alone honour him? Lud's was a story made up by the medieval scholar Geoffrey of Monmouth, already discounted as early as the sixteenth century by historian John Stow as an attempt to aggrandise the city's history, by '...interlacing divine matters with human'.[514]

Ackroyd's recuperation of the fable of King Lud is not a passing whimsy, but characteristic of his antiquarian predilections, and central to his theme of an 'underlying identity', '...the permanent and unchanging nature of London...reaffirmed in the very face of change'.[515] If it sounds too awkward of England, at least we can sing 'there'll always be a London'. It is pointed that Ackroyd's admirers, like Will Self, have baulked at the scope of his latest book *Albion: The Origins of the English Imagination* – it is acceptable to affirm the eternal London, but eternal England is too much to swallow. Emotionally, Ackroyd, Mayor of Londonostalgia, appeals to history to underline his conservative faith in continuity. But as history, this is very poor scholarship – the subordination of historical truth to Heritage London.

Londonostalgics owe a debt to 'psychogeography' – Situationist Guy Debord's '...the study of the precise laws and specific effects of the geographical environment...on the emotions and behaviour of individuals'. [516] Stewart Home and Tom Vague perfected a punk psycho-geography that soaks up the local colour, as in Vague's Notting Hill tales of Crippen, Rachmanism and race riots.[517] The psychogeographer's method is to wander the town, without a pre-planned route, like Walter Benjamin's footsore flaneur, dwelling on the idiosyncratic and esoteric corners. According to Phil Baker, Ackroyd's *London* '...is underpinned by an ultimately irrationalistic psychogeography, claiming that the character and atmosphere of different London districts inhere over time by an echoic haunting process'. [518] Iain Sinclair brings in another influence in the 1960s Earth Mysteries school which revived the idea that Ancient monuments are joined by ley-lines, unmarked connections across the countryside, with magical powers.

LONDON'S ESSENCE?

The very idea of a history of London is full of pitfalls. The mere persistence of the formal tag 'London' masks what is largely discontinuous. The fact of settlement emanating from the same spot over two millennia disguises the fact that the different settlements played quite different roles in each era. Making 'London' the subject tempts scholars to sum up the essence of London – but these are always artificial definitions. Porter and Inwood alight on the 'multi-cultural' London. But this is a retrospective re-ordering of the real events. London's '...successive waves of immigration' are alike only in that they happen one after the other. London's medieval Jewish population were a source of tax-revenue, when money-lending was forbidden by church law. The Hanse, and Lombard traders of the sixteenth century were granted monopolies **because** trade was largely alien to rural Britain. Jewish immigrants in the 1890s came to work, not trade, but their conditions were quite distinct from those of West Indian and Bengali migrants recruited to fill menial jobs in the 1950s. 'Multi-culturalism' is above all a contemporary label designed to assimilate a whole range of distinct conflicts into one story, of growth into maturity. It also obscures the fact that London's population was for the most part drawn from the surrounding countryside, in the nineteenth century.[519]

Ackroyd identifies another candidate for the post of London's essence, fixing on the '...organic continuity of its financial life' as a defining feature

515] Peter Ackroyd, London: The biography (London, Vintage, 2000) p 120 and 122

516] Guy Debord, Introduction to a Critique of Urban Geography (1955) posted on http://library.nothingness.org

517] Tom Vague, London psychogeography: Rachman, Riots and Rillington Place (London, Calvert's Press, 1998)

518] Phil Baker, 'Secret City: Psychogeography and the End of London', in Joe Kerr and Andrew Gibson, editors, London: From Punk to Blair (London, Reaktion books, 2003) p. 328

519] Stephen Inwood, The History of London (London, Macmillan,1998) p 412

520] Peter Ackroyd,
London: The biography
(London, Vintage, 2000)
p 34

521] Peter Marsden, Ralph
Merrifield, and Dominic
Perring, cited in Stephen
Inwood, The History of
London (London,
Macmillan, 1998) p 27

522] Tacitus, quoted by
Stephen Inwood, The
History of London
(London, Macmillan,
1998) p 18

523] Stephen Inwood, The
History of London
(London, Macmillan,
1998) p 100

524] Peter Ackroyd,
London: The biography
(London, Vintage, 2000)
p 481

525] William Maitland,
cited in Stephen Inwood,
The History of London
(London, Macmillan,
1998) p 391

of London.[520] Trading London seems to be a plausible essence. But actually London was created as an administrative centre of the Roman Empire, where the circulation of goods was principally through taxation, not trade. Then London prospered through the tribute exacted on the surrounding countryside. 'The archaeologists' view, expressed by Peter Marsden, Ralph Merrifield and Dominic Perring, is that London's heyday as a great centre of population and commerce did not last much beyond the Hadrianic fire of about AD 125, and that from AD 150 onwards it survived mainly as a centre of government and officialdom, without strong economic roots.[521] Tacitus describes the way the British Londoners enjoyed Roman baths, language, banquets and togas: 'They spoke of such novelties as "civilisation", when really they were only features of enslavement.' [522] London's specialisation as a trading centre – which actually isolated it from a predominantly rural nation – came later. In the twelfth century Boston, not London, was Britain's leading port.[523] It is of course true that with the ascendance of trade London dominated mercantile Britain, though it subsequently lost out to West Coast cities like Liverpool and Bristol in the Atlantic Trade, and to northern cities in the industrial revolution of the nineteenth century. The problem with an assertion of continuity is that it misses out the real stuff of history – change.

LONDON MYTHS

The Londonostalgics, though, are not interested in history, but myth, and the mythic London they create is perverse. It is a myth-making that revels in the violent and sordid. Ackroyd in particular draws on all the hysterical, church-led accounts of the East End slums to paint a terrible – read 'titillating' – picture of the great unwashed. There is a difference between Ackroyd and his sources, though. Victorian Philanthropists like Mayhew exaggerated the degeneration of the slums out of a sense of fear. Ackroyd, with the advantage of distance, glory's in the mob's supposedly primal energies, as he does the London crowd and Bartholomew's Fair. Later historians like Gertrude Himmelfarb have pointed to the shortcomings of Ackroyd's Salvation Army version of the 'residuum', but their qualifications are unknown, or even un-useful to him. He repeats the blood-curdling stories of the eighteenth century Mohock Gang slashing noses and rolling people downhill in barrels, [524] even though William Maitland discredited the stories as a newspaper invention at the time.[525]

Celebrating the lawlessness of the mob, Ackroyd also finds room for the radicals' version of Londonostalgia. He sketches an apparently unbroken line of dissent running from Wat Tyler to the offices of the *Morning Star* concentrated in Clerkenwell, while the radical tradition in the East End apparently extended down from the London Corresponding Society of the 1790s to George Lansbury's Poplar rates revolt in 1919.[526] Stephen Inwood also indulges this fancy, seeing a history of revolt stretching back to the fifteenth century, when London Aldermen resisted the imposition of the King's choice of Mayor: 'The episode is a reminder that John Lilburne, John Wilkes and William Lovett, London radicals of later centuries, were inheritors on an anti-oligarchic tradition with an obscure but ancient pedigree.'[527] The image is one that the movement rock musician Mick Farren invokes in his memoirs, when he writes of

> '...a noble, if disgruntled, pedigree of churls and malcontents, a continuous guerrilla Bohemia, and endless Children's Crusade, Peasants' Revolt and Beggar's Opera winding down the centuries on a trail of chaos and disorder, through Nihilists and Anarchists, Pre-Raphaelites and Romantics, all the way back to the twelfth- and thirteenth-century troublemakers like the Cathars and Adamites, Robin Hood and Merlin, the interdicted Dionysians and the persecuted Bacchae.'[528]

This is a dream that is peculiarly inappropriate to London, though. As Stephen Inwood's own researches show eloquently, there is no continuity between medieval conflicts with authority, and the democratic agitation of the eighteenth century. More pointedly, the later moments of working class agitation were often much weaker in London than in the provinces. Only one in every 100 Londoner's signed the People's Charter of 1839, compared with more than half of the people of Birmingham – and London's softness was a talking point to delegates at the Convention that year. On other occasions, such as the 1889 Dock Strike, it was London that stood out against the rest of the country for its radicalism. More recently the novelist Will Self supposed that London was intrinsically liberal in its attitudes – which might be true of some parts of Islington, but overall the European Elections in June 2004 saw a majority for the Conservatives in Greater London, in a campaign where almost all candidates competed for the title 'tough on crime'.

526] Peter Ackroyd, London: The biography (London, Vintage, 2000) p 461 to 474, 680 and 681

527] Stephen Inwood, The History of London (London, Macmillan, 1998) p 84

528] Mick Farren, Give the Anarchist a Cigarette (London, Pimlico, 2002) p 401

529] Peter Ackroyd, 'London luminaries and Cockney visionaries' in The Collection (London, Chatto and Windus, 2001) p 316, 348, 342, and 349

530] Gareth Stedman Jones, 'The "Cockney" and the nation', in Gareth Stedman Jones and David Feldman, editors, Metropolis: London histories and representations since 1800 (London, Routledge, 1989) p 278

If London is not radical, it has another possible identity, Cockney London. Ackroyd sang the praises of the 'Cockney visionaries' in his lecture at the Victoria & Albert Museum on 7 December 1993. And while insisting that '...I am not adopting some variant of London jingoism', and '...this is not some quaint Cockney pride of the old sort', but '...the spirit of London, the Genius of London', he means that 'Cockney' is something weird and spiritual. His ambition to uncover a spiritual dimension among the English comes up against the 'pragmatic "English" character' that has dominated these islands since the fifth century, which Ackroyd read in Maureen Duffy's *England: The Making of a Myth* that he reviewed for the *Sunday Times* in 2001. But in the following year Ackroyd re-wrote English history as mystical and dreamy in *Albion: The Origins of the English Imagination*. For the most part, then, the qualities of the Cockney visionaries are projections of Ackroyd's own preoccupations onto the Cockneys – a feeling for light and dark, of heterogeneity, and the persistence of place. He sees music hall as an expression of 'London genius' (though 'Down at the Old Bull and Bush' was written in New York). Ackroyd wants to put the Music Hall performer Dane Leno up in his pantheon of Cockney visionaries with William Blake and Charles Dickens: 'When we contemplate Dan Leno dressed up as Mother Goose, we may be considering something very pagan indeed'. [529] Mother Goose as pagan survival? Hardly. The Cockney that Ackroyd celebrates is not an enduring spirit of the capital, but a cruel caricature of relatively recent construction.

'Cockney' is an insult, from a 'cock's egg', meaning something queer, then an effeminate man, until it was stuck onto the people of the East End. Shakespeare's Cockney '...in pure kindness to his horse, buttered his hay'. The historian Gareth Stedman Jones explains the emergence of the modern Cockney. [530] The word was used disparagingly by the *Blackwood's Edinburgh Magazine* of Leigh Hunt and his collaborators, whom they dubbed the 'Cockney School of Poetry', in 1817, an insult they later extended to Keats (who '...was a cockney and the cockneys claimed him for their own' according to *Blackwood's* in 1826). The archetypal Cockney then was not a proletarian, but a vulgar businessman, like Peter Makemoney in Pierce Egan's 1839 novel *Pilgrims of the Thames*. The reduction of Cockney-dom to the lower orders could be seen in E.J. Milliken's sketch 'Arry, which ran in Punch between 1877 and 1890. On 11 May, 1878 'Arry amused *Punch*-readers with a song: 'I say we're the

new 'Arry-stocracy, not arf a dusty one, hay?' The sentimentalisation of
the Cockney comes later, when the Empire depended on the East Ender
for its defence, and is well expressed by Kipling:

'For it's Tommy this and Tommy that an'
'Chuck 'im out, the brute!'
But it's 'Saviour of 'is country', when the guns begin to shoot.'[531]

Already in 1912, novelist Edwin Pugh was singing Cockney praises:
'The Cockney, you see...is the supreme type of Englishman: in his sturdy
optimism, in his unwavering determination...to make the best of things
the way they are...an in his supreme disdain of the outsider'.[532] Though
seemingly more generous, this is just as vicious a caricature as 'Arry,
one that praises the cockney for his loyalty to the powers-that-be.

East end memoirs written before the 1950s rarely use 'Cockney'
as a self-description, preferring, if anything, East Ender. Dock leader
Jack Dash, a pioneer of East End nostalgia still only refers to himself
as a Cockney in childhood, dropping the implied condescension as
he turns to his adult years. Only in defeat did Londoners embrace the
derogatory title, led by 'Rockneys' Chas'n'Dave, Mike 'Runaround'
Reid and the rest of the cast of *East Enders*.

Londonostalgics might speculate that the Cockney accent is a
survival of East Saxon. The theory was first put by Samuel Pegge in his
Anecdotes of the English Language – 'Chiefly regarding London and its
environs – whence it will appear that the Natives of the Metropolis have
not corrupted the language of their ancestors' – in the 2nd Edition of
1810. But the real meaning of those double negatives and sounded
aitches is the affectation of talking like the toffs – the airs and graces
of people who knew they were at the bottom. George Melly chuckles
at the 'Mayfair Cockney' spoken by young Rada trainees, but those
actresses were retailing a bad imitation of a bad imitation of
themselves.

Allied to the Cockney caricature is the myth of the Blitz: ' 'We can
take it' was one of the most often recorded comments by those who
had been bombed out of their homes', writes Ackroyd.[533] 'They were
proud of their own sufferings', he thinks. Michael Moorcock pours scorn
on the official defences, but has Josef Kiss say '...the ordinary people
pulled the city through'. Moorcock quotes Arthur Mee: 'The Londoner,
proud Cockney, became a warrior', and '..."London can take it" became

531] Rudyard Kipling,
Barrack Room Ballads
(London, Macmillan, 1921)
p 9

532] Edwin Pugh, City of
the World (London,
Thomas Nelson, 1912)
p 315

533] Peter Ackroyd,
London: the Biography
(London, Vintage, 2000)
p 739

534] Michael Moorcock, Mother London (Harmondsworth, Penguin, 1988) p 375 and 386

535] Angus Calder, The Myth of the Blitz (London, Jonathan Cape, 1991) p 233

536] Humphrey Jennings, quoted in Angus Calder, The Myth of the Blitz (London, Jonathan Cape, 1991) p 180

537] Ernest Bevin, quoted in Angus Calder, The Myth of the Blitz (London, Jonathan Cape, 1991) p 84

the common man's cry'. [534] But 'We can take it' was not an innocent remark, it is a line from a Ministry of Information film, *London Can Take It*. An American reporter Quentin Reynolds wrote the script: 'I can assure you, there is no panic, no fear, no despair in London Town...London can take it'. Strangely, Reynolds tried out this line first in Germany, not London, as a reporter on *Colliers Weekly Magazine* between 1933 and 1940. 'Trained to take it' was first an article about German preparedness for a British bombing campaign. [535] *London Can Take It*'s director, Humphrey Jennings, was a left-wing contemporary of W.H. Auden and Christopher Isherwood at Cambridge and the GPO film unit, whose condescension to ordinary people was often commented on. 'Some of the damage in London has been pretty heart-breaking', Jennings wrote to his wife in October 1940, '...but what an effect it has had on the people!'

> *'What warmth – what courage! What determination ... a curious kind of unselfishness is developing...We have found ourselves on the right side and the right track at last!'* [536]

Jenning's revelation was shared by much of the British elite. As Ian Maclaine describes in his *Ministry of Morale*, the elite expected a moral collapse on the part of the public, actually just an unconscious projection of their own inner fears. When the expected collapse did not happen, the government and the Ministry of Information reacted the other way, reading great fortitude into the doughty Cockneys. 'We can take it!' was the formulation of that response, an act of ventriloquism, where the establishment assumed the right to speak for the people (even though all party political contestation had been suspended for the duration). The coercive meaning of 'We can take it' is illustrated in Ernest Bevin's confrontation with Communist shop stewards in Coventry on 14 November 1940: 'The trouble with you people is – you can't take it', he said, provoking uproar in what was, after all, the most heavily bombed of all Britain's cities. [537]

Put in the mouths of Londoners, 'we can take it' rings hollow – many did pull London through but they did not have any choice in the matter. And though the MOI was impressed by the lack of panic, tens of thousands of people tramped off into the Kent countryside during the first raids, without any real direction. On 3 March 1943, 173 people were killed in a panic crush on the steps of the Bethnal Green underground station,

though no bombs fell on East London that night.[538] Nina Masel,
reporting for the Mass Observation project described the bombings of
7 September 1940 as 'unplanned hysteria':

> 'The press versions of life going on normally in the East End are
> grotesque. There was no bread, no milk, no electricity, no gas, no
> telephones ... The press version of people's smiling jollity and fun are
> a gross exaggeration.'[539]

Pointedly, 29,890 Londoners could not 'take it', but were killed outright,
with a further 50,000 seriously injured; 116,000 houses were destroyed
outright, and 288,000 badly damaged. A third of the Port of London
Authority's warehouses were destroyed.[540] 'Finsbury's huge pre-war
industrial workforce never recovered from the bombing of its factories
and workshops' and the City of London lost 40 per cent of its industrial
workers – part of the reason that today both are non-industrial districts.
Between 1938 and 1947 London's population fell by 20 per cent to
3,245,000. The London boroughs most hit by the blitz suffered the
greatest population loss: Bermondsey, Finsbury and Southwark each
lost 38 per cent of their population, Poplar, Shoreditch and the City lost
about 45 per cent and Stepney lost over half. [541] London did not take it,
but was substantially depopulated and destroyed by the blitz, to be
re-made as another kind of settlement after the war.

For the Londonostalgics, the blitz is all part of the myth of London,
though the contemporary stress is more on the horror than the hero-
ism. Drawn to the dark side, Peter Ackroyd, spurred on by Iain Sinclair,
revels in the supposed history of necromancy in London. Preoccupied
with the marginal figure of Elizabethan magician John Dee, divining
ancient runes in the pompous churches of architect Nicholas
Hawksmoor, Sinclair and Akroyd insist on drawing imaginary ley-lines
between them, and all over London.[542] Ackroyd thinks that '...the city
itself remains magical; it is a mysterious, chaotic and irrational place
which can only be organised by means of private ritual or public
superstition'. [543] Though, surely, the London Underground and Traffic
Control centre have done more to organise London than necromancy,
or even religion in more recent times. Iain Sinclair resurrected the nineteenth century 'Hermetic Brotherhood of Luxor' and its fantasy that
Hawksmoor's interest in Egyptian motifs was evidence of an interest
in the occult. But the pyramid supported by roman columns, topped by

538] David Widgery, Some
Lives! A GP's East End
(London, Sinclair
Stevenson, 1991) p 34

539] Nina Masel, Mass
Observation, quoted in
Angus Calder, The Myth of
the Blitz (London,
Jonathan Cape, 1991) p 133

540] David Widgery,
Some Lives! A GP's East
End (London, Sinclair
Stevenson, 1991) p 34

541] Stephen Inwood,
A History of London
(London, Macmillan, 1998,
p 809 to 810, and 812

542] Peter Ackroyd,
'Nicholas Hawksmoor –
his Churches', in Lud Heat
and Suicide Bridge
(London, Vintage, 1995)
p 18 and 19

543] Peter Ackroyd,
London: The biography
(London, Vintage, 2000)
p 216

544] Robert Gray, A History of London (London, Hutchinson, 1988) p 229

545] Peter Ackroyd London: The biography (London, Vintage, 2000) p 226, 233, 273

546] Michael Moorcock, Mother London (Harmondsworth, Penguin, 1988) p 344

547] Peter Ackroyd London: The biography (London, Vintage, 2000) p 562 and 566

King George on a Church Spire in Bloomsbury only demonstrates Hawksmoor's absurd appetite for the grandiose. It is hard not to think that Hawksmoor was chosen for the Sinclair/Ackroyd treatment **because** he was less well known, and so easier to elaborate, than more interesting teacher, Wren. If Hawksmoor's churches seem a bit spooky, it might be because they were generally empty, being part of an artificial oversupply created by the Church Building Act of 1711: 'Vast edifices in the slums, outposts of the establishment set in the midst of extreme distress, [that] were rarely filled'.[544]

Ackroyd writes of 'The Burden of Mystery', 'Atavistic remembrance' and '...the essential paganism of London'.[545] It would be easy to lose sight of the fact that London has for most of its existence been a pious, Christian city. Underground agitation against the established church – suppressed in the sixteenth century – sought to reduce, not expand its superstitious elements. The attraction of 'magic' amongst the Londonostalgics is puerile, doodling in fantastic connections across the ages, where real ones are missing. Ghost story writers like H.P. Lovecraft and M.R. James showed us that you could hold the reader's interest by alluding to occult practices without describing them. In history, though, this is just obscurantism.

A weirder theme is the recurring fantasy of 'a forgotten troglodytic race that' in Michael Moorcock's version '...had gone underground at the time of the Great Fire, whose ranks had been added to periodically by thieves, vagabonds and escaped prisoners, receiving many fresh recruits during the Blitz, when so many of us sought the safety of the tubes.'[546] Ackroyd cites this passage as fantasy, but one shared by the war-time government, which feared the creation of a subterranean race in the Blitz. He should have added that these fears were absurd – and that Moorcock's character is in the grip of a schizophrenic delusion. Instead Ackroyd is drawn to the 'mysterious' world of London's sewers, where '...the figure of the underground man is so potent'.[547] Joseph Bazalgette's 1868 sewers were a triumph of rationalism – substituting brick-lined tunnels as carriers of waste, for the Thames and its tributaries. But they are turned instead into the setting for a Gothic horror story.

This is what the French call **nostalgie de la boue**, or Beckett, sniffing the turds of history. Beckett's description of a land where '...history's ancient faeces [...] are ardently sought after, stuffed and carried in processions. Wherever nauseated time has dropped a nice fat turd', he continued, '...you will find our patriots, sniffing it up, on all fours, their faces on fire'.[548] 'Since childhood I have been interested in the less salubrious areas of London – Wapping, Spitalfields, Limehouse – and in the air of dilapidated gloom which they embody'.[549] It is a perversion he shared with Dickens, who, according to his friend and biographer John Forster, '...had a profound attraction of repulsion to St Giles'.[550] Gertrude Himmelfarb noted that for the Victorian philanthropists, 'the same words – 'residuum', 'refuse', 'offal' – were used to denote the sewage waste that constituted the sanitary problem and the human waste that constituted the social problem'.[551] Today, ghettoes are once again identi-fied with sewers – historian Tristram Hunt adopts the term 'residuum' without irony in his Building Jerusalem[552] – except that what repelled the Victorians attracts the Londonostalgics.

It is easy to slip into the mode of thinking where dark and dangerous means exciting – or grubby means interesting. But you should check yourself before adopting the implicit values of **nostalgie de la boue** entirely. If the stairs to your cellar are dark, and dangerous, you should put the light on and tread carefully. When your shirt is a little grubby, change it.

These themes of the mob, the occult and the underground, are central to the nostalgic idea of London. It is worth asking what the resonance of these themes is. It is the passing of a way of life. Though 'eternal London' is an appeal against change, it is also nostalgia for what has already passed away. The London yearned for is a mythical one of gentleman gangsters in the East End, cockney street traders, the mingling of high and low in the Elizabethan crowd and the spirit of the Blitz. What real activity is imaginatively re-invented as occult ritual hidden from view undertaken by an ancient, underground race? It is the world of work. London's manual work is passing away from the silk weavers of early 19th century Spitalfields, to the Bryant and May Match-girls (whose poisonous factory has been turned into the fashionable Bow Quarter apartments) to the 10,000 jobs at the Beckton Gas and Light Works in 1900, the 27,000 registered London Port Workers in 1947 reduced to a fraction and relocated to Tilbury and Southampton by 1967, and the 30,000 workers at Ford's Dagenham plant, now closed.

These are the race of 'troglodytes' that haunt London. They have been cleared away in the transformation of London into a city dedicated

548] Samuel Beckett, First Love, 1973, p.30 and 31

549] Peter Ackroyd, 'London luminaries and Cockney visionaries' in The Collection (London, Chatto and Windus, 2001) p 378

550] John Forster, quoted in Stephen Inwood, A History of London (London, Macmillan, 1998) p.524

551] Gertrude Himmelfarb, The Idea of Poverty (London, Faber and Faber, 1984) p 356

552] Tristram Hunt, Building Jerusalem: The Rise and Fall of the Victorian City (London, Weidenfeld and Nicholson, 2004) p 23

553] Hugh Pearman,
Sunday Times, 30 May
2004

554] Michael Moorcock,
Mother London
(Harmondsworth,
Penguin, 1988) p 377 and
378

555] Iain Sinclair, London
Orbital – a walk round the
M25 (London, Penguin,
2003) p 20

primarily to business services (844,500 workers) and retail (500,000) compared with just 250,000 remaining manufacturing workers, concentrated mostly in the Lea Valley or Park Royal. 'There's a lot to be said for poignant dereliction,' writes Hugh Pearman, regretting the redevelopment of Paddington. 'I love it: the old, now silent factories, the rusting railway sidings, the buddleia sprouting from the walls and the birches shouldering through the pavements.' [553] But this is poignant in the same way Roman ruins are – the sentimental pleasure of reflecting on the downfall of a once mighty race.

The changing employment structure corresponds to a changing sociology. Where the seventies saw a flight out of the impoverished inner cities to the suburbs, the nineties saw a reverse movement, the gentrification of inner London that Lord Rogers celebrated as a renaissance. The vacated shells of industrial London were turned into expensive apartments or art galleries. With rising house prices it was working class London that was being driven to the suburbs.

The Londonostalgics pour scorn on the new Londoners, who, says Moorcock's *Joseph Kiss*, come '...from the Home Counties...They're driving out most Londoners and taking over our houses, street by street...I know people born in Bow who've had to move as far as Stevenage to find a house they could afford. And who's getting the house in Bethnal Green, my boy?' [554] Sinclair agrees:

> 'Waltham Abbey and the inhabitable pockets of Epping Forest were white Cockney on the drift, the tectonic plate theory. Hackney becomes Chingford, Notting Hill relocates to Hoxton. ... Cabbies, always awkward sods, had uprooted years ago: try finding one who did not grow up in Bethnal Green and who doesn't now live in Hertfordshire or Essex.' [555]

But surely it is the new, gentrified Londoners who are the natural audience for Londonostalgia? Blue plaque London is a cornucopia for the heritage merchants. Ackroyd is writing copy for tour guides, and signage for the London Dungeon. Shoreditch's Victoriana makes an attractive venue for graphics designers who hope the lingering historical stench will lend their studios a bit of local colour.

Who else are these tales of cheeky Cockneys written for, if not the Mockneys that have taken their place? The psychogeographers chose to wander without a destination, letting the geography impact on the psyche, as thoughts run unbidden. Street wise, world foolish. But wandering without purpose is the privilege of a leisure class. Sinclair, Ackroyd and Vague are just churning out the fat, obscure books that meander through time and space to fill up the yawning leisure time of the new Londoners. Londonostalgia is the imaginary re-appropriation of a disparate history.

Immigrants from other parts of the country often move into the city to be part of the latest wave of London's history. Londonostalgia is only possible because 'London' is history – notwithstanding its claims to eternity. Having burst its bounds, there really is no recognisable unit called London that can be parcelled together under one name any more. The green belt cannot contain the sprawling suburbs. Like all cities, London owes its origins to that original division of labour between town and country, but with intensive farming, more and more land is becoming available as London expands outwards in the way that Ford Madox Ford anticipated. But as it expands, it ceases to be anything like London. Rather the growth is the growth of the South East, spurred on by the shift from Atlantic to European trade. London has dissolved as its boundaries expand and become more porous.

For more than a century, the London of the Londonostalgics has been a fraction of the administrative London. Victorian London outnumbers medieval London by more than six to one. Since 1965 Greater London has incorporated Essex boroughs like Walthamstow, and other 'railway suburbs'. The Londonostalgics jeer at the suburbs. 'Barret Hutches...'Kennels', 'Lego Homes', 'They come in kits,' according to Iain Sinclair. But for all that bitter condescension, London's suburbs are where most of its population now lives. Put another way, they do not live in London at all, but Stevenage, Shepperton, or even Oxford and Brighton, commuting sometimes to work or play in the central heritage zone.

CHAPTER TWELVE

EASTWARD HO! – RETRO-CHIC & INERTIA IN THE THAMES GATEWAY, DOCKLANDS & THE CITY FRINGE

JUNE 30TH, 2004, A BARGE ORGANISED BY THE DEPARTMENT OF CULTURE
Media and Sports, leaves the Savoy Pier near Westminster Bridge carrying
Lord Rogers of Riverside, assorted developers, journalists, including the
design critic Stephen Bayley, Mark Brearley of the Greater London
Authority down the Thames, to Thurrock, epicentre of the Thames
Gateway development. We are going to hear the Culture Secretary Tessa
Jowell tell us that in Thurrock, 'Culture is at the heart of regeneration'.
The priority of the arts over development is emphasized by Housing
Minister Keith Hill's apologies for not being able to make it. Also absent
are the people of Thurrock, whose future some 300 dignitaries have
assembled in the Tilbury Cruise Terminal to discuss. 'One hardly knew
such places existed', says a bemused Bayley. Our little boat flew the
pennant of *Tate* (never 'the Tate') courtesy of Nicholas Serota,
reinforcing the impression that we have come to civilise the natives.

The Culture Secretary Tessa Jowell is emphatic that '...we want to
avoid the pitfalls of regeneration' such as '...the Hoxton effect, where
regeneration becomes gentrification'. She is full of ideas about heritage:
'As we can see with the Baltic Exchange in Newcastle the re-use of
historic buildings has a positive effect for regeneration.' Any conflicts
between the government and Lord Rogers seem to have been forgotten,
as she flashed him a warm smile on the way to the podium. In her
speech, she emphasized the common ground between the
Deputy Prime Minister and the chairman of the Urban Task Force:
'As John Prescott has said there is no urban renaissance without
good design.'

In his presentation, Sir Richard gave a nod towards design, before plunging into some alarming mathematics designed to show that 304,000 households could be crammed into the 38,000 hectares of derelict land, running along 43 miles of the Thames at 80 to the hectare. Of course he had his sums wrong: at that density 38,000 hectares would accommodate three million households, not three hundred thousand. But then that is the Urban Task Force's agenda: if there must be more homes, stack them high, to keep the countryside pristine. Pile them up down here, in the flood planes of the Thames Gateway, out of sight, if they must be built at all. Did Roger's dodgy maths reveal a subconscious fixation with the numbers? Perhaps, but there really is no need to build so densely. In any event, he need not have bothered. The underlying message of the day seemed to be that there is no intention to house 304,000 homes, let alone three million.

The 'Visionary Brief in the Thames Gateway' is being dissipated fast, as the event begins to look like a workshop on sustainable living at the World Social Forum. The Dutch artist Jeanne van Heewijk, is reporting back from her 'one-day charette' ('an intensive, multi-disciplinary brainstorming workshop where visionary ideas are encouraged') with 'spectacularist' Keith Khan. They think that development must take place over an eleven year time-cycle, and that before there is any volume building, '...ten innovative prototype houses' should be made by a teams of one architect, one potential resident, one artist and one ecologist. No, this is not a 'how many to change a light-bulb' joke. Instead of dismissing this proposal for the impractical, time-wasting job-creation scheme that it is, the Culture Secretary said it was 'inspiring', and endorsed it. Three hundred and four thousand houses? At this rate you would be lucky to have ten, custom built, eco friendly wigwams sinking into the Rainham Marshes in eleven years. As the charettes reported back, the phrase 'volume building' was only used as a swear word, the negative of 'environment', 'culture' and 'design'. But volume building is precisely what is needed – if we are serious about building millions of new homes. In the audience, volume builders shrank back into their seats, the uncultured villains of the piece, gloomily calculating the costs of sub-contracting the design to an ecologist, an artist, an architect and a resident to be, factoring in an eleven year wait, before concluding that they could do better business elsewhere.

The gloomy vision seen at the Thurrock event belies the general view of what the government's policy is towards house building. In October 2004, plans to build 478,000 homes got more coverage than any previous action by the East of England Regional Assembly, a body few of us knew existed. But the legend that John Prescott plans to concrete over the countryside lives on in this and other announcements about thousands and millions of new homes. On closer inspection, though, the inertia seen in Thurrock is evident throughout. Numbers and plans are announced, but the years pass by without any obvious expansion in new housing starts. The BBC's rural affairs correspondent commented on the Regional Assembly's plan that 'broad unease' had not grown into angry opposition among residents because they cannot yet say '...this is going to happen in a field near me'. [556] No indeed, actual plans are scarce, but pronouncements frequent and alarming to opponents of new homes, without offering a roof to those who need one.

The local authorities charged with developing the London end of the Thames Gateway meet with business as the Thames Gateway London Partnership. Their London Thames Gateway Development and Investment Framework (TGDIF) sets out its suggested action plan to 2007 in the document *Creating Sustainable Communities*. But the arithmetic is unimpressive:

> The ultimate potential of the Thames Gateway could be in excess of 150,000 new homes.

> The TGDIF aspires to 91,000 units by 2016.

> Government minimum target is for 59,500 units by 2016, which is an average of 4,125 per year.

> Assuming 4,125 units per year, 21,000 new homes need to be constructed by the end of 2007 (for TGDIF vision, 32,500 homes needed by end 2007)

> There are already, approximately 18,000 homes committed for delivery by end 2007.

556] 'Regional panel backs housing plan', BBC Online, 15 October, 2004, posted on http://news.bbc.co.uk

There is a lot of aspiration, but only 18,000 homes committed for delivery by the end of 2007. Since the Thames Gateway development has been the centrepiece of the ODPM's plans for new homes, it is disappointing to hear that at the outside the London end of it is expected to enlarge the housing stock by just 91,000 units – or less than three per cent of the four million new homes originally mooted for 2016. Just 0.45 per cent will be built by 2007.

The new homes committed by 2007 are:

THAMES GATEWAY, LONDON END

6,400	in the Isle of Dogs;
600	in Lewisham & Catford;
2,900	in Woolwich;
1,400	in Greenwich Peninsula;
400	in Hackney Wick;
1,150	in the Royals Area;
400	in East Beckton;
400	in Barking Town Centre;
700	in Thamesmead;
350	in Belvedere & Erith;
900	in New Cross;
2,400	in Deptford & Greenwich.

In Thurrock 4,327 were built between 1998-2003, with a further 5,303 planned by 2016.

In Cambridge 2,582 homes have been built (mostly in Cambourne and Hampton Town) with a further 9,930 planned (mostly in Cambourne Abode and Hampton Town).

All of which is no doubt welcome, but a long way from meeting the demand for new homes, and with the lion's share of the new building put off into the future. So what has gone wrong? Something of the answer can be found in the TGDIF investment plan, which sets out some of the practical constraints, most pointedly the Crossrail network (first mooted in 1991, but whose £10bn. funding was not agreed till 2003, making completion before the 2012 London Olympics unlikely) and upgrades to the Docklands Light Railway. Even power lines and pylons are not yet in place, and spending of £160 million on schools, £67 million on health care are needed. To meet government targets for social housing, the ODPM must make £388m in grants. And if the lack of infrastructure is not enough of a disincentive to developers, the plan budgets for a 'Planning Gain' surcharge of £5,000 for each unit to pay for the infrastructure that is not there.

The planning consultations of the Thames Gateway London Partnership verge on the surreal. At one 'move' (like a 'charette', with prodigious quantities of red wine poured in) organised by the London Development Agency, the ever playful Will Alsop sketched out huge rectangles across a map of the region, parcelling it up into different zones – each to be dedicated to a different style, or activity. As Alsop became more animated Lord Rogers' brow knitted tighter, until eventually he tutted, '...that's all very well, but we mustn't let the public see any of these drawings'. Rogers' fear that expectations of actual house building might be engendered was decisive. The architects' input at this level is for the most part, pointless. They are not town planners, and the project is not about individual buildings, still less the prestige ones that Rogers and Alsop are known for. (If only they would deign to design a spacious terrace, or some attractive semis or bungalows, the kind of thing that people want to live in, they might have something to offer.) The point of the consultation is just activity to substitute for the decisions that the Thames Gateway London Partnership are avoiding.

The houses will never be built in the Thames Gateway unless the government gets right behind the development. Glossy brochures are not enough. Setting out to tax development before it begins with 'Planning Gain' agreements is setting up a financial disincentive before the project starts. Instead government should be building the infrastructure now to make the developments attractive to investors. But most of all, it needs to take the issue out of the hands of the culturati, including the architects, the artists, the DCMS, the environmentalists and all the other small-is-beautiful fanatics who simply do not want to see the houses built.

DOCKLANDS – LEARNING TO HATE GROWTH
The ambiguity towards developing the Thames Gateway replays the controversy over an earlier development project, the London Docklands

557] Ian Jack, Before the Oil Ran Out (London, Vintage, 1997) p 275 and 277

558] David Widgery, Some Lives! A GP's East End (London, Sinclair Stevenson, 1991) p 219

559] Ian Jack, Before the Oil Ran Out (London, Vintage, 1997) p 280

Development Corporation (LDDC) founded in July 1981 by the Environment Minister Michael Heseltine. From the outset, the LDDC was embroiled in conflict over the future of Docklands, with the Conservative government turning it into a beacon of free enterprise, while their radical critics such as the Labour-controlled Greater London Council denounced it as undemocratic, and a haven for yuppies.

"Toffs Out!" "Yuppie Scum go Home!" In the spring of 1987, journalist Ian Jack went to the opening ceremony for a housing development at Watermint Quay, with TV East Enders Lofty (Tom Watt) and Michelle (Susan Tully). But it was the demonstration by the anarchists who called themselves Class War that made the story. Their spokesman, Swansea University graduate Ian Bone, explained that the Isle of Dogs would be "the Alamo" for the working class. 'It's too late for Islington and Stoke Newington. We've lost them to the gentrifiers. But we've got to hold the Isle of Dogs.' [557]

East End GP, the late David Widgery, echoed Bone's sentiments in his 1991 memoir, calling the development of Docklands '...a species of social apartheid': 'Islanders encountered the LDDC when it was taking away their communities, closing down local firms, buying up homes and cafes by compulsory purchase, shooing them off their imposing buildings and knocking down their homes to build motorways nobody wants.' [558] Local activist Ted Johns told Ian Jack that 'In Docklands we're seeing the kind of laissez-faire capitalism that hasn't been seen in this country since Queen Victoria'. 'Greed is being made into a shining virtue.' Like Ian Bone, Johns saw the Isle of Dogs as '...the last Cockney village in London'. [559] Widgery voiced a common complaint that the new wealth brought no jobs for local people because '...the new commercial firms bring their own staff with them'. He reports '...it is said of the red brick road along Marsh Wall that not a single brick was laid by a local.' In proportion to the hurt felt on behalf of the 'indigenous' Islanders, the incomers are dismissed to the point that their very existence is doubted. David Widgery pooh-poohs the development as if it were all a mirage: 'A high proportion of the houses and offices have never been occupied,' – bought as investments not to live in. 'Butler's Wharf can't sell enough flats to cover its interest charges.' And '...by the recession of the 1990s...Canary Wharf's 12 million square feet of office space was distinctly hard to let.'

'The owners are either subletting or absent most of the time in their weekend homes, living invisibly behind high security in their refuge-with-a-view, insulated from anything outside of the front door. Children, if there are any, are packed away at boarding school, health problems sorted out by private subscription, and groceries bought over the phone by computer.'[560]

One substantial complaint against the LDDC was that it was free from local democratic control. The legislation that created this pioneer model of Urban Development Corporation (the same model that is now being used to develop the Thames Gateway) gave it extraordinary powers as the sole planning authority particularly with respect to compulsory purchase. With its boundaries drawn around vacant land, it was answerable to no electorate. The Greater London Council, under its radical leader Ken Livingstone, tried to have the LDDC plan stopped in the courts on the grounds that it had failed to accommodate the GLC's own development plan for London. They failed, but the boroughs of Greenwich, Newham and Southwark Council appealed.[561] The GLC's challenge was accompanied by protests and decorated with agit-prop montages by Peter Dunn.[562]

It is true that the re-development of 'Docklands' symbolises the defeat of organised labour, since the land made available for development is the land vacated by the closure of the up-river London docks: the 245-acre site of the Royal Group built between 1855 and 1920, now home to the University of East London, London City Airport and the Excel centre; The West India Docks opened in 1802 on the Isle of Dogs, the site of Britain's highest tower block at Canary Wharf; Surrey Commercial Docks opened in 1807, now home to '... the largest new housing development in the whole of London.'[563]

Despite their ideal location, London's docks were dependent at first upon legal monopolies, always challenged by competition from northern ports, and later by the rising costs of navigating ever-larger boats upriver. None the less, '...the nineteenth century Port of London was still the biggest in the world, both in volume of goods and dock area, taking most of the Far Eastern trade, half of the Caribbean and a third of the Baltic, and dealing with vast quantities of dried fruits, wine, tea, grain and wool.' While dockers struck for their 'tanner' in 1889, a parliamentary commission criticised shareholders basking '...in the sunshine of their

560] David Widgery, Some Lives! A GP's East End (London, Sinclair Stevenson, 1991) 217 to 221

561] S.K. Al Naib, London, Canary Wharf and Docklands (London, Research Books, p 67

562] www.cspace.org.uk/cspace/archive/docklands/photo.htm

563] S.K. Al Naib, London, Canary Wharf and Docklands (London, Research Books, 2003) p 98

564] David Widgery, Some Lives! A GP's East End (London, Sinclair Stevenson, 1991) p 211 and 212

565] Spitalfields Housing and Planning Rights Service, Bengalis and Housing Planning in E1: An update report, 1984, quoted in Keith Tompson, Under Siege: Racial Violence in Britain Today (Harmondsworth, Penguin, 1988) p 124

566] John Mason, 'Ted Johns', Guardian, 12 May 2004

annual ten per cent'. [564] But dwindling returns persuaded the owners to sell up to the Port of London Authority in 1909. Dockers were rewarded for their loyalty in the Second World War by regularisation of work under the 1947 Dock Labour Scheme – but at the same time pallets, containerisation, roll-on roll-off methods that were developed during the war were used to break the dockers' militant organisations. Immediately after the war, London's docks boomed, as Britain's share of world trade had been temporarily boosted by the eclipse of its rivals, but fell back in the 1960s. Work was moved downriver to Tilbury, or to Folkestone and Southampton. Not just the docks, but associated industries, like the McDougall grain silo on Millwall Dock, a big employer in Cubitt Town, and Tate & Lyle which had employed 30 000 at its model village, Silvertown in 1955 closed its Plaistow Wharf refinery in 1967. In 1970 Ted Johns, then a Tower Hamlets councillor, led the Isle of Dogs in a 'Declaration of Independence' from the mainland, catching the attention of a media eager to interview the Islands' new 'President', and drawing attention to their declining services. Hostility to outsiders has an unfortunate resonance in Tower Hamlets given the influx of Bengali immigrants filling a vacuum left by departing East Enders. In 1984, an internal report found that '...effectively the GLC has picked out certain estates on which it will make offers to Bengalis, and is keeping others almost exclusively white'. [565] This unofficial apartheid policy was quietly carried on first by the Labour Council in Tower Hamlets, and then more explicitly by the Liberal Democrats, who formalised a preference for local people, the 'sons and daughters' policy. When Bengalis were re-housed on the Island, the British National Party played on local resentments, winning the Millwall seat for Derek Beacon in 1993. Ted Johns threatened to run against the official Labour candidates unless more homes for local people were pledged [566] – a concession to indigenism that succeeded in winning the Millwall seat back from the BNP eight months later.

The impact of the dock closures on East London was terrible. But pay attention to the years: the docks were closed in 1968. The London Docklands Development Corporation was not created until 1981. The working classes in East London had already been defeated, their workplaces abandoned and their communities impoverished, long before Michael Heseltine set up his office in the old Fred Olsen shipping shed on the east side of the Millwall Inner Dock. In the preceding decade, the Labour government had done nothing to stop the descent. One industrial dispute that did impact on Docklands in the eighties started when the new owner of the Times, Rupert Murdoch, moved his printworks into the area, at Wapping in 1986. Though they might have seen this as new development, many local residents identified with the skilled printworkers who had been robbed of their jobs in the move to the computerised works. Hundreds of police attacked protesting print-workers to ensure that Murdoch's presses rolled. I saw a police officer in riot gear floored, when a cast iron rail struck the centre of his round shield, to which a chorus of local women shouted, 'one-hundred and eighty!' (the top score in the game of darts). In the wake of that bitter strike, working class activism was turning into an underdog resentment that decried all success.

The redevelopment under the LDDC really did turn the fortunes of the 'Docklands' around. A population of 39,000 in 1981 had increased to 65,000 by 1994. Even in 1992, the workforce had increased from 27,000 to 51,500.[567] Businesses moved in to take advantage of the tax breaks, first Olympia & York, the developers of Canary Wharf Tower, then Merrill Lynch moved its HQ there (though only after Olympia & York agreed to buy up their office lease in the City), followed by Texaco in 1989. One Canada Square is the address of the *Independent* (floors 18-19), the *Telegraph* (floors 11-16, as well as its premises in the South Quays) and the *Mirror* (floors 19-24). Westferry Printers in the old Surrey Docks prints the *Telegraph*, the *Express*, the *Star*, the *Guardian*, *Observer*, *Financial Times* and the *Sport*. The one national paper not printed in Docklands, ironically, is the one that started it, the *Times*, which is moving its printworks out to Glasgow.[568] The HSBC Tower, completed in 2001 brought its 8,000 staff under one roof. Bank of New York, Bank of China, International, Bank of Montreal, Barclays Capital, Citibank, Morgan Stanley, Credit Suisse First Boston, Bear Stearns International and Coutts & Co. are just some of the residents at Canary Wharf.

The recession of the early nineties did indeed cause problems for the LDDC. Excessively indebted, Olympia & York went into receivership in May 1992, such that Canary Wharf Ltd had to be created independently. The shopping and tourist centre at Tobacco Dock also folded after failing to bring in sales. But by 2001 total occupancy of Canary Wharf was 98 per cent.[569] Terence Conran's work on Butler's Wharf might have hit problems in the early years, but by 2004 it was cited as an '...outstanding

567] S.K. Al Naib, London, Canary Wharf and Docklands (London, Research Books, 2003) p 140

568] 'We're on the move', The News – the newspaper for everyone at News International, October 2004

569] S.K. Al Naib, London, Canary Wharf and Docklands (London, Research Books, 2003) p 86

570] Royal Institute of British Architects, 'Memorandum to the Select Committee on the Office of the Deputy Prime Minister', 26 January 2004

571] S.K. Al Naib, London, Canary Wharf and Docklands (London, Research Books, 2003) p 94

572] David Widgery, Some Lives! A GP's East End (London, Sinclair Stevenson, 1991), p 227

573] Pat Bagshaw, interview with the author, 19 November 2004

574] Hansard, 5 June 1991

575] Rising East Online, posted on www.uel.ac.uk

example of a commercially-developed regeneration project'. [570] Nor was the new housing exclusively for the rich, with assisted housing schemes in Surrey Docks, Beckton, Wapping and the Isle of Dogs. According to the University of East London professor S.K. Al Naib, '...queues at sales offices were a common site for both upmarket riverside conversions in Wapping and assisted housing schemes in the depths of Surrey Docks'. [571] Those that lost their homes in the building of the Limehouse Link Road succeeded in getting themselves re-housed in the attractive Barleycorn estate, as well as Timber Wharves Village and Devons Road, nearby, after the local tenants association protested. [572]

Employment prospects were certainly changed by the transformation of Docklands. There are no jobs for Dockers, for a start. Even by 1992, finance and banking jobs were up to 16 400 from 1450 ten years before. Four thousand people worked on the construction of the Canary Wharf Tower. In 1999 the Royal Docks Community School opened in its state of the art facilities near the old Albert Dock, funded with £5.2 million from the London Docks Development Corporation – only to have the teachers pelted with eggs by the locals. 'Were they hostile to the LDDC?', I asked Head Pat Bagshaw. 'To authority of any kind', she told me, darkly. Bagshaw rattles off the list of her 50 first languages spoken in the school, from Latvian to Somali, with something like pride. But she describes the host community as 'Very East End', with a tone that hints of disapproval. [573]

In 1991 the Conservative minister Michael Portillo twitted the Labour opposition: 'Antipathy to enterprise has guided Labour Members in their opposition to the regeneration of docklands. They opposed the creation of the LDDC. They carp about the immense achievements of the development there.' [574] Ken Livingstone, then Member of Parliament for Brent East, insisted that he was always behind redevelopment, and that anyway, it was the Tories who were the ones who had stood in the way of his plans to extend the Jubilee line there. The left was moving on from its outright opposition to Docklands. They started a Journal of 'East London Studies', Rising East, '...to engage with the future development of East London ...the biggest zone of regeneration in Europe'. [575] On 4 July, 2000, the new Mayor of London opened the £40 million Docklands Campus of the University of East London. But while New Labour got with the Docklands programme, radical resentments still remained. In the Cubitt town and Blackwall council election in 2003, Ted Johns' son

Terry stood as an Independent and took support away from the far left Socialist Alliance, drawing complaints from their election agent Paul McGarr, that Johns '...pandered heavily to racism,' and '...stressed that he was the "only born and bred Islander"'. [576] McGarr learned his lesson, and when he won support in the neighbouring Millwall ward on the Respect ticket in 2004 he boasted:

> *You cannot do well electorally in Millwall without winning significant support from the white working class. That is precisely what Respect did. Our local activists have been at the centre of a series of successful campaigns over the years, saving a local health centre, post office and community centre.* [577]

Indigenism, it seems, is the key to the protest vote on the Isle of Dogs, but Paul McGarr's supporters gave it a more acceptably radical twist by complaining about '...an influx of people, from the fairly affluent to the very rich', instead of an influx of Bengalis. [578] 'Respect' did beat the Labour Party into third place, but it was the Tory Party that won the seat, '...the first time the Conservatives have made gains in Tower Hamlets for over 100 year' according to Party Chairman Liam Fox. [579] Truth to tell, it was the conservatism of the left that made the running on Docklands.

DOWN ON THE DOME, LOVING THE VILLAGE

To approve of the Millennium Dome, wrote Andrew Marr in 1998, is to be '...a member of the most reviled and outcast minority on these islands, harried through the streets, silently pitied by generous-minded relatives and the object of sniggering derision at parties.' [580] Certainly, that was the experience of Ben Evans, the 'scruffy mockney' in charge at the New Millennium Experience Company, who said '...you get beaten up over it – socially as well as in the press – a lot of my friends have had a go at me about it.' [581] And that was before the Millennium. The sub-headings on the *Sunday Times'* mid-year assessment, 'Dome and Gloom', summed up the general mood: 'Going for Broke Zone', 'Airhead Zone', 'Brave Face Zone', 'Droning On Zone', 'One Dull Day Zone' and 'Snooze Zone'. Author Iain Sinclair played soothsayer:

> *'It was very perceptive of New Labour to nominate Bugby's Marshes as the site for their monumentally expensive folly. Where better to greet the millennium than this ravished swamp with its history of plague, pestilence and pillage?'* [582]

576] Kambiz Boomla and Paul McGarr, Report on the Blackwall and Cubitt Town By-Election, 2003

577] Paul McGarr, interview, 'It was a stunning result for Respect in Millwall', Socialist Worker, 18 September 2004

578] Alice Livingstone Boomla, 'The New Battleground Against Blair', Socialist Review, September 2004

579] 'Stunning Success in Tower Hamlets', Conservative News, 10 September 2004

580] 'True Confessions of a Social Outcast', The Independent, 7 January 1998

581] Ben Evans, interview with the author, November 1999

582] Iain Sinclair, 'All change. This train is cancelled', London Review of Books, 13 May 1999

583] Roger Bate, 'Ban Luddites, not Chlorine', Wall Street Journal, 22 July 1998

584] 'Greenpeace Welcomes New PVC-Free Millennium Dome', Press release, 22 August 1997

585] Peter Mandelson, House of Commons written answers, 27 October 1997

586] George Monbiot, 'The House Trap', Guardian, G2, 4 February 1998

Under-ambition damaged the Millennium project. First the Dome itself was subject to perverse constraints. First Greenpeace lobbied to have the Polyvinyl Chloride (PVC) roof replaced with a more 'friendly' material, PTFE, a Teflon-coated fabric material – though the objections to PVC are just junk science,[583] and the cost was many times higher. More perversely, the material change changed the Dome's life-span. Greenpeace's objections were not strictly scientific. 'PTFE was not one of Greenpeace's chosen solutions to the problem of using a toxic PVC coated fabric', according to a press release, '...but one main benefit is that it will have a much longer life than PVC.' And '...this will change the whole concept of the dome away from being part of the plastic throwaway culture of the 20th century to being a permanent part of the regeneration of north Greenwich in London.'[584] And Peter Mandelson, the Minister without Portfolio agreed: 'The reason for the change was to give the dome a greatly-enhanced lifespan, thereby assisting delivery of the government's aim to ensure an enduring legacy from the millennium.'[585] But the whole point of the Dome's original conception was that it was indeed disposable. Who wants to see the Christmas decorations in January? The Millennium, in its nature, is a passing moment, not an enduring legacy. Look at the Millennium Dome, today – shabby, empty, a hangar for visitors to the European Social Forum, but for the most part, a white elephant. Greenpeace, you were supposed to throw it away; that is the whole point.

The argument over the Millennium Dome crystallized into one between parsimony and celebration. Britain's puritans listed the things that the money ought to be spent on, before wasting them on having fun: hospitals, the North of England, the environment, settling on one thing that ought to get built, homes. The radical comedian Mark Thomas floated a homeless woman in a balloon over the Greenwich site, calculating how many homes could be built for the cost of the Dome (but not how many for the cost of making the television programme). Environmentalist George Monbiot pitched in:

> 'No luxury development should be permitted until basic needs have been met. In other words, affordable housing should come before office blocks, superstores, executive flats and millennium domes.'[586]

All well and good, you might think. More homes: that is what we need. But the cautious and parsimonious spirit in which the new homes were planned undermined the possibilities of development in the area. Like the Dome itself, the tendering for the Greenwich Millennium village was influenced by the strength of the reaction against Grand Schemes, and not for the good.

Two interesting, but ultimately contradictory ambitions were written into the tender. The first, overwhelmingly positive, was the ambition to use the development to pioneer prefabrication, as a way of increasing productivity in house-building, so reducing costs. The second, was a reaction against the supposed short-comings of the previous stage of the development of Docklands, the disruption to community. This exigency, to build not just houses, but communities, was actually absurd. Though architects often imagine that buildings make communities, the truth is you cannot make communities out of bricks and mortar, or wood and glass either. None the less the architect chosen for the Greenwich Millennium Village Ralph Erskine was known for his 'community-friendly' designs.

The physical manifestation of the desire that we should all love one another is Ralph Erskine's Greenwich Millennium Village. It is all higgledy-piggeldy, brightly painted in red and yellow, wooden boards, full of idiosyncratic twists and turns, barrel-roofs and other non-standard shapes. This Amsterdam/Ikea cuteness is supposed to make everybody feel warm about each other. It has an eco farm. It promises a '...new way of living', no less, with a focus on design and the relationship between people and their environment. The development's website presents the Millennium Village through the eyes of a child. 'Hi, my name is Max and I live in the Millennium Village. Come with me and meet some of the people:

> 'There's Alice, I sit next to her at school, she looks down on the
> ecology park and she can see the two swans that live there...Oh how
> embarrassing that's my dad' he plays football in the park, but
> 'I don't think they are very good because mum told dad they aren't
> fit enough and dad needs to go on a diet.'

Patronising does not begin to say it. The Greenwich Millennium Village in conception is a kind of Scandinavian Early Learning Centre hell. The Deputy Prime Minister welcomed new residents at the Ralph Erskine-designed Greenwich Millennium Village personally. To show that this was not just more riverside yuppie flats, but a real community, Erskine

587] Amanda Dennison, interview with the author, 25 November 2004

built in a combined school and health centre, except that an old school, Anandale had to be relocated from the centre of Greenwich to the peninsula to provide the children – and spookily, it has kept its old catchment area.[587] In other words, Ralph Erskine's Potemkin Village recruits children from Greenwich to act the part of the local community. A few parents objected at first, but most changed their minds when they saw the quality of the facilities. Around ten of the families in the Village proper send their children there, and of those, the majority are in the 20 per cent of new homes that earmarked for social housing. Like other attempts to reinvent the village in the town, such as the B001 estate in Malmo, Sweden, Erskine's Greenwich peninsula is overwhelmingly upper middle class.

More problematically, Erskine's non-standardised designs defeat the other ambition of the site, that it should take advantage of the new techniques in prefabrication. Fortunately for him, his office, too small to take on the implementation of the design, did not carry the can. The implementation architects, EPR, defeated by the difficulties of turning Erskine's Dingly-Dell into an assembly kit were blamed instead. A new team of architects taken on to replace EPR avoided the problem by quietly forgetting all about prefabrication, with a big hike in costs.

The development of the Greenwich site could have taken advantage of a Millennium Experience to build some competitively built homes that really would have contributed to easing the housing shortage. Instead the eclectic Millennium Village remains too much of a unique project, carefully nurtured, absorbing vast amounts of resources for all of its claims to ecology, to ever be a model for more growth. Instead it makes a virtue of its small-scale tweeness. The underlying ethos is not so much Millennium Homes as Millennial Homes. After all, at the current rate of replacement, each home in England will have to stand for a thousand years – at least! The Greenwich Millennium Village exemplifies the feeling that, if we really must build some new homes, let it just be once for all time, on a containable space, and how ideal, that it should be an outcrop surrounded by water, hemmed in, without the possibility of extending any further.

THE CITY FRINGE

While Docklands and the Millennium Dome only made people flinch, there was another model of regeneration that seemed to recommend itself: the rise of the 'City Fringe'.

In the 1980s the City of London expanded by nearly four times encroaching upon the old market at Broadgate in 1985, as it has done upon Spitalfields since. Criticism that the dynamism of the City was essentially isolated from other parts of the London economy preoccupied policy-makers from the late 1980s. The growth of the City contrasted badly with the de-industrialisation of East London, with the closure of the Docks in the 1960s and the decline of the furniture-making industry.

Interest in the City Fringe, the area abutting the City of London in the southern end of the London Boroughs of Camden, Islington, Hackney and Tower Hamlets, grew as a response to the contrast. Surely the wealth of the City ought to have a spin-off effect on other parts of East London? In the 1990s, with the encouragement of the boroughs and the City Fringe Partnership, signs of a dynamic within the City Fringe could be seen, though not always as envisaged.

The expansion of the City encouraged property developers to refurbish warehouses and other industrial spaces as office spaces. However, supply of office space outstripped demand, as the recession of the early nineties hit the City. It took six years without new development for vacancy levels to return to the optimum eight per cent. In that time the oversupply of converted office space engendered different kinds of development than those anticipated: the rise of the urban loft.

On the edge of the City bars and restaurants, their facades gilded with neon, have sprung up all over the district, usually in the ground-floor units of new residential blocks converted from unused office space.

> *'Fifteen thousand new homes have been created within a mile and a half of here in the past three years', says David Salvi of Hurford Salvi Carr Estate Agents. 'Of those, at least 50 per cent have been bought by single people. As a result the bars are alive in the evenings. The social life is good but it's definitely for unencumbered living.'* [588]

The growth of residential occupation in the fringe was not encouraged by the boroughs, who did favour work-live spaces, only to find these gradually giving way to straightforward residential. The residential profile of the City Fringe itself is intriguing. The agglomeration of expensive flats indicates a new influx of city-dwellers. Many are owned by City workers. Further north, the East London boroughs were home to artists and designers. The coalescence of the financial and cultural elites on the borders of the City of London represented a sea change in the

588] David Salvi, quoted in Jay Rayner, 'We want to be alone', Observer, 16 January 2000

589] Anthony Sampson, The New Anatomy of Britain (London, Hodder and Stoughton, 1971) p 478

590] Liz Malone, in correspondence with the author

luxury housing market. In the 1960s stockbrokers lived in Mayfair or Chelsea,[589] and artists and writers in Hampstead or on Camden's Gloucester Terrace. But the Mayfair set never could reconcile themselves to the influx of Arabs, and Hampstead's distance from commerce belongs to another era. In those days only an impoverished white working class lived in Shoreditch, cheek-by-jowl with an influx of Bengali immigrants. Today, those areas are the sites of luxury developments as the attraction of Henley-on-Thames palls for City brokers, drawn instead to Richard Rogers' model of urban living. The artists, too, are attracted, not repelled by the City's mammon.

Artists have gravitated to East London to take advantage of large and cheap industrial spaces since Bridget Riley first squatted the Ivory Shed in the West India Docks in 1967 – a model followed right up until 1980 when Andrew Logan and others squatted Butler's Wharf in 1980. Today the artists' scene adds to the character of Shoreditch and Hoxton Square.

Alongside the growth in residential living there has also been an increase in new media and creative industries that is being analysed by the City Fringe Partnership's Liz Malone. From an initial analysis of the Shoreditch and Spitalfields areas, around 1550 of 7000 businesses listed in Yellow Pages could fit the very broadest definition of creative industries, from 18 Art Galleries, through 180 ladies clothing wholesalers, 42 internet services and 125 graphic designers [590].

The knowledge economy and creative industries are considered to be at the cutting edge of industrial policy by both the DTI and Foreign Office. But in the fringe, they are a minority, if one with a high profile. There is evidence of a fairly high churn of enterprises, with relatively small investments of venture capital pursuing innovative products. Characteristically such businesses have a short-term approach: their leases are generally less than five years. They are lean businesses occupying on average between 1,000 and 2,000 square feet and employing five people. Just over half recruit by word of mouth, and virtually none use an employment agency (though employment agencies themselves number 110 in this part of the 'fringe'). They are businesses with a modest turnover, of between a quarter and a half a million pounds.

Taking advantage of the low rents these new media/creative industries have secured space at an average of £15 per square foot compared to an average of £20 throughout the fringe and of £50 per square foot in the City proper. The relative success of the fringe could be forcing the initial wave of entrepreneurs out. This was what Tessa Jowell called one of the pitfalls of regeneration, '...the Hoxton effect, where regeneration becomes gentrification'. The more successful design companies based in Clerkenwell (where rents are £30 per sq ft) are moving to Shoreditch – but not just to take advantage of the rents.

The Department of Trade and Industry are particularly interested in evidence of new media 'clusters', where suppliers and clients gravitate into close geographical proximity, creating a virtuous circle of growth. There is some evidence of this clustering taking place. In particular, new media/creative industries in the fringe surveyed by Malone say that their suppliers – such as reprographic houses, photographers and so on – are close by. With clients too location is important. Among the most important clients are those from the City itself, who make up a sizeable minority. According to the designers, City clients enjoy coming to the Bohemian atmosphere of Shoreditch and Hoxton. 'It's a day out for the clients', one that might well end up in a bar like the Canteloupe. Other clients tend to be from West London or out of town. Interestingly, though, workers in the new media and creative industries are unlikely to live in the City Fringe, though they do socialise there during the week.

Characteristic of the chaotic development of the City Fringe is the seven-acre site of the old Truman brewery, home to a number of innovative internet and new media companies, as well as the Vibe Bar. Without proper planning applications, the spaces have been unattractive to established businesses, but that is changing as more investors see the attraction of such a large space so close to the City.

Attractive a model as the City Fringe is for the region's boosters, it really is a failure in terms of housing. Riverside apartments catering for the top end of the market are attractive, for sure, but they are too small in number to make any dent in the overall shortfall. The re-purposing of bespoke office space as lofts is a salutary reminder to the developers of the pressure of unmet housing needs. Along with the offices, the many warehouses re-made as flats seem to recommend themselves as a model of environmentally low-impact dwellings. According to Tessa Jowell '...the re-use of historic buildings has a positive effect for regeneration'. [591] No doubt it is just these kinds of warehouse conversions that many architects have in mind when they talk up the possibilities of housing people on brownfield sites. But far from following the Urban

591] Tessa Jowell, speech, 'A visionary brief in the Thames Gateway', 30 June 2004

592] S.K. Al Naib, London, Canary Wharf and Docklands (London, Research Books, 2003) p 94

593] James Heartfield, Need and Desire in the Post-Material Economy (Sheffield, Sheffield Hallam University Press, 1998) p 7

594] James Heartfield, Great Expectations: the creative industries in the New Economy (London, Design Agenda, 2000)

595] Jess Cartner-Morley, 'Where have all the cool people gone', Guardian, G2, 21 November 2003

Task Force's arguments for compact living, most of these conversions represent the power of cash to conquer greater individual living space. 'It is a somewhat ironical thought', writes Professor Naib, '...that many loft dwellers are living in a 2,000 square foot space that in their parents, and grandparents days was the oppressive workspace for perhaps 200 people and dockworkers!' [592]

The rise of East London as a Bohemian quarter was surprising. Somewhat sceptically, I wrote at the time that the cultural renaissance was a '...flower growing on a dunghill of deindustrialisation'.[593] 'Best place to grow a flower', the artist Patrick Hughes rightly chided me. But the great expectations that the government invested in the creative industries were overblown. [594] By 2003, the headline was 'Hoxton Square? It is now!' [595] The biggest problem is that the renaissance in the City Fringe offered a soft option for development. Instead of new building, the experience in Shoreditch seemed to suggest that the new conditions could be satisfied in the shell of the old buildings. And of course, the graphic designers and internet startups adored those old East End premises, thronging with historical resonance. These were solutions for a relatively small minority, though, which left the greater number of people without homes. The belief that one could achieve regeneration by boosting the cultural sector, though, would have a pernicious influence on urban policy for some time.

CHARLES LANDRY AND THE CREATIVE CITY

Charles Landry, consultant with Commedia, and a collaborator with the think-tank Demos developed the idea of the Creative City, drawing largely on the experience of London's reviving East End.

The idea of the Creative City restores the City to pride of place in urban geography, even though most people no longer live in cities. Landry's 'Creative City', though, is distinct from the nineteenth-century industrial city. Indeed it is contrasted to it. The nineteenth century city is a place demarcated by the division between town and country, specifically by the recruitment of industrial workforces from the countryside. By contrast, Landry's 'creative city' theorises the re-conquest of de-industrialised city centres by elites, which he calls creative or knowledge workers. Implicit in the account is the evacuation of the working classes from the city centre, which is understood as a meritocratic result of competition.

Landry's account privileges the creative sector, because this can identify '...whatever turns out to be the next growth sector'. 'Knowledge industries', writes Landry, '...require urban settings that project space, openness and social interchange.' Having set up the importance of proximity for nurturing the creative sector, Landry goes on to explain how this fits into the hollowed out nineteenth-century city. The urban settings that project space, openness and social interchange are on hand: 'Ironically, this is often provided by redundant industrial buildings around the urban core' – like the factories on Great Eastern Street, turned to artists and designers' studios. Landry pays obeisance to finance and the state alike: 'In the centre are high value services like finance, business, retail, and civic and political or cultural institutions' (that's the City of London, and Westminster). And then '...the inner urban ring provides supply services to the hub – printers, couriers, catering.' And '...it is usually the home of the less well-established creative and knowledge industries – such as design and Internet companies, young multimedia entrepreneurs or even artists – that provide the buzzing atmosphere on which cities thrive, experimenting with new products and services' (that is the 'City Fringe').[596]

Landry thinks of his account as a theory of the City, as we have seen cities today are nothing like the defined redoubts of the past. British urban settlements, particularly in the South-East of the country, are derogatorily known as urban sprawl, or what Will Alsop more positively calls 'super-cities'.[597] Landry's version of the creative city seems to envisage something like a return to the renaissance city, with more than a presentiment of Sir Richard Rogers' pedestrianised Urban Renaissance. Landry's account works, though, by relegating the less 'buzzing' and 'experimental' to the margins, just as they are actually moved out to the suburbs. 'For those with the education and portable skills – the portfolio workers – the city offers excitement, freedom and energy; for those without such personal assets it has only hopelessness, impotence, discomfort and squalor.' Optimistically, Landry thinks that the answer is retraining, so that we can all be portfolio workers. Attractive as the idea of portfolio working is to those portfolio working consultants, all the studies of changing workforces have failed to find any significant shift towards this exotic lifestyle (indeed, even the policy wonks are tempted by more permanent job status in time).

596] Charles Landry, The Creative City (London, Earthscan, 2000) p 35

597] Will Alsop, Supercity (Manchester, Urbis, 2005)

Landry's Creative City generalises the experience of a tiny proportion of the people that live in the Greater London Conurbation, the culturati, the professional hangers-on, clinging to the fringes of high finance and government. Noticeably, Landry's account stops short at the 'inner urban ring', of support services, which would be Clerkenwell, Hoxton and Shoreditch in the East, Soho and Pimlico in the West, Camberwell in the South; but what about Newham, Croydon, Southall, Wimbledon or Enfield? These centres of population are not welcome in the 'creative city', because the people there are not web-designers or image consultants. 'How does the urban manager encourage new investment and development while safeguarding the interest of people by-passed or made unemployed by the change?' Leaving to one side his patronising division between the achingly trendy and the tragically left behind, Landry has no answers to the problem. He is anxious about the '…"sink estates" where nearly everybody and everything is pulled down'. But all he has to say is that '…solving these interconnected problems to avoid creating "dual cities" is not the responsibility of any single department or the public sector alone'. One gets the feeling that his objection to the "left behind" in the "Sink Estates" is that they threaten to "pull down" his café society utopia.

Not surprisingly, Landry has almost nothing to say about housing people. 'Housing and land use present some of the most intractable problems', he volunteers, but new building exists as a distant thought on the horizon 'How well is the housing stock holding up? Is there enough? And are there sufficient resources to maintain quality?' The changes that Landry envisages are mostly tinkering, like 'individual housing extensions' or '…changes in patterns of use', but the question does not detain him very long. In fact he is irritated by the problem, which does not seem to fit into his model of regeneration as acculturation. He yearns to go 'Beyond Planning as Land Use', complaining that planning '…in the urban context is nearly exclusively associated with land use and development control'. Pity poor Charles Landry, banging his head against a brick wall, trying to persuade the planners that planning is not about planning but about nurturing creatives, like him: 'It remains difficult to get conventional planners to understand that "my" experience is powerful and felt and may have nothing to do with land use.' 'If land use planners are to maintain a predominant role', he threatens, '…it is essential that they understand more about culture, history or social dynamics'.

Get with the programme, guys! Or better still, move aside to make room for people who can really tell you how to make a latte: 'If [the planners] role is to be reduced to an equal status with other disciplines, these forms of knowledge can be present in a team.'[598] Landry's proposal to demote the land-use obsessed planners arises because he is not really interested in development, in the sense of new building, but the more restricted experience of gentrification, by occupying the emptied working spaces of declining industry. The "Creative City" is substantially a schematic representation of the "culturally-driven" improvement of the East End of London, albeit one that is presented as a universal rule. But Landry's model was applied to provincial capitals beyond the South East, subtly changing in its features as it was reproduced outside of its original conditions.

598] Charles Landry, The Creative City (London, Earthscan, 2000) p 29, 31, 35, 37, 247, and 248

CHAPTER THIRTEEN

LOOK NORTH – CAPTIALS OF CULTURE & THE NORTH SOUTH DIVIDE

GLASGOW'S DESIGNATION AS EUROPEAN CITY OF CULTURE IN 1990 IS A CUTE JOKE.
Every Scot knew that it was Edinburgh that was the Athens of the
North. But Glasgow's bid drew attention to the way that the city had
changed, after the long decline of its shipbuilding days. 'This was the
funeral service for Glasgow's old image', said council Leader Pat Lally.

The promotion was modelled on the "I♥New York", which Ad Exec
John Struthers, or Consultant Michael Kelly, re-worked as "Glasgow's
miles better".[599] The slogan played on "miles" and "smiles" with 'Mr Happy,
on loan from Roger Hargreaves and his *Mr Men* books' as icon.[600]
The promotion of the cultural claims of Glasgow followed on, and was
not as daft as it first sounded. Emerging from under Edinburgh's Royalist
shadow, Glasgow's solid Georgian centre was rediscovered to be very
grand indeed. Pointedly, Lally had cut his teeth as head of housing in the
council, provoking some hostility from the old guard for his willingness
to shift local authority stock into Housing Association control – hostility
which helped fuelled the controversy which lost him that post after his
office was charged with favouritism. The Council's desire to shed
responsibility for its ageing housing stock was a background theme in
Lally's career, all the same. While struggling to raise £3 billion to repair
housing stock, the council splashed out a £40 million programme for
the City of Culture, including a £2 million fee for Saatchi & Saatchi.

In conflict with central government over funding for housing and
the imposition of the Poll Tax, Lally's Labour administration sought
constructive engagement with the Tory enemy in the Scottish Office.
Their differences were buried in the promotion of a Garden Festival

599] Pat Lally, Lazarus
Only Done it Once
(London, Harper Collins,
2000) p 39 and 49

600] Ian Jack, Before the
Oil Ran Out (London,
Vintage, 1997) p 206

601] Pat Lally, Lazarus Only Done it Once (London, Harper Collins, 2000) p 47 and 49

602] Ian Jack, Before the Oil Ran Out (London, Vintage, 1997) p 208

in 1988: 'The government's policy was the festival should promote the regeneration of derelict land'. Lally built upon his predecessor Jean McFadden's success in promoting "Mayfest", a cultural re-working of the traditional worker's May Day, which took off, as much as a respite from the bitterness over the city's industrial decline. Cooperation over the Cultural City bid was a welcome "in" to Scottish affairs for a Conservative government that had not one MP north of the border. When Glasgow won the contest, Edinburgh's Lord Provost Dr John McKay denounced the decision as '...political and vindictive'.[601]

As well as the garden festival, the Georgian architecture, and Lally's Jazz Festival, there was also a striking literary and artistic scene in Glasgow. Writers Alasdair Gray, James Kelman, Tom Leonard and Agnes Owens; painters Ken Currie and (London-born) Peter Howson were all contributing to a thriving cultural life. Unsettlingly, for the Glasgow bid, though, they were mostly very dark, if not morbid artists. Currie and Howson tended to paint broken down muscle-men, the cast-offs of the industrial age, heavy on the shadows, and James Kelman's heroes were of a similar ilk, drunks, vagrants, on the Kerouac (or Trocchi) model of the outsider, while Owens' were hardened, bitter, even. Though the bid was supposed to be about coming out of the shadow of declining, industrial Glasgow, the writers and painters were still feeding off the sentimental resonance of that twilight.

In regeneration the Glasgow renaissance was more marked for its interest in renovation than new building. In 1984, the city's 22 Housing Associations had spent £185 million in the renovation of 10,000 of Glasgow's ubiquitous tenements. The craze for renovation was a reaction against the previous experience with some hastily built estates in slum clearances, consolidated in the Housing (Scotland) Acts of 1969 and 1974, which '...substituted the idea of "housing treatment areas" for slum clearance'. Ian Jack found the result to be '...sparkling [sic] sandstone outside and large and lofty rooms within' that '...stand as a reprimand to the city's years of heavy petting with Le Corbusier and Basil Spence'. Drafty and damp flats, in my experience, with dark and uncared for entrance halls. But most of all the city had been tutored in the ideals of make-do-and-mend rather than new building, which was a recipe for an ageing housing stock that stored up problems for the future. [602]

The award of City of Culture in 1990 was seen as the realisation of the city's ambitions, but it is, all the same, a problematic model of regeneration. At its core was a preoccupation with preservation of architectural sites: the regeneration of the Queens and Princes Dock, and the near universal sandblasting of blackened sandstone into a perky yellow, and, look here's Rennie Mackintosh's Glasgow School of Art, and have you seen the tea-rooms? On television, Robbie Coltrane and Emma Thompson tried a little too hard to make Glasgow rock-nostalgia look lively in the Bafta-winning BBC2 Series *Tutti Frutti*, screened in 1987.

Unfortunately for the boosters, the Glasgow artists, long-schooled in knocking success down south, did not like the suggestion that it would visit itself on their city. A pious Farquhar McLay saw a "Shameless Endorsement of Greed": 'We know the year of culture stinks – and why it stinks', he wrote. 'It is more a question of art sponsoring big business, promoting the new tourist drive and giving aid and comfort to the shallow ethos of yuppie greed.' The biggest clash between the artists and the administrators came after the latter effectively dismissed the curator of the People's Palace museum, Elspeth King, a move opposed by the key figures on the Glasgow cultural scene, including Gray, Kelman, Pat Kane and Billy Connolly. Council leader Lally growled back at '...these dilettanti, and the'...well-heeled authors and critics', and, in fine philistine form, boasted that:

> '...it is the intention of the City Council and our Colleagues on the Strathclyde Region...to use the title [Cultural Capital of Europe] to the maximum advantage – we are going to milk it for all its worth.[603]

The differences between the "Workers City" version of Glasgow and Pat Lally's were not as great as at first appears. Though McLay, Gray, and Kelman appealed to the city's working-class history, they were themselves artists rather than labourers. It was just that their art took the old Glasgow working class culture for its subject-matter. So Elspeth King's pamphlet *The People's Palace and Glasgow Green* lauds '...Glasgow is the birthplace of the labour movement in Scotland, and the Green was its cradle'. But it also contains some very contemporary reflections on public art and leisure, ending in a celebration of the same 1984 folk-festival that became Lally's model for the 1990 Year of Culture.[604]

But for all his ranting, the champion of what Lally called '...pathetic, factless, plank-walking anti-1990ism', Farquhar McLay did score a hit

603] James Kelman, 'Storm in the Palace', in Farqhuar McLay , editor, The Reckoning: Beyond the Culture City Rip Off (Glasgow, Clydeside Press, 1990) p 52

604] Elspeth King, The People's Palace and Glasgow Green, (Glasgow, Richard Drew, 1985) p 66 and 114

605] Farqhuar McLay, editor, The Reckoning: Beyond the Culture City Rip Off (Glasgow, Clydeside Press, 1990) p 87

606] James Kelman, 'Art and subsidy', in Farqhuar McLay, editor, The Reckoning: Beyond the Culture City Rip Off (Glasgow, Clydeside Press, 1990) p 130

607] Dolan Cummings, In Search of Sesame Street: Policing civility for the twenty-first century (Sheffield, Sheffield Hallam University Press, 1999) p 25

when he charged that '...with Saatchi & Saatchi's help they revamp the image and leave the reality untouched'. [605] The real test would be whether the Year of Culture changed Glasgow for the better.

There was good evidence that the City Centre raised its game, but less that people's homes improved. But then, that was always the point. Cultural regeneration of the kind that Charles Landry would later formularise was always about tarting up the shop-front. James Kelman's scepticism is pertinent, when he recounts that '...Art is not the product of "the cultural workforce", a term I first discovered in 1990 and which seems to refer to those who administer public funding and/or private sponsorship for "arts initiatives" '. [606] The hope was there that the rising tide would lift all ships, as the Reaganites used to say, but that was by no means certain. It was the case that the abating of the economic recession in the 1990s took some of the sting out of the regional problems, but substantially regeneration had been reinterpreted from a change in material conditions to an improvement in cultural life. For the people of Glasgow, the important initiatives from on high after 1990 were not better resources, but more intrusive policing of communities. In 1997, Hamilton became the test-bed for the "Child Safety Initiative" – which is to say, the curfew on younger people. [607] It seemed like it was easier to rebuild Glaswegians' behaviour than their homes.

For outside, though, the lesson looked quite different. The remarkable leap from declining industrial city to European Capital of Culture was one that any provincial town would envy. The programme was invented by former-actress and Greek culture minister Melina Mercouri, who was no doubt pleased to see Athens named the first European Capital of Culture in 1985. The advantages being identified as a Capital of Culture were better known on the Continent than in Britain, as Florence (1986), Amsterdam (1987), Berlin (1988) and Paris (1989) all discovered. After 1990, Britons too could see the cultural effect in practice. Growing interest clogged up the process, and nine cities were named centres of culture in 2000, after which the contest was handed over to countries on a rotating basis, with Britain nominating the European Capital of Culture in 2008. A circular from the Department for Culture, Media and Sport issued before the choice lectured '...culture is central to the life of a city, given the demonstrable links it has with regeneration, social inclusion, education and business'. Demonstrable links? We beg to differ, but the demonstration that the DCMS was thinking of was Glasgow.

HOW BRITAIN BECAME A CULTURAL ECONOMY

Britain was dubbed a "knowledge economy" in a Department of Trade and Industry report in 1998. The report was written by *Financial Times* journalist Charles Leadbeater for the then industry minister Peter Mandelson. Leadbeater's subsequent book *Living on Thin Air* indicates the thinking behind the report:

> 'We are all in the thin-air business these days...most people
> in advanced economies produce nothing that can be weighed:
> communications, software, advertising, financial services.
> They trade, write design, talk, spin, and create; rarely do they make
> anything'. [608]

It was not a good omen for British industry, including the construction industry. In an internal memo leading up to the DTI publication, it was acknowledged that there were few ideas around, so the theme would have to be "knowledge economy". That the DTI should showcase the arguments of the "knowledge economy" was by no means a foregone conclusion. Under the previous minister, Margaret Beckett, the DTI had maintained its Thatcherite reputation as the "Ministry for Closing Things Down". Beckett's evident paralysis as industry minister was revealed from the very first problem that the Blair administration met: the withdrawal of Japanese manufacturing investment from the North-East. Her isolation from the centre of power doubtless added to her inability to act. By contrast, Mandelson as industry minister was well-liked by his department as a proactive head who led the office in a rumba through new policy initiatives. But there were a few steps on the way to Mandelson's brief reign at industry.

Judging by his extensive spinning on the issue, Mandelson did not want the industry portfolio, but rather Chris Smith's job at the Department of Culture, Media and Sports (DCMS). Why? The DCMS is the unexpected success story of the Blair administration. Britain's first "out" MP scored well in placing New Labour at the heart of an apparently booming "creative Britain". Ministers were to be seen at the Brit Awards, among the Young British Artists and the literati. While Beckett made lonely visits to closing factories, Smith took Blair to meet the head of Factory Records. No wonder Mandelson wanted DCMS. Blair, of course, understood that there was no reason to take Smith off a succeeding brief. When Mandelson went to the DTI, he took the "creative Britain"

608] Charles Leadbeater, Living on Thin Air: The New Economy (London, Penguin 2000) p 18

609] Prime Minister Tony Blair, quoted in Jeremy Myerson, Britain's Design Industry: the Design Workshop of the World (London, Foreign and Commonwealth Office, 1998) p 3

610] Nicholas Serota, 'Save him for the nation', Guardian, 8 March 2001

611] Patricia Hewitt, quoted in Anneke Elwes, editor, Creativity Works (London, Routledge, 2000) p ix

612] Patricia Hewitt, Institute of Public Policy & Research Manufacturing Project Speech, Tothill Street, London, 23 September 2002

613] Centres for Social Change: Museums, Galleries and Archives for All (London, DCMS, 2000) p 8

model with him. Acknowledging that she was no longer the workshop of the world, Tony Blair boasted that '...we can say with pride that Britain is the "design workshop of the world" – leading a creative revolution.' [609] The Tate's Nicholas Serota aired an interesting rumour when he pleaded that the DCMS be protected: '...news has emerged that the government may be planning to abolish the department and pass the creative industries – cinema, pop music and broadcasting, as well as the arts – into the tender care of the huge Department of Trade and Industry'. [610] Such an idea could only be floated because of the way that the DTI had incorporated the "creative Britain" policy originally formulated at the DCMS. Unfortunately the bias to the knowledge economy was making the more traditional industries feel left out. Chancellor Gordon Brown was moved to reassure the seemingly abandoned manufacturing sector that '...of course creativity is not confined to any one sector of the economy'. [611] You too, can be creative! It was only much later that the new Trade and Industry Minister Patricia Hewitt acknowledged that the policy was a mistake. 'Quite inadvertently', she said, as though it had all been an accident, '...we let the impression build up that we were only interested in something called the "new economy" – the dotcoms, the internet and all that. And that we weren't interested in traditional manufacturing – which was part of the old economy. With no future in the modern economy.' With the benefit of hindsight, Ms Hewitt added, '...this is nonsense.' [612]

As economic policy, it perhaps was indeed nonsense. But in the heady atmosphere of the late nineties the claims for the arts expanded even more widely. Not only were the arts imagined to be the solution to economic regeneration, but to the problem of social exclusion, too. The Department of Culture, Media and Sport published a document Centres for Social Change: Museums, Galleries and Archives for All in May 2000. There it was argued that museums '...can play a role in generating social change by engaging with and empowering people to determine their place in the world, educate themselves to achieve their own potential, play a full part in society, and contribute to transforming it in the future'. [613] The magical powers of the arts were inflated to undreamed of regions. The writers Charles Leadbeater and Kate Oakley go so far as to suggest that '...cultural entrepreneurs can play a critical role in promoting social cohesion and a sense of belonging'. Why? 'Because art, culture and sport create meeting places for people in an increasingly diversified,

fragmented and unequal society' – meeting places that once were
'...provided by work, religion or trade unions'. [614]

More recently, a number of researchers have drawn attention to the
shortcomings of this argument, not just in terms of their exaggerated
views of the potential of the arts, but also the problem of adopting an
instrumental approach for the arts themselves. Warwick University
researcher Elenora Belfiore was the first to spell out the difficulties, in a
'...critique of instrumental cultural policies and social impact studies in
the arts'. As well as unpicking some of the more ostentatious claims for
the economic and social contribution the arts make, Belfiore indicates

> '...the main problem created by the argument that the arts are a
> source of urban regeneration, or that public subsidy is in fact an
> "investment" with specific, measurable social returns, is that the
> arts became entirely instrumental. Degraded to the function of
> mere tool, arts become a matter of "value for money".' [615]

Munira Mirza, who surveyed local authority cultural policies at the
University of Kent puts it more bluntly: 'The instrumentalism of cultural
policy tends to devalue the specific content of the product.' [616]

THE CULTURE VIRUS

Charles Landry identifies "Formula Thinking" as chief among the
barriers to action in pursuit of creative cities. 'City marketing is concerned
with identity and distinctiveness, yet common formulae emerge
from urban publicity.' Landry bemoans the fact that in the brochures
'...if you replaced one city name by another you would not know the
difference". [617] More than anybody, though, it was Landry who was
responsible for turning the supposed Cultural Renaissance in East
London into a template that could be reproduced in cities across the
country. He even sets out the formula in *The Creative City*, complete
with a "Conceptual toolkit" and a "five-stage plan" for creating a creative
city. Between East London's revival and Glasgow's nomination as
Capital of Culture, the case for recreating the model all over the country
became unassailable – though ultimately self-defeating.

Up and down the land local authorities and Urban Development
Corporations got the culture virus, and started drafting policy documents
"bigging up" their creative industries. These were not entirely deluded –
there always was some evidence to identify of a nascent cultural economy.

614] The Independents
(London, Demos, 1999)
p 17

615] Eleonora Belfiore 'Art
as a means of alleviating
social exclusion: does it
really work? A critique of
instrumental cultural
policies and social impact
studies in the UK',
International Journal of
Cultural Policy, Routledge,
2002, Vol. 8 (1)

616] Munira Mirza,
'Culture and social
inclusion: Examining the
ideology behind
contemporary local
government cultural
strategies in the UK',
unpublished paper
provided to the author,
September 2004

617] Charles Landry, The
Creative City (London,
Earthscan, 2000) p 43

618] Max Hanna and Marcus Binnney, Preserve and Prosper: The Wider Economic Benefits of Conserving Historical Buildings (London, SAVE Britain's Heritage, 1983) p 99

What is more, the growth in personal consumption, a long-term economic trend, but one that reasserted itself as the economy overall picked up could be felt in the growth of urban night life. The impression that the cultural economy is revitalising the country is reinforced by the transformation of decaying industrial sites with new bars, galleries and cyber-cafes. In Glasgow, Manchester, Birmingham and East London, canal-side developments have re-purposed the shells of industrial heritage as cafe society.

But was the "creative city" model all that different from the Heritage Industry that had taken off in the 1980s? Then Max Hanna and Marcus Binney proposed the basic idea of making money from cultural sites in their pamphlet *Preserve and Prosper: The Wider Economic Benefits of Conserving Historical Buildings*: 'The main economic benefit will be derived from transport, accommodation, catering and retail businesses.' 'In this context', they add candidly, '...the historic building is a classic example of a "loss leader"'. [618] The Prime Minister might have down-played Britain's taste for pageantry, but the same hope that tourism would boost growth was continued in the "creative city". The problem was that "cultural regeneration" was becoming a displacement activity for new building. A preoccupation with branding cities was turning into a substitution for real development.

MANCHESTER'S POSTMODERN FLANEURS

In Manchester, academic Justin O'Connor, having researched French intellectuals for his doctorate ending in 1988, knew all the postmodern buzz-words of the emerging study of culture industries, and secured the job of writing the report for the City Council. O'Connor took a page out of Charles Landry's book and talked up the obvious signs of a booming retail sector:

> 'Shops, cafes, bars, restaurants, clubs – people watching, people meeting; the construction of lifestyle identity through consumption; postmodern flaneurs – whatever we call it – these are as essential an indicator of a lively city as the large cultural institutions.'

"Postmodern flaneurs"? Perhaps we should call it window-shopping Manchester. But O'Connor has a harder job persuading us that employ-ment in the cultural industries will transform the city. After all it might be true that '...the City Pride area accounts for 75 per cent of all North

West employment in radio and TV', but that is the North West for you. More realistically, '...de-regulation and the commissioning system' favoured '...the more global distribution systems based in London'. In other words, London took Manchester's business, not the other way around. 'Granada's regional base is now weakened'. In fact, Granada, which has been broadcasting since 1956, merged with Carlton TV in 2003 after the failure of their OnDigital joint venture. With the company's Headquarters and most of its productions already in London, the Quay Street complex is to close. Acknowledging that '...Media is becoming globalised and centralised', O'Connor is left arguing that '...part of the answer lies in the profile of Manchester itself and the image/vibrancy of the local scene' [619] In other words, Manchester could be a location for programme makers, rather than a base. This is a rather more subordinate role than originally flagged up, the Manchester scene as exotica for jaded London palates. Since O'Connor's report, the BBC relocated staff to Manchester – though whether they can recreate the regional bias of the Corporation in the face of its employees' tendency to gravitate towards London has yet to be seen.[620]

Suspecting that it would be difficult to talk up the cultural component of Manchester's wealth creators, O'Connor did the obvious thing and formulated an '...expanded definition of cultural industries' – or what we used to call "empire building". But even this attempt founders on the facts. His estimates show just 5310 people working in cultural industries in Manchester, one twentieth of the number working in London. And as a share of the workforce, cultural jobs are just two per cent, less than in London (3.3 per cent) Cardiff (2.1), and just a little higher than in Southampton (1.9). As a share of the industry as a whole, the cultural industries sector is just 3.7 per cent of the North West region, compared with, five per cent of the South East, and more than seven per cent of London, but the same as Yorkshire and Humberside. And where other regions' cultural industries sectors, like East Anglia's or Humberside's, were growing, the North West's was contracting.[621]

While the council was trying to find evidence for Shoreditch in Manchester, the Department of Trade and Industry was doing the less doctrinaire survey of what business clusters actually existed in different regions of the country. In the North West they found the important industries were chemicals (including soap and detergents in Trafford, and photographic chemicals in Macclesfield, as well as associated

619] Justin O'Connor, 'The Cultural Production Sector in Manchester, research & strategy, Summary, Report', Manchester City Council, Economic Initiatives Group 2001, p xxvi

620] 'The BBC needs a convincing regional strategy', Financial Times, 13 December 2004

621] Justin O'Connor, 'The Cultural Production Sector in Manchester, research & strategy, Summary, Report', Manchester City Council, Economic Initiatives Group 2001, p xxv, 16, 21 and 24

622] DTI, Business Clusters in the UK – A first assessment (London, DTI Publications, 2001) section 5, North West, p 60 and 63

623] Justin O'Connor, 'The Cultural Production Sector in Manchester, research & strategy, Summary, Report', Manchester City Council, Economic Initiatives Group 2001, p 25

624] Manchester City Council, Housing Strategy, Objective 1, posted on www.manchester.gov.uk

research at University of Manchester Institute of Technology), pharmaceuticals, Aerospace, especially BAE Systems, which employs 30,000 people across the region, 34 per cent of the country's mail order industry is based in the North West, including Manchester, Bolton and Preston, a growing furniture upholstery and wholesaling sector, based in Trafford and Bolton, and one fifth of the country's paper and paperboard manufacture (21,000). But the DTI found that '...by regional standards the North West has a reasonable presence in the creative and media industries', '... however, total employment remains small'. But then, as the report politely says, 'for most regions of the UK, and for most the creative industries, the position can, at best, be described as "embryonic".' Or again, '...outside London and the South East...the cluster must be considered aspirational'. [622]

On the more objective measure, then, Manchester just was not one of Charles Landry's "creative cities". Justin O'Connor, grappling with the facts, suggested hopefully that '...there are historic connections between the manufacturing sector and the cultural industries which should be explored as a matter of priority rather than opposing "old" to "new" industries.' [623] But the lack of practical evidence for Manchester's status as an especially creative city did not stop the City Council from pursuing the Landry model. On the contrary, it was a useful diversion to concentrate all the regeneration efforts onto the retail sector, especially in the centre of Manchester, where an IRA bomb destroyed the Arndale Centre in 1996. While 67 per cent of local authority housing fails to meet the decent homes standard, and the surrounding conurbation is among the most run-down in the country, Manchester has a shiny new Centre for Urban Culture, the glass, fin-shaped tower called Urbis. Indeed, the Council's central goal is not to deal with the mass of run-down housing surrounding the city, but '...a shortage of high quality, high value homes' in the centre.[624] Concentrating on cultural regeneration turns out to mean concentrating on servicing the wealthier parts of the city.

EUROPEAN CITY OF CULTURE, 2008

The habit of exaggerating the cultural component in regional development echoed the general push towards reproducing the Creative City model in the provinces. The Scottish Enterprise Creative Industries team, of course, found that '...Scotland may be UK's main creative industries region outwith London/SE'. [625] But few noticed that its new environment altered the specific meaning of Charles Landry's "creative city" template. Landry, after all, was talking primarily about private enterprise, concerned with governmental authorities in so far as they could encourage it. Re-planted in northern soil, The Creative City plan became a case for Grand Projects, mostly subsidised by government, or funded with lottery money.

In Walsall, the lottery paid for £15,750,000 of the £21 million costs of the New Art Gallery opened in 2000. Architect Adam Caruso says '...we approached the building as a public building'. But that is not quite the effect that comes to mind. The gallery is a Bauhaus Bastille that towers over the town, but without much relationship to it. Inside the austere building is built too large, throughout. Rather like the outsize furniture and set in the Laurel and Hardy film *Brats*, the effect is to make you feel child-size. Museum Director Peter Jenkinson says that the Victorian Town Hall was the last good building, '...everything since then in Walsall has been decrepit'. [626] But when I was there, the pedestrian shopping centre, with its eighties rounded arch was full of life, while a handful of earnest arty-types shivered in a room in the drafty New Art Gallery, wondering how we could "connect" with the people.

The competition for the UK nomination for the European Capital of Culture in 2008, awarded to Liverpool in 2003, drew out some of the problems with the reproduction of the model. The other towns that put themselves forward were Belfast, Birmingham, Bradford, Bristol, Cardiff, Canterbury, Inverness, Milton Keynes, Newcastle-Gateshead, Norwich, and Oxford. All the entrants, by now, had learned Glasgow's trick from 1990: '...you did not think of us as a city of culture, then think again'.

"'Ah, Glasgow" you can almost hear the politicians sigh', wrote the art critic Jonathan Jones. [627] But by now the trick was a little hackneyed, and the basic formula was on show. These cities aimed to showcase their unique attributes, but ended up performing the same dance, showing off the same steps. Even when they were emphasizing their idiosyncrasies the competing cities were uniformly acting out the part of "character". 'If you don't pick Belfast', joked the former paramilitary leader Gerry Adams, '... don't come back'. [628]

Newcastle-Gateshead's prestige projects ought to have won the contest, if it had really been about raising your game in cultural terms.

625] Scottish Enterprise, Creativity and Enterprise: Scotland's creative industries (Glasgow, Scottish Enterprise, 1999)

626] Rosie Millard, The Tastemakers (London, Thames and Hudson, 2001) p 219

627] Jonathan Jones, 'Come friendly bombs...', Guardian, 8 January 2000

628] Miranda Sawyer, 'Bigger than the Beatles', Observer, Review, 8 June 2003

629] Anna Minton,
Northern Soul: Culture,
creativity and the quality
of place in Newcastle and
Gateshead (London,
RICS/Demos, 2003) p 5

630] Rosie Millard, The
Tastemakers (London,
Thames and Hudson,
2001) p 220 and 221

631] Anna Minton,
Northern Soul: Culture,
creativity and the quality
of place in Newcastle and
Gateshead (London,
RICS/Demos, 2003) p 10

Anna Minton investigated the project for the Royal Institute of
Chartered Surveyors. But her view that Newcastle and Gateshead
'...offer a clear example of successful transformation from coal city to
culture city, underpinned by a dynamic form of urban entrepreneurship',
is not entirely justified.[629] The city's Millennium bridge, the Sage music
centre and Baltic (no, not "the Baltic", just Baltic art gallery), are all
remarkable structures – but they are examples of public art, not of private
enterprise. A great brick warehouse, Baltic was once part of Joseph
Rank's baking business, counterpart to the Solent, Atlantic and Ocean Mills,
it was known as the Baltic Mill for its location. Rosie Millard remembers
that when she lived opposite, it was reputed to hold the European
Community's sugar mountain. Following the landmark success of Anthony
Gormley's Angel of the North, Norman Foster's Sage music centre was
funded to the tune of £70 million from the lottery, disbursed by the arts
council, the European Development Fund, One North East (the Regional
Development Agency), and Gateshead Council; Baltic won funds of
£33.4 from the lottery/Arts Council, plus another £12.3 million from the
European Development Fund, English Partnerships, Northern Arts and
the local council; on top of which, it has revenue funding of £1.5 million
a year. As Millard says, '...clearly, no one wants Baltic to run aground'.[630]

Anna Minton hints at some of the problems. On the one hand
'...house prices in fashionable Gosforth are among the highest in the
country', as cultural renaissance corresponds to city centre gentrification.
'In sharp contrast, a couple of miles away in Newcastle 's West End,
it is possible to purchase a house in Scotswood or Benwell for under
£10,000.' The sharp differences suggest '...the dangers of a two-speed
economy', and '...whether or not communities here are feeling the
benefits of the city 's cultural renaissance is a question frequently
posed by critics of culture-led regeneration.'[631] Seeing above-average
employment in the service and leisure industries as a positive factor,
Minton wonders why it runs alongside high unemployment and
decline. But the two are complementary, not contradictory. With other
job prospects limited, the straitened people of Scotswood or Benwell
serve up lattes at Baltic's café to the pampered residents of Gosforth.

In 2000 Rainbownetwork reported that '...civic chiefs in Newcastle
are trying to bring in the so-called "pink dollar" by encouraging
Americans to invest in the city's gay nightlife.' Promoting Newcastle
as '...a top international holiday destination in the specialised

gay market,' [632] seemed a bit optimistic, though, and one correspondent warned that '...outdoor cruising and cottaging are not advisable on Tyneside – you have the twin hazards of police surveillance and queer bashers'. [633] Indeed, Sussex University researcher Darren Smith calculates that the North East is the least gay part of England or Wales.[634]

Chris Donald, founder of that great Geordie institution, *Viz* magazine is sceptical of the attempts to market Newcastle as "Britain's answer to Bilbao", arguing that most of the money comes in from "beer tourism", and '...if you ask the people who live here, lots of them haven't been to any of the new arts centres'. Donald's comic-book character Art Carbuncle imagines he sees artistic statements in the everyday trappings of working class life. Playwright Alan Plater makes the point that '...if you cover your waterfront with wine bars, you will make it look pretty much the same as everywhere else'. [635]

While Minton notes the limitations of the "creative city" model, the gentrification of the city centre, and the forcing of residents out, she is unduly scathing of previous, more muscular models of regeneration. She dismisses the 1960s council leader T. Dan Smith's '...grandiose vision for Newcastle, of which little was ever realised...inspired by the concept of a "Brasilia of the North"'. Smith's subsequent jailing on corruption charges puts those ambitions in the shade, (his crime was to sell influence in council planning decisions, through his public relations companies Dansmith Ltd and T Dan Smith Associates).[636] But the contrast between then and now is stark:

> 'We are concerned, however, not only with the extent but the quality of industrial growth. It is not enough that we should aim to have sufficient jobs to match the manpower available. We must aim at achieving a much larger share than in the past of modern-science based and capital-intensive industries which show high productivity and provide well paid employment with a high skill content... We cannot be content that the region should become the home of factories engaged on assembly work. It must have its proper share of research and development units and of administration.' [637]

The difference between today's gratitude for low-productivity, service sector jobs, and the National Economic Planning Council's aspirations to for the most productive skills and technology base is clear. Is it

632] Newcastle aims high', Rainbownetwork, 28 June 2000, www.rainbownetwork. com

633] 'Gay Newcastle', Rainbownetwork, 6 December 1999, www.rainbownetwork. com

634] 'Are you the only gay in the village?', BBC Online, www.bbc.co.uk

635] Vanessa Thorpe, 'Now true Geordies mock the Tyne's "art revolution"', Observer, 25 June 2005

636] Raymond Fitzwalter, Web of Corruption (London, Granada, 1981)

637] Northern Economic Planning Council, Challenge of the Changing North (Newcastle upon Tyne, NEPC, 1966) p 55

"grandiose" to want to see investment in the region of a quality that would better the lives of the people that live there? The ambitions of the sixties foundered ultimately not on T Dan Smith's personal weaknesses, but the slow-down in economic growth. As prospects were frustrated, so too were expectations lowered. Planning had its problems, but the anti-development mood that followed only helped reconcile people to less.

One example is Ralph Erskine's Byker estate. Usually celebrated as a model of community-sensitive development, this was also a case of humbling the aspirations of the planners – and not necessarily for the better. The original Byker Terraces were heavily damaged in the Second World War, by German bombers aiming for the shipyards. The redevelopment of Byker was late, though, at a time when the shine had come off the post-war developments. In particular, the kind of "comprehensive redevelopment" that T Dan Smith's council favoured was faulted for destroying communities. But to build the modern Byker estate, half the residents were moved out to Killingworth New Town, and the other half were moved into Byker Wall, the curved wall of flats, originally built to dampen the sound of a motorway that was never built. Running down the valley side, below the wall are smaller homes, with their Erskine-trademark wooden shutters, individualised design, and plenty of landscaping. These houses were quite popular, with their personal scale and walkways separated from driveways. The wall, too, has its charms, though overall the estate has more than its share of social problems and remains predominantly council-owned. Today, the brightly-painted wooden features are faded and weather-worn. Beatrix Campbell, the radical journalist and anti-paedophile campaigner lives there.

Byker is a listed building, now. The estate is supposed to embody the good "community architecture" alternative to the bad days of "comprehensive development". But the thinking behind Byker is confused. Erskine thought that he was building not just houses, but a community. The Byker community though is something of a myth. It is a conservative idea to think that people stay in the same locale generation in and generation out. Communities are not precious flowers, nurtured by architects or designers. They make themselves, and unmake themselves, and remake themselves again. If anything binds the estate together, it is a feeling of being hard done by. But the belief that it was the job of the developers to build communities instead of houses was a first step in the retreat from building homes altogether. A preoccupation with the supposed fragility of community made planning departments behave far too gingerly with residents. The end result is Newcastle and Gateshead today, where redevelopment no longer involves building homes at all, just beautifying the city centre.

Let me not be misunderstood. Baltic, the Sage and the Millennium Bridge are excellent. But people need homes to live in. In Newcastle, there might not be the same pressure on the housing stock, but many of the city's residents need new homes. The "creative city" formula is not another kind of redevelopment, it is a substitute for redevelopment.

LIVERPOOL, CITY OF COMPLAINTS

'Liverpool is a handsome city with a tribal sense of community. A combination of economic misfortune — its docks were, fundamentally, on the wrong side of England when Britain entered what is now the European Union — and an excessive predilection for welfarism have created a peculiar, and deeply unattractive, psyche among many Liverpudlians. They see themselves whenever possible as victims, and resent their victim status; yet at the same time they wallow in it.' [638]

Boris Johnson's editorial in the *Spectator* (possibly written by Simon Heffer), caused uproar. Above is quoted the meat of the argument, but the particular flash-points were the *Spectator*'s assertions that the city had gone overboard in its public expressions of grief for Ken Bigley, the local man executed by Islamists in Iraq, and that the deaths of 96 Liverpool Football Club fans at Hillsborough in 1989 might have been in part their own fault. Both were guaranteed to provoke outrage among the Scousers. [639]

Johnson's position as editor was compromised by the fact that he is also a Conservative MP for Henley, and was shadow arts minister. Tory leader Michael Howard insisted that he recant: 'I have asked Boris Johnson to visit Liverpool next week and to apologise in person.' A contrite Johnson said '...I have been stunned by the hurt this article has caused. I will be going as soon as I can next week to apologise in person for the offence I have caused, and to listen in a spirit of complete humility to local people.' [640] Of course, the over-sensitive Howard reinforced any

638] Boris Johnson, Spectator, 16 October 2004

639] 'Hackwatch: Beyond the Whinge', Private Eye, 29 October 2004

640] Telegraph, 17 October 2004

641] Guardian, 18 October 2004

642] Guardian, 16 October 2004

643] Guardian, 18 October 2004

644] Guardian, 20 October 2004

645] Guardian, 20 October 2004

sense of outrage that there might have been, and Johnson betrayed his editorial independence by acquiescing. But once the media show was on the road, Liverpool lived up to the accusation of victim-status.

Johnson's visit proved to be an exercise in rehearsing the City's wounded pride. In an open letter, Jane Wolstenholme, the editor of the *Liverpool Daily Post* wrote

'On rare occasions somebody will write an article about Liverpool that is so outdated, breathtakingly unfair or just plain unpleasant that we cannot allow it to pass unchallenged. Congratulations: your leader in this week's Spectator passed the test.' [641]

Council leader Mike Storey refused to meet Johnson, while local MP Peter Kilfoyle said that '...to single out Liverpool as somehow being psychologically flawed is absolutely outrageous'. [642] Sensing that the city was in danger of scoring an own-goal, Alan Bleasdale, writer of the television series *The Boys from the Black Stuff* warned: 'We should be careful of making too much fuss: he may be coming up here to prove a point.' Then, laying claim to the moral high ground, Bleasdale advised '...the people of Liverpool should listen to what he says and treat him with the compassion, dignity and generosity we're famous for'. Adding, in the true voice of the outraged '...we don't need to sink to his level'. [643] Another local playwright, Jimmy McGovern, feeling some ownership of the Hillsborough tragedy having written it for television, let slip that, in essence, Johnson's editorial was right about Liverpool's distinctivness: 'Our so-called mawkishness is a rallying round, an expression of grief.' McGovern only insisted that it was the southern stiffness that was pathological, not the other way around. 'We're a Celtic city here, and we have our way of death which is different from the anal English way.' [644] Ged Starkey, a local nightclub owner put it more prosaically: 'We're a city that rallies round and gets over what happens to us, and let's face it, we've got a lot to get over.' [645] All of which seemed to confirm the *Spectator*'s original point: 'They see themselves whenever possible as victims, and resent their victim status; yet at the same time they wallow in it.' Of course, the point is that Liverpool is hardly exceptional in its chosen role of victimhood. This is a common manoeuvre in all appeals for public finance today, a hollowed out remnant of the socialist case for a fair share.

The peculiar impact of the Johnson episode in Liverpool's history was not only that it confirmed the point of the article, but also that it

threatened to undo the city's success in winning the City of Culture
nomination the previous year. UK culture secretary Tessa Jowell
announced that Liverpool had beaten its rivals – Oxford, Bristol,
Newcastle-Gateshead, Birmingham and Cardiff – to be the British
nomination for European Capital of Culture. The competition is credited
with winning billions of pounds to redevelop run-down cities, but in
Liverpool's case it looks a bit like a consolation prize. 'The city instinctively
knew...that the Glasgow experience 10 years earlier was exactly the
model for Liverpool', runs the first bid document, but could the underdog
trick be pulled off a second time?

Liverpool's bid, run by Sir Bob Scott (previously best known for the
failed Manchester Olympic bid) did not know whether to argue that
Liverpool was truly a great centre of culture, or to plead that the city
was most in need of a boost. Liverpool's claim to be a centre of culture
is dubious. That most talk about the Beatles – a group that disbanded
more than 30 years ago – is a sign of the bleakness of the city's cultural
profile. Actually, the Beatles' iconic status is a curse to the arts in
Liverpool, which still languish under the band's memory. More prosaically,
the bid points to 16,000 Merseyside jobs in the creative industries,
4.7 percent of the total – which sounds good, except that the Department
of Culture Media and Sport calculates that six per cent of all jobs
nationwide are creative, and, in any event, the Policy Studies Institute
puts Merseyside's total at just 4,750. [646] In 1988, John Myerscough found
just 2,648 employed in cultural industries, including 170 making the
now cancelled Channel 4 series *Brookside*, 130 working in cinemas,
150 in pop bands, and seventeen authors – though at that time only six
were working on the festival gardens and none at the Albert Docks.[647]

When the Department of Trade and Industry surveyed business
"clusters" in the North West, Liverpool's computer gaming sector was
the only creative industry big enough to show up on the radar (with 700
people working for Psygnosis). It is true that the "cultural" redevelopment
of the docks and waterside has improved Liverpool, but on a template
that is copied from other major cities. Most of all it centres on re-fitting
historic buildings more than making new ones. It was the company
Urban Splash that pioneered the project. According to local author Linda
Grant: 'The aim is to turn Liverpool city centre into a place for urban
living and working, with the conversion of old warehouses, schools and
factories into loft and office accommodation (in much the same way as

646] Justin O'Connor, The
Cultural Production
Sector in Manchester,
research & strategy,
report commissioned by
Manchester City Council,
Economic Initiatives
Group 2001, p 16

647] Economic
Importance of the Arts in
Merseyside (London,
Policy Studies Institute,
1988) p 17, 19, 22, 24

648] Guardian, 10 July
1999

649] Peter Taafe and Tony
Mulhearn, A City that
Dared to Fight (London,
Fortress Books, 1988) p
120, 147, and 222

650] Liverpool Star, 11 April
1985

central Manchester has been transformed in recent years).' [648] In the
1990s, when you walked around the renovated Albert Dock, you could
just hear the sound of seagulls, and the occasional hoot of a foghorn.
If you waited long enough, you could learn the sequence of subliminal
port noises, which were being played on a long tape loop.

In fact, the underlying message of Liverpool's bid, and the reason
for the bid's success, is that the city needs the economic boost: '...more of
a scholarship than a cup', says the bid document. Liverpool has for decades
been complaining about its victimisation at the hands of an uncaring
southern establishment. As Britain's Atlantic trade fell while its
European trade expanded, this west-facing port declined, feeling the
recessions of the 1970s and 1980s very badly. Liverpool's own resources –
a patrician elite first made rich on the slave trade, a working class
divided along sectarian lines – were not equal to the challenge.
Dominated by Tory politicians for decades, the Town Hall was briefly
home to the radical left Militant Tendency, who took over a defunct
Labour Party in the 1980s. The Militant council did manage to build
5,000 council houses between 1983 and 1987. But even that late challenge
to "Tory Rule" emphasised all the worst characteristics of Merseyside:
special pleading, a parochial regionalism, and a sense of outraged
victimisation.

In their account of Militant Liverpool's struggle against Westminster,
A City that Dared to Fight, Peter Taafe and Tony Mulhearn pander to the
stereotype: '...the mood of "us against the world" ': 'In the case of
Liverpool, the government acted in a particularly arbitrary and unfair
fashion', they protest, as if Mrs Thatcher's administration had gone easy
on other cities. 'A picture of Liverpool working people as "workshy, drug-
addicted and incorrigible scroungers" was presented to the national
media', they claim, though in point of fact, Militant was responsible for
some of that perception itself, having blamed criminal gangsters, not
police repression, for the rioting in Toxteth in 1981, and generally shown
off the city's wounds to win sympathy. [649] A poll by the Liverpool Star
found that 90 per cent of Liverpudlians thought that the government
did not care about the people of Merseyside.[650] Liverpool's victim identity
was reinforced by the belief that the city was punished for its truculence,
while nearby rival Manchester was rewarded with new investment.
'Liverpool has had a difficult recent past', acknowledges the bid document.
And, noting that "Objective One" European funding is coming to an end,

suggests '...Capital of Culture status would be the perfect exit strategy to Objective One'. The Cultural designation was always in danger of being seen as compensation rather than celebration.

Liverpool's unique cultural signature dwells precisely on that sense of victimhood. Hippy romantics outside of Liverpool, the Beatles' reflections on their hometown set the melancholic tone for maudlin sentimentality in *Penny Lane* and *Eleanor Rigby*. TV Playwrights Alan Bleasdale and Willy Russell, filmmaker Terence Davies, novelist Linda Grant and the Mersey beat poet Roger McGough all dwell on the down-trodden side of Liverpool, managing quirky humour at best, and feelings of depression (Grant) or suicide (Davies) at worst.

Not surprisingly, the reaction of Liverpool's literati has been mixed, as was Glasgow's. The artists' doom-laden instincts sit unhappily with the local authority's boosterism. Jimmy McGovern parodies the city's catchphrase:

> 'This is Liverpool Eight, the only place which you really can describe as "The World in One City", It's the Harlem of Britain: there's a black man living there called O'Riley, there's Irish and Welsh, Somalis and West Indians – and look at it. Bricked up for demolition. It's the "Capital of Culture" on its arse – fucked up by these bastards wanting to knock it all down for development, investment and whatever they can get out of it. That's not culture, that's vandalism.'[651]

American film-maker Alex Cox was also sceptical. He believes that the kind of urban redevelopment cities like Liverpool want is often at the expense of "real" people. Smart new loft apartments, museums, galleries and cafes are for a moneyed and "cultured" middle class.[652] In 2002, I debated the City of Culture bid with Sir Bob Scott, who conceded that '...no scheme works twice', that is, that Liverpool would not be able to reproduce Glasgow's success. But he rejected my argument that the creative industries would not turn Merseyside around.[653]

The relationship between civic culture and the arts has been strained before. In 1963, at a civic reception of some 300 people at the City Art Gallery at John Moores University, a drunken Roger Hilton badgered the portly council leader John Braddock incessantly to know when he would get paid for the new painting being honoured. Dinner, and Hilton, took their toll on City Boss Braddock, who collapsed with heart failure, having to be dragged out of the hall on the back heels of his tall chair by porters.[654] The festivities, though, were not interrupted by the

651] Guardian, 20 October 2004

652] Jonathan Glancey, 'Bright lights, big city', Guardian, 29 March 2003

653] Laura Davies, 'Winning bid will not bring wealth', Liverpool Daily Post, 8 June 2002

654] Patrick Hughes, interview by the author, 28 November 2004

655] David Ward, 'City of
Tattered Dreams',
Guardian, 9 March 2006

656]
www.artscouncil.org.uk

civic leader's death. In those days artistic patronage was a decoration on development, not a substitute for it.

As a counter to Jimmy McGovern's glum, Sir Bob's bid emphasises the dumb. Nervously it acknowledges that '...in truth the city cannot emulate, say, Salzburg, the home of Mozart and all that is respectable, perhaps even comfortable, in high culture' (though note that snide use of "comfortable"). So instead of being stuffy and exclusive, Liverpool's cultural claims play to the lowest common denominator. One project, "2008 bottles", has school children fill sweet jars with anything that represents culture to them. The artists, though, have a tendency to frighten the horses, and Yoko Ono's vast, close-up pictures of women's bodies displayed on St Luke's Church provoked complaints from local people. But the missing centre of Liverpool's City of Culture status was underlined by the reluctance of its Director Robyn Archer to re-locate from her native Australia, until eventually she resigned in July 2006.

Just as it dumbs-down the culture, the Liverpool bid retreats from the regeneration. Too much of Liverpool's plans depend on re-fitting old buildings. Pointedly, even the showpiece new architecture, like Will Alsop's ten storey "cloud", a curvilinear "diamond fist" known as the "fourth grace", was dropped...after the bid had been won. The proposed £65m new Museum of Liverpool was refused a grant by the lottery fund, and will not now be open for 2008.[655] The proposed £170m new tram system has not been built. New building takes a second place to refurbishment – an unfortunate lesson from Liverpool's status as Capital of Culture.

CULTURAL OVERLOAD

Arts researchers Josie Appleton and Kunal Dutta identified 53 new arts centres (or major extensions of existing centres) funded with lottery money, '...to a total cost of £471,451,587, nearly half a billion pounds'. Some were plain eccentric, like the National Centre for Carnival Arts (£3,000,000) in Luton, which aims to '...[disseminate] best practice within the carnival community'. [656] But many, as Appleton points out were simply commercial venues, pragmatically dressed up in an "arts" shell. The Galeri Creative Centre in Wales (£3,075,436) offers '...office and workshop space for rent and rooms for hire', and the Lowry Centre in Manchester (£83,526,000) includes shops, a cinema complex, restaurants and bars., while '...the paintings by L.S. Lowry are cramped in a low-ceiling gallery at the top of the building'.[657] This subtle retreat from the art part of the arts centre is perhaps a response to the overheated preoccupation with the arts that came to a head around the turn of the Millennium.

The mounting disquiet over the Millennium Dome and opening night wobbling of the Millennium Bridge were the first signs that perhaps the country was being oversupplied with cultural venues. There were increasing signs that not all of the new ventures being funded by the National Lottery could be sustained. The Office of National Statistics guestimate of Museum attendance in 1998-99 of 81 million was drastically reduced by the Museums and Galleries Commission to 65 million the following year. By 2004 public attendance at "high" cultural institutions has fallen nationally by 20 per cent in 10 years.[658]

Sheffield's National Centre for Popular Music opened in 1999 with an £11 million grant was forced to close for lack of interest. The premises were handed over to the Sheffield Hallam University Students' Union in 2003. The Earth Centre, at Denaby, near Doncaster, opened in April 1999 with £60 million lottery money. Its aim was to '...make sustainable development and green economics fun' and kept 400 acres of organic farm fertilised with visitors' sewage, but failed to live up to visitor predictions, and was closed. In Cardiff, a £9 million Centre for the Visual Arts was closed in November 2000 after 14 months, having failed to get visitors. In Newport, a planned Arts Centre ran into trouble when developers uncovered the remains of a sixteenth-century ship. Terry Underwood, who had championed the development said '...we need an arts centre. And if there's a boat underneath, so what?' But 6,000 people signed a petition preferring the ship to the Arts Centre, persuading the Welsh Assembly to try to save both.[659] Subsequently, Newport Council has said that it cannot save the ship, provoking more protests.

The quiet world of museums and arts centres was becoming more hysterical, under the hothouse of National Lottery funding and cultural regeneration. Within months of each other two Museum Directors in the North West killed themselves under pressure to achieve results – on 1 October 2000, father of three, Lea Parkinson (32) could not cope with the stress of his job as director of the Lowry Arts Centre he had opened the previous April, and threw himself off of its tower at Salford Quays;[660] on 8 March 2001, Sir Richard Foster (59) head of the National Museums and Galleries on Merseyside, who had been knighted in the Millennium honours list, drowned himself off a Dorset beach, feeling that he was

657] Josie Appleton, 'Where's the Art in that?', Spiked-online, 8 December 2004, posted on www.spiked-online.com

658] Guardian, 20 October 2004

659] 'Newport's medieval ship', South Wales Argus, 23 August 2002

660] 'Suicide verdict on Lowry organiser', Lancashire Evening Telegraph, 13 April 2001

661] Martin Wainwright, 'Museum director's stress led to suicide', Guardian, 20 April 2001

662] Beatrix Cambell, BBC Radio Four, 'Start the Week', 1 November 2004

663] Guardian, G2, 27 October 2004

not on top of his job, and that there was a lack of leadership.[661] Back in London meanwhile, a Charities Commission investigation has found that the Tate had broken the law, buying paintings to the value of £600,000 from one of its own trustees, Chris Ofili – the kind of insider-trading that businessmen go to prison for.

Today, the oversupply of public art is beginning to look like a menace to life and limb. In July 2006 two women were killed and 12 people seriously injured in County Durham by an inflatable structure, Dreamscape, made by artist Maurice Agis broke free of its moorings. In March of 2005, local authority architect Gillian Beckingham faced charges of manslaughter when seven people died from legionnaire's disease spread by the Forum 28 Arts Centre air conditioning system, after she cancelled a service contract. Meanwhile in Carlisle an artwork featuring a 16th-century curse has been blamed for everything from foot-and-mouth disease to the relegation of Carlisle United.

NORTHERN PRIDE

Contributing to Radio Four's Start the Week, Newcastle-based writer Beatrix Cambell talked up the special characteristics of the North of England. Rejecting the '...lamentable myth of the North' that it is always in decline; Campbell pointed to a "palpable resurgence". The special characteristics of northern-ness she thought were a sense of public space, public art, conviviality and congregation. But of course the positive case for the North, '...the first thing that the North is, is not the South'. The South's "proximity to power", Campbell suggested, was corrupting, whereas the North's distance from it, a kind of identity.[662] Elsewhere she wrote '...the South is power, wealth, the political centre, a self-absorbed and complacent locale from which the North, for good reason, feels estranged'. The importance of the Northern sense of the underdog was underscored when she suggested that '...the North is a metaphor for class'. Up North '...I still feel the working class is the majority class; full of resilience, stamina and wit'. [663]

The focal point for this latest discussion of northern-ness was the referendum campaign for a regional assembly in the North East. Unlike previous administrations, this Labour government has lent its support to regional devolution, supporting the Scottish and Welsh Assemblies. The North East was to be the first elected English regional assembly and a central plank of the government's devolution campaign. Stars like

"Robocop" and Middlesborough Mayor Ray Mallon, and long-distance runner Brendan Foster, lent their support. Labour's politicians, including London Mayor Ken Livingstone, got on the train north. In Sunderland, Chancellor Gordon Brown dismissed opponents of the assembly as nothing more than '...a bunch of London Tories'. [664]

But it was not London Tories who delivered the verdict on the assembly. Instead, Labour's heartland voters rejected their own local assembly by a staggering 78 per cent of the vote. Of course there were specific local reasons: people in Middlesborough did not feel any great affection for those in Newcastle, and feared domination from that centre. But then the vote lost in every single local authority area. It is also true that the disaffection with politicians is so great that they were suspicious of so pointedly top-down a proposal and campaign. The Scotsman's leader argued that '...Thursday's vote suggests an earthy, northern two-fingers to the government from an electorate increasingly cynical about Mr Blair in general, and the government in particular.' [665] But that would be to interpret the vote against the assembly as an assertion of regional pride, which seems too clever by half. *The Scotsman*'s Murdo Macleod and Brian Brady got closer to the truth when they crowed over the non-appearance of '...the mythical "Geordie nation"':

'For more than a decade, centre-left politicians have happily rehearsed the glib claim that theirs is a more distinct regional identity than can be found elsewhere. This from a region comprising some 2.5 million people, in areas as geographically and socially diverse as the inner-city areas of Newcastle and Sunderland, to the Durham and Northumberland coal-fields and the swathes of countryside beyond – let alone its ambiguous relationship with Cumbria... More questionable was the assumption that this "Geordie identity" automatically translated itself into a desire for greater political independence.' [666]

Macleod and Brady were right to point to the questionable case for political identity in the North East. But the contrast that they have in mind is that of Scotland and its "thousand years of history". Looking back at the Scottish Assembly referendum, even when the project of devolution was at its high point, only 45 per cent of the electorate voted for the Scottish Parliament.[667] Is Scottish identity that much more rooted than Geordie identity? Television executive Stuart Cosgrove

664] Guardian, 27 October 2004

665] The Scotsman, 6 November 2004

666] 'Auf wiedersehen, Prescott', Scotland on Sunday, 7 November 2004

667] 'Scots say "Yes" to home rule', 12 September 1997, posted on http://news.bbc.co.uk/on thisday/

668] Observer, 13 February
2005

669] 'Divided Britain',
Labour Party News,
June 1987

surely had a point when he argued that Scottish identity was
unduly morbid:

> 'The Scots prefer failure – whether that's the failure of the national
> football team, the failure of industries, the failure of the parliament.
> They almost obsess over it. They also love the culture of poverty.
> They indulge the culture of poverty. The rise of the Scottish Socialist
> Party is a case in point. They don't seem to be able to imagine
> themselves out of this culture.' [668]

The idea of regional identification has always been wrapped up with
the region's attitudes to the centre, and generally one of complaint. The
high-point of Scottish agitation for devolution was during the eighties
and early nineties, when Scotland was most at odds with the overwhelmingly southern-based Conservative government. So, too, did the
idea in England of **North** against **South** become more pertinent when it
appeared that the South was irredeemably Tory, and the North solidly
Labour. After a third crushing defeat in the elections of 1987, Labour's
officers reflected on the state of the country: 'Hardly ever can any
election results have shown a nation so deeply divided between the
South and the North, between the haves and the have-nots, between
those in work and those out of work.' [669] Here is the argument that
Campbell put, that the North is hard done by, the South venal. But note
that this is an excuse. The Labour Party was trying to explain away its
inability to address the aspirations of people south of the Wash.

In 2004's referendum, the powers-that-be tried to connect to the
people beyond the South Eastern core by appealing to a presumed
regional identity. As the Chancellor's comment about "London-based
Tories" showed, they were willing to press the negative identification of
the North – not the South – to make that connection. But they failed.
The people of the North East simply have no such positive identification.
And just as they are voting at the polls, so are they voting with their
feet. Demographers Daniel Dorling and Bethan Thomas point out that
outside of London, all major cities are declining in population, and that
'...the population of the UK is slowly moving to the South'.

Dorling and Thomas's analysis of the 2001 Census drew criticism
from regional dignitaries. Bob Kerslake, chief executive of Sheffield City
council, and a champion of the lobbying group Core Cities insisted that
'...there is already evidence of a turnaround in the last five years and

every prospect of things getting better'. Denton and Reddish MP Andrew Bennet, Labour chairman of the Commons local government, housing and planning committee also claimed that '...in the regeneration of cities, the government's proposals are working well', while admitting that there were "horrendous" problems.[670] It is not hard to see why the census should be so problematic for champions of a Northern resurgence.

> 'At the start of the 21st Century, the human geography of the UK can most simply be summarised as a tale of one metropolis and its provincial hinterland... On each side of the divide there is a great city structure with a central dense urban core, suburbs, parks and a rural fringe. However, to the south these areas are converging as a great metropolis, while to the north is a provincial archipelago of city islands.'[671]

The decline of the North has at least been contained by a relatively buoyant economy, rather than being experienced as the disaster of de-industrialisation that it was in the 1980s.[672] The divergence though, is difficult to wish away. Most pointedly, what growth is taking place in the North owes more to government spending that it does to private initiative. The public spending share in output is 52.6 per cent in the North West, 61.5 per cent in the North East, and 54.9 per cent in Scotland.[673]

For housing, the importance is clear. With the provinces suffering greater or lesser degrees of depopulation, houses have to be cleared. In 2002 government plans to demolish up to 880,000 homes in northern England and the Midlands were announced.[674] Gateshead, Newcastle, Blackburn, Manchester, Hull, Sheffield, Liverpool, Stoke-on-Trent and Birmingham are all earmarked for substantial demolitions. In Liverpool alone, the council has to cope with 28,000 derelict homes.[675] Simon Jenkins bemoaned the fact that under the Pathfinder plan 100,000 Victorian terrace houses in the Welsh Streets area of Liverpool are to be knocked down, especially as they comprise the '...sort of buildings about which the government's Islington friends would purr were they in London'.[676]

To some, the contrast between empty homes in the North of the country and the prospect of new building in the South is just too provocative. Green Party's London leader Darren Johnson says that it is '...particularly ludicrous to have every single scrap of land in London and

670] 'North scorns study of gulf with South', Guardian, 1 July 2004

671] Daniel Dorling and Bethan Thomas, People and Places: A 2001 Census Atlas of the UK (Bristol, The Policy Press, 2004) p 183

672] David Smith, North and South (Harmondsworth, Penguin, 1989)

673] David Smith and Claire Newell, 'Britain's northern 'soviets' swell on Brown handouts', Sunday Times, 28 May 2006

674] Jonathan Leake, 'Prescott plans big knockdown in the north', Sunday Times, 6 October 2002

675] Helen Carter and Faisal al Yafai, 'Demolition planned for thousands of homes', Guardian 27 June 2003

676] Simon Jenkins, 'We should give thanks for what has been saved from the Great Satan', Guardian 18 November 2005

677] Darren Johnson, Green Party Press Release, 17 March 2004

678] Ros Coward, 'Regeneration Games', Guardian, Society, 30 October 2002

679] Richard Rogers and Richard Burdett, 'Let's cram more into the city', in Marcial Echenique and Andrew Saint, editors, Cities for the New Millennium (London, Spon, 2001) p 13

the South East being eyed up by developers, when the populations of other regions, such as the North West and the North East, are actually declining'. [677] Ros Coward protests that '...in the North-West, vast tracts of urban land lie derelict, while in the South-East...our countryside is under ever-increasing threat'. [678] Richard Rogers takes a similar view, but using the coded proposition that '...regional balance is critical to achieving a sustainable economy'. This is in the context of bemoaning the "divided country" of the North and the Midlands with the '...bulk of redundant industrial land' and the South-East' where the '...greatest pressure for new housing development' is felt. [679] Though he is cautious to spell it out, "regional balance" could only mean relocating people up North. No doubt the chaotic workings of the economy do create unplanned waste and blight, but the critics need to take care. Is anyone really suggesting that people should be moved up North? Infamously Westminster Council housed its homeless out of borough, paying more outlying regions to take on the social problem. More recently the government imposed resettlement schemes on asylum seekers, forcing them into unwelcoming estates in Glasgow and elsewhere. Surely, everybody understands that in a free society you cannot direct people where to live, like Stalin did the Chechens in 1944.

The shifting economic geography of Britain is not something that we can hold up our hands to like Canute and wish away. It is something that has to be worked with. For cities and towns outside of the South East that can mean some profound challenges. It is not easy to manage a downsizing without it appearing to be a rout. But the demolition of old houses ought not to be seen as a disaster, so much as an opportunity. Britain's ageing housing stock needs renewing, and that means demolition, as well as building. Though Simon Jenkins presumed to speak up for the "local community" of the Welsh Streets area of Liverpool, Irene Milson and Mary Huxham of the local tenants and residents association saw things differently:

> 'Far from it being "wrought" on them, residents in this neighbour-hood have been campaigning to be included within the Housing Market Renewal Pathfinders plan for over four years. The decision was supported in a survey of all Welsh Street residents, with a 72 per cent majority in favour of a clearance. ...The campaigners, conservationists and critics don't have to deal with 125-year old properties that are damp, decaying and expensive to heat –

*let alone with collapsed Victorian sewage systems now over-ridden
with rats.'*[680]

680] 'Demolition is the
best thing for these damp
and decaying homes',
Guardian 21 November
2005

In principle, there is nothing wrong with the population concentrating
itself more densely in one part of the country than another. It is not as
if it will tip up and sink. No doubt a perfectly planned society would
achieve things less chaotically, but until then we need to manage
change, not wish it away.

CHAPTER FOURTEEN

WHEN AND WHERE TO BUILD

WE LIVE IN A "MAKE DO AND MEND" SOCIETY BECAUSE WE ARE NOT BUILDING enough new homes. Near constant refurbishment of cramped and crumbling housing is glorified as a way of life to be aspired to. When homeowners can't afford to pay for builders a lot of DIY becomes necessary, but is turned into a virtue. Older houses, tending to be more spacious, are often seen as more attractive by those "unfortunate" enough to live in relatively new homes. But Georgian and Victorian housing also need the greatest amount of laborious upkeep. Even modernist housing is now old and in need of increasing care. Dating modernism rather too neatly as occurring between 1914 and 1939, the curators of the V&A exhibition *modernism – designing a new world* (without capital letters) were sponsored by Habitat, who clearly understand the home improvement market potential of "modern" as the flip side to "traditional". [681] Homes built as a solution to slums, then damned as "Jerry-built" when hastily constructed for the urban poor, are, today, lovingly "restored", despite any lack of space and light, or their anti-social acoustics. As the trend spreads through suburbs too, Britain is now into every kind of period house restoration.

The "make do and mend" ethos is also applied to the utilities and amenities that existing and new households need. Instead of population growth being anticipated with infrastructural investment, excuses are made. 'Water resources, energy, transport and green spaces are being taken for granted, so we must re-think the way we live', lectures Nick Reeves, executive director of the Chartered Institution of Water and Environmental Management. Throughout his collected essays in

[681] Christopher Wilk, editor, modernism 1914 – 1939 – designing a new world (London, Victoria & Albert Publications, 2006)

682] Nick Reeves, In My View, The Condition We're In – Collected Writings (London, CIWEM/Aqua Enviro Technology Transfer, 2006) posted on www.ciwem.org

683] Nan Fairbrother, New Lives, New Landscapes; Planning for the twenty-first century (New York, Alfred A Knopf, 1970)

684] John Stewart, 'Building a Crisis - Housing Supply in Britain', July 2002, posted on www.hbf.co.uk

The Condition We're In, Reeves imagines the "dangers" of urbanisation, population growth, consumer attitudes and economic development.[682] The only danger is in environmentalists like Reeves telling us to make do without. When the South East suffers from a lack of running water we do not consider that this might be due to the fact that we are using an infrastructure designed for millions fewer people, who bathed once a week, and washed their clothes in a tub. We do not plan where to build new reservoirs; instead we impose bans on watering our little pieces of Britain, outside our outmoded homes.

These low aspirations, and our lack of imagination, are so powerful that new houses are built to look like old ones, and our lives squeezed into them. The desire to live in spacious accommodation and drive about is damned as culturally, politically and technically backward. Often spurious environmental arguments are whipped into moralistic fear-mongering of the lowest order.

But this is the twenty first century. While the South East population continues to expand we cannot continue to bury our heads in the idea that this process can be stopped. Our society possesses the technical and cultural know how backed by the wealth to create a new living environment. We do not have to behave nihilistically or "concrete over the countryside" to build a beautiful and comfortable place for us and our children to live in. We can create a new landscape for our new lives. We always could.[683] We might today. We could build instead of make do and mend.

This book began with a selection of official estimates, and made the point that at current rates of house building we have to refurbish every home for 1,500 years.[684] To reduce that figure to 100 years we need to build half a million homes every year over the next decade, because we need to anticipate:

> New household formation recognised at 200,000 per annum – currently

> Additional housing, to relieve overcrowded families and anticipate greater immigration, at, say, 34,000 per annum – an underestimation

> Housing stock replacement on a 100 year cycle at 266,000 per annum – a low rate of renewal

Building five million new homes in Britain in the next 10 years is not a problem: it is a tremendous opportunity.

236

But is that going to be enough? In certifying residential buildings the Building Research Establishment says that '…the life expectancy of the structural system and inaccessible elements or components shall not be less than 60 years.' The BRE sensibly allow for parts of those homes with shorter life expectancies – the bits that we use intensively, wear out and get tired of like kitchens and bathrooms, but also windows and doors, and roof and facade – to be '…identified in the installation and/or user manuals'. [685] So at 60 or 100 years that is still a lot of refurbishment of all the non-structural and accessible construction. But at 60 years life expectancy the logic of building half a million homes a year falls apart. If we build to the BRE standard, we will still have a housing problem because we needed to build more. The lower the design life of the structure, the more homes we need each year.

Let us put those earlier estimates of five million "100 year" homes in 10 years aside, and consider a Britain where homes have, say, a 65 year design life cycle. Also we can consider a "London Supercity" within the national picture, consisting of the South East, London, Westwards out to Oxford, and the Southern most populated part of Eastern England. In 2001 the South East of England accounted for about 13.8 per cent, London for 12.4 per cent, and Eastern England as a whole for 9 per cent of total households. Looking at figures from the Office of National Statistics *Regions in Figures* series for population estimates and projections,[686] and household type,[687] the London Supercity might comprise about 35 per cent of total households, which will reach about 28 million by 2016.

To replace that stock every 65 years requires 430,000 homes per annum, of which about 35 per cent, or say 150,000 could be built in the London Supercity. The remaining 280,000 could be distributed throughout the rest of the country. But to allow for household growth 200,000 homes a year are required in addition to the stock rotation. That means at least 630,000 homes are needed each year (430,000 stock replacement and 200,000 household growth)

Again if 35 per cent of those homes built to increase, as opposed to replacing housing stock were in the London Supercity that would be another 70,000 homes in the South-East. But due to migration and immigration the demand for new homes in these most popular regions undoubtedly exceeds this percentage, reducing the demand in other areas of the country by possibly 15 per cent.

685] Building Research Establishment, LPS 2020:2006 – Loss Prevention Standard for Innovative Systems, Elements and Components for Residential Buildings (Garston, BRE Certification, 2006) posted on www.redbooklive.com

686] Office of National Statistics, Population Estimates and Projections, by sub-region, Regions in Figures (Newport, ONS, 2005) and posted on www.statistics.gov.uk

687] Office of National Statistics, Table 7.1, Households by type, Spring 2004, Regions in Figures (Newport, ONS, 2005) and posted on www.statistics.gov.uk

688] Ian Abley, 'If London is so great, why not build more of it?', Rising East Online, University of East London, December 2005, Issue Number 3, posted on www.uel.ac.uk

Assuming 250,000 homes per annum are required in the London Supercity (150,000 stock replacement, 70,000 household growth, and 30,000 as a London weighting) then how many will be on brownfield or greenfield sites is a question of housing density (whether these homes are to have gardens) and of preferred location. The more "living space" people want, and the more people want to move out of existing urban areas, the fewer homes will be built on brownfield. These sites can be used for other things such as playgrounds, parks, nature "corridors", and even the odd museum or gallery. Also, within the London Supercity the Thames Gateway must be made attractive as a location, and that will require an ambition for development.

A Thames Gateway of 1.2 million homes is entirely possible in the decade up to 2016 to add to the estimated 600,000 households already living in the allocated growth area. Only 120,000 new Gateway homes in total are currently planned to 2016. In the Gateway area of 80,000 hectares, assuming 75 per cent is developed at densities that range anywhere from one up to 100 homes a hectare, it is possible to consider a Thames Gateway of three million households.[688]

The London Supercity requires a total of 250,000 homes per annum, of which 100,000 are new homes for new households. But an ambitious Thames Gateway alone could realise 120,000 new homes every year for the next 10 years. That raises the potential to demolish 20,000 of the worst existing stock every year in a programme of de-densification throughout the London Supercity.

That de-densification would reduce the requirement for 150,000 replacement homes to 130,000 per annum. Not only does that allow the worst stock to be taken off the market entirely, and space made over where there is overcrowding, but it recognises that over 10 years the 1.3 million replacement homes required throughout the London Supercity could be substantially planned as replacement stock. In other words, minimal new land would be needed to replace existing stock unless people wanted to lower existing densities still further to allow for new settlements outside of the Thames Gateway. That is clearly a question of development control in a democracy. But perhaps only 20 per cent of the housing outside of the Thames Gateway might be required to be on greenfield sites to allow for some further de-densification and new growth areas (such as around Cambridge and the M11 corridor)

So up to 2016 it would be possible to have 80 per cent of the
1.3 million homes required in the London Supercity outside of the
Gateway on brownfield sites, the rest on greenfield (beating all ODPM
and CPRE targets) and without necessarily increasing existing densities
at all – provided the Thames Gateway is 10 times more ambitious than
is currently planned.

That is 120,000 new Thames Gateway homes on both greenfield and
brownfield land, 104,000 brownfield replacement homes and 26 000
greenfield homes every year in the London Supercity. Taken over
20 instead of just 10 years, the Thames Gateway would reach a target
of 2.4 million new homes by 2026, to transform the 0.6 million homes
built there already into a three million Eastwards expansion of London
at the full range of development densities. Such a scale of development
would also encourage redevelopment of the 0.6 million existing
Gateway stock as a positive spin off. That same 20 year period would
see 2.6 million of the most dilapidated housing stock in the London
Supercity replaced, with a further 400,000 homes cleared and not
replaced, to provide better landscaping and urban design.

The rest of the country could variously enjoy 20 years of 380,000
homes being built every year outside of the London Supercity, allowing
30,000 of the worst stock to be demolished without replacement each
and every year. The new and replacement housing would all be at
various densities and variously built on brownfield or greenfield sites,
according to local demand and development control.

That overall picture depends on building an ambitious Thames
Gateway of 3 million households in 20 years, enough for about 7 million
people, effectively matching the existing population of all the London
Boroughs taken together. That would be the key to the London
Supercity, which at a rate of 250,000 homes each year would
mean the building of five million homes in 20 years. It remains
the case that:

**Building five million new homes in Britain in the next 10 years
is not a problem: it is a tremendous opportunity.**

But those homes might not last 100 years, or might not be able to
accommodate a century of social change in Britain. So let's build more:

**So let's build the London Supercity, with the Thames Gateway at
its centre.**

689] DETR, The Government's Response to the Environment, Transport and Regional Affairs: Seventeenth Report - Planning Policy Guidance 3: Housing (London, HMSO, 2000)

Let's build five million homes in 20 years in the South East, London, Westwards out to Oxford, and the Southern part of Eastern England.

Of those five million, 48 per cent (2.4 million) might be built new in the Thames Gateway, and outside of that growth area 41.6 per cent (2.08 million) to replace stock on brownfield land and 10.4 per cent (0.52 million) newly constructed on greenfield sites. That would be accompanied by the planned and compulsory clearance of the worst existing stock in the London Supercity, returning developed land to new landscaping. The difference between new landscaping and greenfield development being 120,000 homes over 20 years. At a spacious 10 homes a hectare (suburbia is 20 to 30) that means only 12,000 hectares of additional land will be built on in 20 years, or 600 hectares each year. After the 20 years is up, and the Thames Gateway built, a different plan will be needed, of course.

Let's build a total of 12.6 million homes nationally over that 20-year period, at a rate of 630,000 per annum. A rate of building that outstrips any record for annual house production in Britain. How that is done requires every sector of construction to produce homes on an unprecedented scale, that last structurally for at least 65 years, and are designed to be refurbished, if not upgraded, several times over that period

That would take us to the end of the first quarter of the twenty-first century. We would have planned to replace Britain's ageing housing stock for a changing demographic with greater aspirations for living space, while accommodating annual household growth, and all on a realistic Design Life cycle. That will reduce the laboriousness of indefinite refurbishment and end the narrow density prescriptions of planning policy guidance.

WHAT IS THE ALTERNATIVE?

Currently existing homes have to last anywhere between 1,000 and 1,500 years, depending on whose estimates are taken. With annual national production recently averaging at around 180,000 we are building about 450,000 too few homes every year, all forced to be built at densities to meet PPG3,[689] and with an emphasis on microflats. If an ambitious Thames Gateway is not pursued, catching the public imagination through a transformed landscape, then five million homes are still needed throughout the South-East, London, Westwards out to Oxford, and the Southern half of Eastern England. The opportunity to use the Thames Gateway to meet housing need and minimise the uptake of greenfield land for the next 20 years will have been missed.

After those two decades, we will still need to find other and better ways to build more widely in the London Supercity, but at least by then we will have recognised that London is larger than we think.

THE END OF THE DIVISION BETWEEN TOWN AND COUNTRY

In the nineteenth century Utopian Socialists envisaged the end of the antagonism between Town and Country coming as a result of the abolition of capitalism. But things did not work out like that. All the same, the geographic expression of proletarianisation, the division between the town and the countryside, has lost most of its technical rationale.

If the fundamental monopoly over land has persisted, technological change has undermined much of the reason for the division between Town and Country. There are two important changes. The first is the continuing revolution in agricultural output, which has made it less and less necessary to keep so much of Britain under pasture and the plough. The second is the transport revolution that has made the distance that people can cover in their daily commute greater by the decade.

Increased yields have made much of Britain's farmland redundant. That is no small thing, since fully three-quarters of Britain is earmarked for agriculture. Now farmers are leaving the business, and seeking to get rid of their land. The tell-tale statistic released by the government in the wake of the foot and mouth crisis is that even in the countryside proper, agriculture is not the main source of wealth. The losses to tourism and leisure industries during the foot and mouth crisis were greater than those to agriculture (tourism and leisure lost £4.5 billion, agriculture £3.1 billion).[690] The vacuum left by vacant land is a powerful pull factor for new developments.

At the same time the way people travel makes it easier for them to live at a distance from their work. The amount of time people commute to and from work is surprisingly static, about the same time as they did in 1950. But over the same fifty years the distance they travel in that time has increased six fold, from five to thirty miles a day.[691]

690] 'Government Memorandum addressing issues raised in the Framework Document of the Lessons Learned Inquiry', HMSO, March 2002, 2.5.10

691] John Adams, 'Hypermobility', Royal Society of Arts lecture, 21 November 2001

692] Daniel Dorling, Bethan Thomas, People and Places: A 2001 Census Atlas of the UK (Bristol, The Policy Press, 2004) p 157

693] www.rialto.com/fordmadoxford_society/

694] Daniel Dorling, Bethan Thomas, People and Places: A 2001 Census Atlas of the UK (Bristol, The Policy Press, 2004) p 7 and 183

695] http://earth.google.com

696] Guy Davenport, translator, Herakleitos and Diogenes (San Francisco, Grey Fox Press, 1979) p 40

Nor is the transport revolution letting up. Between 1991 and 2001 the share of the population with no access to a car dropped from 20 to 12 per cent.[692]

Land vacated by agriculture and hypermobility; these are the changes that are driving the revolution in living. Far from taking the population into high density cities – that is a solution for a minority only – the main trend is towards suburbs, and exurbs.

Today there is no London, as such. The city has lost all definition, as its outer edges have blurred into the dormitory towns around it. A century ago Ford Madox Ford imagined a London that was a hundred miles across, taking in Oxford in the West, Cambridge in the East, Brighton to the South.[693] In their comprehensive atlas of the 2001 census, *People and Places*, Daniel Dorling and Bethan Thomas observe that '...the metropolis of Greater London...now extends across all of Southern England', and 'from Gainsborough in the north to Penzance in the west' [694]

The Londonostalgics avoid the obvious conclusion - there is no city of London anymore, but a 100-mile radius conurbation. Not the country-side concreted over, but the city liberally interspersed with green spaces (take a look at Google Earth some time: England's green and pleasant land is not in danger).[695] Instinctively radicals will resist the conclusion. They remember how the Tories struggled to frustrate a London-wide authority, and raised a reactionary slogan of a London of villages. But today, you would be hard pressed to deny the fact that London has been disaggregated. Is Southall part of the same city as Walthamstow, or Camberwell? Is central London part of London, or a service/tourist centre serving Europe? And is it not quicker to get to Brighton than Forest Gate?

There is no point bemoaning the end of London's community. Physical proximity was never the real basis of community anyway. The champions of the new urbanism talk about "cosmopolitanism" but it is a word they do not understand. When Diogenes coined the term two and a half thousand years ago, he was not praising city life, but decrying it. It was his rebuttal to the city dignitaries who had exiled his father. His loyalty was not to the city, he said, but to the world: I am a citizen of the world, he said, a **cosmopolitan**[696].

The way that people really relate to one another has precious little to do with the arrangement of their houses, but the activities they engage with. Who seeks out the company of their neighbours? You are more likely to spend social time with your workmates, or fellow enthusiasts of some cultural activity, or other collaborators, in networks that are voluntarily based, not geographically imposed. Nowadays, a lot of time will be mediated through mobile phones and e-mail, as well as "face-time".

Of course it would be a mistake to prescribe dispersed living, just as it was to prescribe high-density dwelling. As a political goal, we should aim for the maximum liberty in choosing where and how we live.

For younger people, cities will carry more attraction. Couples with families might see more benefit in suburbs, or dormitory towns. If you work in media, an inner London suburb makes sense, if only because of the paranoia that you might be missing a story. But if you are in computing, why not part of Cambridge's string of new towns? As a matter of sociological observation, the average trend is going in one direction, and that is towards more dispersed living, the same direction it has been going in for fifty years.

For the "New Urbanists" and Londonostalgics, the dissolution of our urban centres is a melancholy conclusion. But they have mostly drawn the same conclusion. London Orbital author Iain Sinclair has moved to Hastings. Sir Crispin Tickell of the Urban Task Force lives in a Somerset Farmhouse. Lord Rogers does live in London, but not so densely – he has two Georgian terrace houses knocked together in Chelsea. Even Jane Jacobs moved out of Greenwich Village to that great American suburb Canada.

But what is there to be so nostalgic for? The demarcation of Britain into town and countryside has served its purposes, good and bad. It was already redundant at the start of the twentieth century when Britons abandoned farming to concentrate on making money, buying in agricultural goods from New Zealand and other colonies. Then people voted with their feet to re-conquer the countryside with rambles and chalets.

Only the political reaction of world war forced us to return the countryside to agriculture in the generalised paranoia of food security. Only the neurotic policing of Duncan Sandys' Green Belts stopped the wholesale dispersal of the captive populations of Britain's nineteenth century industrial cities.

Over time, though, the underlying trend has reasserted itself. We should help it along, and have suggested two ways for Britain to do that over the next decade:

> Build 5.0 million new homes designed to last 100 years to replace existing housing in a plausible time frame, accommodate household growth, ease the affordability problem, and anticipate greater immigration

> Build 6.3 million new homes designed to last 65 years to do all the same things, but faster, with a strategic sense of the London Supercity, and a commitment to the Thames Gateway within it

Doing either is not a problem: it is a tremendous opportunity. We could live in the land vacated by agriculture, and make a new landscape. It might not be quite as Karl Marx envisaged, but the end of the boundary between the Town and the Country is a liberation, not a loss.

Let's stop making excuses, and build the houses for people to live in.
Let's Build!

BIBLIOGRAPHY

BOOKS AND ARTICLES

Abley Ian, 'A lack of commitment in the Labour "commitment" of a decent home for all', 12 October 2003, posted on www.audacity.org

Abley Ian, 'If London is so great, why not build more of it?', *Rising East Online*, December 2005, Issue Number 3

Ackroyd Peter, *London: The biography*, London, Vintage, 2000

Ackroyd Peter, 'London luminaries and Cockney visionaries' in *The Collection*, London, Chatto and Windus, 2001

Ackroyd Peter, 'Nicholas Hawksmoor – his Churches', in *Lud Heat and Suicide Bridge*, London, Vintage, 1995

Adams John, 'Hypermobility', Royal Society of Arts lecture, 21 November 2001

Adams John, 'Social consequences of Hypermobility', reproduced as an annex to Project On Environmentally Sustainable Transport; Proceedings From The Ottawa Workshop, London, OECD 1999

Alsop Will, *Supercity*, Manchester, Urbis, 2005

Andersen Kristi, *Creation of a Democratic Majority 1928-36*, Chicago, University of Chicago Press, 1979

Ashworth Herbert, *The Building Society Story*, London, Franey & Co., 1980

Baker Phil, 'Secret City: Psychogeography and the End of London', in Joe Kerr and Andrew Gibson, editors, *London: From Punk to Blair*, London, Reaktion books, 2003

Balanyá Belén, **Doherty** Ann, **Hoedeman** Olivier, **Ma'anit** Adam and **Wesselius** Erik, *Europe Inc.*, London, Pluto, 2000

Balen Mischa, *Land Economy: How a rethink of our planning policy will benefit Britain*, London, Adam Smith Institute, 2006

Barnett Anthony, *Iron Britannia*, London, Allison and Busby, 1983

Barnett Anthony and **Scruton** Roger, *Town and Country*, London, Jonathan Cape, 1998

Barr Emily, *Plan B*, London 2005

Bate Roger and Julian Morris, *Fearing Food: Risk, Health and Environment*, Oxford, Butterworth-Heinemann, 1999

Beckett Samuel, *First Love*, 1973

Ben-Ami Daniel, *Cowardly capitalism: the myth of the global financial casino*, Chichester, John Wiley & Sons, 2001

Berman Marshall, *All that is Solid Melts into Air: The experiences of modernity*, London, Verso, 1983

Blunden Andy, 'Social Solidarity vs. Social Capital', posted on http://werple.net.au/~andy/works/

Boorman John, *Adventures of a Suburban Boy*, London, Faber and Faber, 2003

Briggs Asa, *Victorian Cities*, Harmondsworth, Penguin, 1968

Brown Lester, and Christopher Flavin, editors, *State of the World Atlas*, London, Earthscan, 1999

Calder Angus, *The Myth of the Blitz*, London, Pimlico, 1992

Carey John, *The Intellectuals and the Masses: Pride and Prejudice among the literary intelligentsia, 1880-1939*, London, Faber and Faber, 1992

Cassidy John, *Dot.con – The Greatest Story Ever Sold*, London, Allen Lane, 2002

Crossman Richard, *Diaries of a Cabinet Minister, Volume One, Housing Minister*, London, Jonathan Cape, 1975

Danielson Michael N., *The Politics of Exclusion*, New York, Columbia University Press, 1976

Dash Jack, *Good Morning Brothers!*, London, London Borough of Tower Hamlets, 1995

Davis Mike, *City of Quartz: Excavating the future in Los Angeles*, London, Vintage, 1992

Davis Philip, editor, *Immigration and Americanization*, Boston, Ginn and Company, 1920

Debord Guy, Introduction to a Critique of Urban Geography 1955 posted on http://library.nothingness.org

Diogenes 'Fragments' in *Herakleitos and Diogenes*, Guy Davenport translator, San Francisco, Grey Fox Grey Fox Press, 1979

Donovan Nick, **Pilch** Tony, and **Rubenstein** Tracy, *Geographic Mobility*, London, Performance and Innovation Unit, 2002

Dorling Daniel and Bethan Thomas, *People and Places: A 2001 Census Atlas of the UK*, Bristol, The Policy Press, 2004

Dorril Stephen and Robin Ramsey, *Smear: Wilson and the Secret State*, London, Fourth Estate, 1991

Dyos H.J., 'Railways and Housing in Victorian London', *Journal of Transport History*, 2, 1955

Eagleton Terry, *The Function of Criticism, from the Spectator to Post-structuralism*, London, Verso, 1997

Easterbook Greg, *The Shape of Dreams to Come: Living, working and changing lifestyles in Britain today*, London, Standard Life, 2004

Eastman Max and Jacob Roisin, *The Road to Abundance*, London, Rider, 1955

Echenique Marcial, 'Mobility and space in Metropolitan Areas', in Marcial Echenique and Andrew Saint, editors, *Cities for the New Millennium*, London, Spon, 2001

Echenique Marcial and **Saint** Andrew eds, *Cities for the New Millennium*, London, Spon, 2001

Echenique Marcial and **Homewood** Rob, *The Future Of Suburbs And Exurbs; Report for The Independent Transport Commission*, Cambridge, The Martin Centre for Architectural and Urban Studies, 2003

Evans Alan, *Bigger, Better, Faster, More – Why some countries plan better than others*, London, Policy Exchange, 2005,

Evans Alan, *Economics and Land Use Planning*, Oxford, Blackwell, 2004

Evans Alan, *Better Homes, Greener Cities*, London, Policy Exchange, 2006

Evans Alan and **Hartwich** Oliver Marc, *Unaffordable Housing – Fables and Myths, London*, Policy Exchange, 2005

Fairbrother Nan, *New Lives, New Landscapes; Planning for the twenty-first century*, New York, Alfred A Knopf, 1970

Farren Mick, *Give the Anarchist a Cigarette*, London, Pimlico, 2002

Ford Ford Madox, writing as Ford Madox Huefor, 'The Future of London', an appendix to W.W. Hutchings, *London Town: Past and Present*, Volume II London, Cassell, 1909

Fuller R.M., **Smith** G.M., **Sanderson** J.M., **Hill** R.A., **Thomson** A.G., **Cox** R., **Brown** N.J., **Clarke** R.T, **Rothery** P. and **Gerard** F.F., Land Cover Map 2000 – Module 7 Final Report, Huntingdon, Cambridgeshire, CEH, 2000

Galbraith J. K., *A Short History Of Financial Euphoria*, Harmondsworth, Penguin, 1993

Gates Richard T., and Frederic Stout, editors, *The City Reader*, London, Routledge, 1996

Giradet Herbert, *The Gaia Atlas of Cities: New Directions for sustainable urban living*, London, Gaia books, 1996

Giradet Herbert, 'A Quarter Century', *Resurgence*, Issue 201, July/August 2000

Giradet Herbert, *Cities People Planet*, London, John Wiley, 2004

Giradet Herbert, *Creating Sustainable Cities; Schumacher Briefing 2*, Fox Hole, Green Books, 1999

Giradet Herbert, editor, *Land for the People*, London, Crescent Books, 1976

Giradet Herbert, *The Gaia Atlas of Cities*, London, Gaia Books, 1996

Giradet Herbert, and **Seymour** John, *Far from Paradise – the story of human impact on the environment*, Marshall Pickering, Green Print, 1988

Gray Robert, *A History of London*, London, Hutchinson, 1988

Green Shirley, *Rachman*, London, Michael Joseph, 1979

Green Shirley, *Who Owns London?*, London, Weidenfield and Nicholson, 1986

Gummer John Selwyn, Foreword, *Household Growth – Where shall we live?*, London, Department of the Environment, 1996

Gunn Simon, and Rachel Bell, *Middle Classes: their rise and sprawl*, London, Phoenix, 2002

Hadjor Kofi Buenor *Another America: the politics of race and blame*, Boston, South End Press, 1992

Hall Peter, *The World Cities*, London, Weidenfeld and Nicolson, 1966

Hall Peter, *The Land Fetish*, London, Town and Country Planning Association, 2005

Hall Peter, and **Ward** Colin, *Sociable Cities: the legacy of Ebenezer Howard*, Chichester, John Wiley, 1998

Hall Peter, with **Thomas** Ray, **Gracey** Harry, and **Drewett** Roy, *The Containment of Urban England: Urban and Metropolitan Growth Processes or Megalopolis Denied*, London, George Allen & Unwin, 1973

Hall Stuart Martin Jacques, editors, *The Politics of Thatcherism*, London, Lawrence and Wishart, 1983

Hardy Dennis and Colin Ward, *Arcadia for All: The Legacy of a Makeshift Landscape*, Nottingham, Five Leaves, 2004

Harrison Paul, *Inside the Inner City*, Harmondsworth, Penguin, 1983

Harvey David, *Social Justice and the City*, London, Edward Arnold, 1973

Hayes Dennis, and Alan Hudson, Basildon: *The mood of the nation*, London, Demos, 2001

Heartfield James, 'Nowhere near enough homes', *Blueprint*, September 2002

Heartfield James, 'People, not architecture, make communities', in Ian Abley and Jonathan Schwinge, 'Manmade Modular Megastructures', *AD magazine*, January/February 2006, Wiley-Academy

Heartfield James and **Abley** Ian, eds., *Sustaining Architecture in the Anti-Machine Age*, Chichester, Wiley-Academy, 2001

Heath Edward, *The Course of My Life*, London, Hodder and Stoughton, 1998

Heffer Eric, *Never a Yes Man*, London, Verso, 1991

Henwood Doug, *After the New Economy*, London, The New Press, 2003

Hewison Robert, *The Heritage Industry: Britain in a climate of decline*, London, Methuen, 1987

Himmelfarb Gertrude, *The Idea of Poverty*, New York, Random House, 1983

Hobsbawm Eric, 'Labour in the Great City', *New Left Review*, issue 166, November 1987

Hobson Dominic, *The National Wealth*, London, Harper Collins, 1999

Howard Ebenezer, *Garden Cities of To-Morrow*, London, Swan Sonnenschein, 1902

Hughes Jonathan, and **Sadler** Simon, editors, *Non-Plan: Essays on freedom, participation and change in modern architecture and urbanism*, Oxford, Architectural Press, 2000

Hunt Ben, *The Timid Corporation: Why business is terrified of taking risk*, Chichester, Wiley, 2003

Hunt Tristram, *Building Jerusalem: The Rise and Fall of the Victorian City*, London, Weidenfeld and Nicholson, 2004

Hutton Will, foreword, Richard Rogers and Anne Power, *Cities for a Small Country*, London, Faber and Faber, 2000

Inwood Stephen, *A History of London*, London, Macmillan, 1998

Jackson Alan, *A Semi-Detached London*, London, Allen and Unwin, 1973

Jackson Kenneth *Crabgrass Frontier: The Suburbanization of the United States*, Oxford and New York Oxford University Press, 1985

Jacobs Jane, *Death and Life of Great American Cities*, New York, Random House, 1961

Jones Gareth Stedman, *Outcast London*, Harmondsworth, Penguin, 1984

Jones Gareth Stedman, 'The "Cockney" and the nation', in Gareth Stedman Jones and David Feldman, editors, *Metropolis: London histories and representations since 1800*, London, Routledge, 1989

Kolko Gabriel, *The Triumph of Conservatism*, London, Collier-Macmillan, 1964

Kurokawa Kisho 'The West, Conqueror and Domesticator of Nature', in The Symbiosis of Man and Nature, of Philosophy of Symbiosis, posted on www.kisho.co.jp

Labour Party *Time for Decision*, Manifesto, 1966

Lawson Nigel, *The view from Number 11* London, Corgi, 1992

Lazare Dan, *America's Undeclared War: What's killing our cities and how we can stop it*, New York, Harcourt, 2001

Leadbeater Charles and Kate Oakley, *The Independents: Britain's New Cultural Entrepreneurs*, London, Demos, 1999

MacCarthy Fiona, *William Morris: A life for our time*, London, Faber and Faber, 1994

Macnaghten Phil, and **Urry** John, *Contested Natures*, London, Sage Publications, 1998

Major John, *The Autobiography*, London, Harper Collins, 1999

Marx Karl, *Capital, Vol.I*, Moscow, Progress, 1974

Marx Karl, *Capital, Vol. III*, London, Lawrence and Wishart, 1984

Marx Karl, *Contribution to the Critique of Political Economy*, London, Lawrence and Wishart, 1981

Marx Karl, *German Ideology*, London, Electronic Book Company, 1998

Marx Karl, *Grundrisse*, Harmondsworth, Penguin, 1973

Marx Karl, *Theories of Surplus Value, Vol. II*, London, Lawrence and Wishart, 1992

Marx Karl, and **Engels** Frederick, *The Communist Manifesto*, London, Verso, 1998

Massey Douglas, and **Denton** Nancy, *American Apartheid: Segregation and the Making of the Underclass*, Harvard, University Press, 1994

McKinnon Alan, 'Life without lorries, The impact of a temporary disruption to road freight transport in the UK', *Commercial Motor*, November 2004

Meller Helen, Patrick *Geddes: Social Evolutionist and City Planner New York*, Routledge, 1990

Moorcock Michael, *Mother London*, Harmondsworth, Penguin, 1988

Morris William, *Political Writings*, Bristol, Thoemmes Press, 1994

Mort Frank, *Dangerous Sexualities*, London, Routledge, 2000

Mount Ferdinand, *Mind the Gap: The New Class Divide in Britain*, London, Short Books, 2005

Mullan Phil, *The Imaginary Time Bomb: Why an ageing population is not a social problem*, London, I.B Tauris, 2000

Mumford Lewis, *The City in History: Its origins, its transformations, and its prospects*, Harmondsworth, Penguin, 1991, orig. 1961

Nairn Ian, *Subtopia*, London, Architectural Press, 1957

Osborn Frederic J., and Arnold Whittick, *The New Towns; The Answer to Megalopolis*, London, Leonard Hill, 1969 first published 1963

P'eng Shu-tse, *The Chinese Communist Party in Power*, New York, Monad, 1980

Patten John, *Things to Come: The Tories in the Twenty-first Century*, London, Sinclair Stevenson, 1995

Pawley Martin, *Home Ownership*, London, The Architectural Press, 1978

Pawley Martin, 'So, Lord Rogers, why shouldn't we build on surplus rural land?', *Architects' Journal*, 24 February 2000

Pawley Martin, 'The sand-heap urbanism of the twenty-first century', in Ian Abley and James Heartfield, editors, *Sustaining Architecture in the Anti-Machine Age*, Chichester, Wiley-Academy, 2001

Pearson Geoffrey, *Hooligan: A History of Respectable Fears*, London, Macmillan, 1983

Phillips Kevin, *The Emerging Republican Majority*, New Rochelle, Arlington House, 1969

Podair Jerald E., *The Strike That Changed New York: Blacks, Whites, And The Ocean Hill-Brownsville Crisis*, New Haven, Connecticut, Yale University Press, 2002

Porter Roy, *Enlightenment: Britain and the Creation of the Modern World*, London, Allen Lane, 2000

Putnam Robert, 'Bowling Alone: America's Declining Social Capital', *Journal of Democracy 6:1*, Jan 1995

Rasmussen Steen *Eiler*, London, Jonathan Cape, 1937

Robertson Scott, J. W. *England's Green and Pleasant Land*, Harmondsworth, Penguin, 1947

Rogers Sir Richard, *Cities for a Small Planet*, London, Faber and Faber, 1997

Rogers Sir Richard, *Introduction, Towards an Urban Renaissance – Final Report of the Urban Task Force*, London, HMSO, Spon, 1999

Rogers Sir Richard and **Burdett** Richard, 'Let's cram more into the city', in Marcial Echenique and Andrew Saint, editors, *Cities for the New Millennium,* London, Spon, 2001

Rogers Sir Richard and **Power** Anne, *Cities for a Small Country*, London, Faber and Faber, 2000

Rosdolsky Roman, *The Making of Marx's 'Capital', Vol. I*, London, Pluto Press, 1989

Rubin I., *A History of Economic Thought*, London, Pluto Press, 1989

Saville John, *The Consolidation of the Capitalist State 1800-1850*, London, Pluto, 1994

Schumpeter Joseph, *Capitalism, Socialism and Democracy*, New York Harper, 1975 first published 1942

Sherlock Harley, *Cities are Good for Us: the case for close knit communities, local shops and public transport*, London, Paladin, 1991

Sinclair Iain, *London Orbital – a walk round the M25*, London, Penguin, 2003

Smith David, *North and South: Britain's Growing Divide*, Harmondsworth, Penguin, 1989

Spalding Francis, *Stevie Smith: A Critical Biography*, London, Faber and Faber, 1998

Stewart John, 'Building a Crisis – Housing Supply in Britain', July 2002, posted on www.hbf.co.uk

Stewart John, 'Building a Crisis – Housing undersupply in England', May 2002

Teige Karel, *The Minimum Dwelling*, London, MIT Press, 2002

Thatcher Margaret, *The Downing Street Years*, London, Harper Collins, 1995

Thomas Keith, *Man and the Natural World: Changing Attitudes in England 1500-1800*, Harmondsworth, Penguin, 1984

Tickell Sir Crispin, foreword, Richard Rogers, *Cities for a Small Planet*, London, Faber and Faber, 1997

Toynbee Arnold J., *The Industrial Revolution in England*, Newton Abbot, Devon, David and Charles, 1969 first published 1884

Uglow Jenny, *The Lunar Men*, London, Faber and Faber, 2003

Vague Tom, *London psychogeography: Rachman, Riots and Rillington Place*, London, Calvert's Press, 1998

Widgery David, *Some Lives! A GP's East End*, London, Sinclair Stevenson, 1991

Wiener Martin, *English Culture and the Industrial Spirit*, Cambridge, Cambridge University, 1981

Wilk Christopher editor, *Modernism 1914 – 1939 – designing a new world*, London, Victoria & Albert Publications, 2006

Williams Austin editor, *Transport in the New Millennium*, Newcastle, Transport Research Publications, 2000

Williams Michael, *The Relations of History and Geography: Studies in England*, France and the United States, Exeter, University of Exeter Press, 2002

Williams-Ellis Clough, *England and the Octopus*, Uckfield, The Beacon Press, 1996 first published 1928,

Wilson A.N., *The Victorians*, London, Hutchinson, 2002

Winter James, *Secure from Rash Assault: Securing the Victorian Environment*, Berkely, University of California Press, 1999

Wolmar Christian, *The Subterranean Railway: How the underground was built and how it changed the city forever*, London, Atlantic Books, 2004

Woudhuysen James, and Ian Abley, *Why is Construction So Backward?* Chichester, Wiley-Academy, 2004

Wright Patrick, *A Journey Through the Ruins: The Last Days of London*, London, Radius, 1992

Young Michael, and Peter Wilmott, *Family and Kinship in East London*, Harmondsworth, Penguin, 1980 first published 1957

PUBLICATIONS CONSULTED

Bank of England Quarterly
BBC Online
Blueprint
Building
Daily Mail
Guardian
Housing Market Analyst
Humanism Today
London Evening Standard
Metropolis Magazine
Municipal Journal
New Statesman
Newsweek
Observer
Private Eye
Property People
Rising East
SF Gate,
Spiked-Online
Sunday Times
Telegraph
Times
Town & Country Planning

REPORTS AND PAPERS OF:

Barker review of housing supply
British Waterways
Building Research Establishment
Campaign to Protect Rural
    England
Committee on Public
    Participation in Planning
Construction Industry Training
    Board
Department for Transport,
    Local Government and
    the Regions
Department of Culture, Media
    and Sport
Department of the Environment,
    Food and Rural Affairs
Department of the Environment,
    Transport and the Regions
Department of Trade and
    Industry
English Heritage
Environmental and Heritage
    Service
Highways Agency
Independent Transport
    Commission
Joseph Rowntree Foundation
Labour Party
Office of National Statistics
Office of the Deputy Prime
    Minister
The National Housebuilding
    Council
Thurrock Urban Development
    Corporation
Urban Task Force